HUMAN RESOURCES FOR TROUBLED CHILDREN

WERNER I. HALPERN, M.D.
Director, Children and Youth Division

STANLEY KISSEL, PH.D.
Chief Psychologist, Children and Youth Division

Rochester Mental Health Center
Rochester, New York

A WILEY-INTERSCIENCE PUBLICATION

JOHN WILEY & SONS New York · London · Sydney · Toronto

To the Generations:
Our Parents,
Our Children,
Our Wives, Edith and Pearl

Library of Congress Cataloging in Publication Data:

Halpern, Werner I
    Human resources for troubled children.

    (Wiley series on personality processes)
    "A Wiley-Interscience publication."
    Includes bibliographies and index.
    1. Child psychotherapy.   2. Family psychotherapy.
3. Child mental health services.   I. Kissel, Stanley,
joint author.   II. Title.   [DNLM: 1. Family therapy.
2. Psychotherapy—In infancy and childhood.
3. Community mental health services—In infancy and
childhood. WS350 H196h]

RJ504.H343   618.9'28'91   75–44290
ISBN 0–471–48908–5

Printed in the United States of America

10 9 8 7 6 5 4 3 2 1

Series Preface

This series of books is addressed to behavioral scientists interested in the nature of human personality. Its scope should prove pertinent to personality theorists and researchers as well as to clinicians concerned with applying an understanding of personality processes to the amelioration of emotional difficulties in living. To this end, the series provides a scholarly integration of theoretical formulations, empirical data, and practical recommendations.

Six major aspects of studying and learning about human personality can be designated: personality theory, personality structure and dynamics, personality development, personality assessment, personality change, and personality adjustment. In exploring these aspects of personality, the books in the series discuss a number of distinct but related subject areas: the nature and implications of various theories of personality; personality characteristics that account for consistencies and variations in human behavior: the emergence of personality processes in children and adolescents; the use of interviewing and testing procedures to evaluate individual differences in personality; efforts to modify personality styles through psychotherapy, counseling, behavior therapy, and other methods of influence; and patterns of abnormal personality functioning that impair individual competence.

IRVING B. WEINER

Case Western Reserve University
Cleveland, Ohio

Preface

There has been a proliferation of intervention strategies to help troubled children during the last 25 years. In this book we give an overview of the major methods available to clinicians responsible for making appropriate treatment plans.

Although a number of related works deal with differing aspects of this topic, they emphasize one area over another such as individual psycho-therapy and behavior modification; or they identify with a particular school of thought such as psychoanalysis and learning theory. Some describe group therapy with children or family treatment exclusively, and do not concern themselves with the use of drugs in the helping process. A discussion of environmental resources such as adoption, foster care, or schools, although recognized as important human resources for troubled children, hardly ever finds its way into books that deal with the whole range of treatment modalities for emotionally and interpersonally handicapped children and adolescents.

This book delineates the diversity of treatment strategies for the practicing clinician who faces the Herculean task of choosing wisely and economically from multiple possibilities. Whenever possible, we mention indications for discriminating among these different ways of intervening with children.

After reviewing the roots of a rich past that gave rise to today's treatment approaches for troubled children in the first chapter, the second focuses on the several useful environmental resources that can be tapped on behalf of the child. Conditions under which separating a child from his biological parents can take place, either permanently or for periods of time with foster parents or in an institution, are considered in detail. Since disturbed children often have difficulty in their school environments, we devote a chapter to an examination of the ways schools can accommodate to a child, while helping him assimilate knowledge and develop skills for self-sufficiency. Two chapters deal exclusively with parents, one emphasizing educationally based strategies for helping parents become more effective in their parenting roles, and the other looking to the more formalized counseling techniques.

Six chapters are devoted to a discussion of more traditional treatment approaches, using a combination of didactic material and illustrative case vignettes. Of these the first three chapters concern the child and his natural social setting. To begin with, we present a view of the classical child guidance tandem approach for parents and child. Family therapy is discussed from the point of view of parent-child negotiations. This is followed by a chapter on group therapy which highlights the importance of peer influence in positive terms.

The two succeeding chapters on psychotherapy and behavior modification concentrate on treatment methods for the individual child, spanning a wide spectrum of techniques such as mutual story telling, the squiggle game, desensitization, and contingency management, among many others. We decided to include a chapter on pharmacotherapy because more and more children are being medicated. There is a considerable increase in the number of nonmedical therapists taking responsibility for the overall management of children; they will be exposed to the uses of drug therapy.

In the final chapter we present some tentative thoughts about making choices for intervention although we recognize our limitations in light of controversial current research findings. We also offer a conceptual model upon which we base our rationale for clinical decision making.

We are grateful to those clinicians and researchers who preceded us and have given us a rich heritage. Our debt to the families who have consulted us is immeasurable because they too have taught us about human experiences. Moreover, working in a comprehensive community mental health center has brought us in contact with diversity in people, in orientations, and in disciplines. We acknowledge the stimulation provided by our co-workers. Special thanks are due to the secretarial staff of the Rochester Mental Health Center, especially Margaret Bilski, Nancy Goldey, Gail Magro, and Eunice Thompson for their assistance in the typing of the manuscript.

WERNER I. HALPERN
STANLEY KISSEL

Rochester, New York
January 1976

Contents

CHAPTER 1

Historical Paths

BEGINNINGS

The writing of a guide to human resources for deviant and troubled children may seem premature or even presumptuous if one keeps in mind that the study of childhood as a serious scientific topic is barely 100 years old (Ariès, 1962; Kanner, 1959; Stone, 1973). Yet, much has happened to the place of the young in human affairs during this time span. From all appearances, there has been a transition from an adult-centered to a more child-centered focus in the social system, mirroring wide changes in outlook about the nature of human relationships and obligations. This attitudinal change arose from the rapidly expanding diversity of experience and dramatically increased choice in a postindustrial world. Society's response inevitably included a kind of schooling of the young for a relevant adult role. It is in the context of this adaptive process that diagnostic and therapeutic efforts were generated on behalf of children.

The position occupied by children in the social order today stands in marked contrast to the plight of their earlier existence when they were subject to such ritual practices as abandonment and sacrificial death. That these extreme acts grew out of beliefs about the universe rather than out of a special animus to children emphasizes the importance of temporal perspective in human survival. At any point in history sanctioned treatments of children have to be looked at through the world view of the times. Although child exploitation, incarceration, and cruel punishment have not disappeared in modern times, there are strong moral and legal deterrents operative that markedly set off the present era from epochs prior to 100 years ago. As a part of the difference in outlook, there has been an enormous growth in the education, habilitation, rehabilitation, and protection services to children. Such functions far transcend the family's previous role in these endeavors. Most

1

explicit is the recognition that if children contain the seeds of the adult's adaptive genius, then special care must be devoted to the young for the fulfillment of this promise. The proliferation of child therapies in the twentieth century has been a constituent part of this philosophy.

That more resources and energies have begun to flow into psychiatric services to children in recent times is best documented by the growth of agencies. While there were less than 100 agencies providing some mental health services for troubled children in 1914, a fivefold increase had occurred by 1927. Among the latter, only 8 of some 500 agencies resembled the modern child guidance clinic (Stevenson and Smith, 1934; Witmer, 1940). Forty years later there were nearly 4000 facilities in the United States providing some form of mental health service to almost a half million children (National Institute of Mental Health, 1968). Of these agencies, 169 were recognized as being exclusively devoted to the emotional needs of disturbed children and their families (American Association of Psychiatric Services for Children, 1972). The National Institute of Mental Health estimate for 1975 is that well over 1 million children will be serviced by mental health facilities (National Institute of Mental Health, 1968). Evidently, population growth alone cannot account for these changes.

Now that some of the scourges of childhood, particularly infectious diseases, have come under control (e.g. poliomyelitis, which during a 20-year span from 1950 to 1970 dropped from 33,300 to 33 reported cases, U.S. Statistics, 1972), a realignment of priorities has taken place, with social and psychological deviance of children getting a greater share of attention.

Overpopulation and crowding are credited with having deleterious effects on behavior, as are the pace and complexity of modern life. More than the danger of infectious disease, life stresses loom as the big survival threat today. The burgeoning numbers of those who seek help from mental health practitioners affirms this point. Consequently, a public mental health view is in the making that attempts to identify psychic and social stress in a period of relative affluence. When people have the luxury of making choices, the psychic effort for arriving at decisions takes its toll.

Children face more risk in this area than do adults. In preparation for their adult roles, children are increasingly exposed to an overabundant experiential diet, starting even in infancy. The modern era, fluid and dynamic in nature, elicits versatile adaptive and maladaptive responses in the young. Thus the therapy enterprise has become increasingly diversified in trying to keep pace with the demands for preventive and corrective programming. This proliferation of techniques, whether psychological treatments, environmental supports, behavior controls, or medical management, raises many questions about the rationale underlying each method. What is appropriate? When? For whom? At what cost? With what effectiveness? If there are many royal roads to Rome, are some shorter than others? Or more attractive? Or more challenging? Or easier? Should each traveler choose his own way? Should he have a tour guide to prevent him from getting lost or one from whom he will gain the appreciation for a richer experience?

When the needs of children and their development are under consideration, must the journey be prepared with special care? Not only are children in the formative stages when the foundations for later maturity are laid down but they are also most impressionable and, presumably, pliable to the imperatives of their coaches. At the same time, the limits to learning readiness that are governed by the principles of ontogeny must be respected (Piaget, 1928). As children are to be programmed for coherence, successive age-appropriate expectations become the means by which their caregivers and tutors exploit readiness at the proper developmental moment in the life of the young. By the same token, corrective steps undertaken during particular growth periods can have maximum impact or none at all, depending on the recognition of readiness for newer levels of organization. Prevention as cure has much relevance here.

Individual differences among children (Gesell et al., 1938; Thomas et al., 1968), once overlooked, now allow for greater diversity in the strategies for adaptive coping. Concomitantly, the clinician is in the position of picking from an assortment of proliferating therapies and is able to tailor the treatment to his young client. He may often feel that there are too many choices and find himself espousing one technique over all others, simply to reduce the complexity to a more manageable effort.

A look at historical antecedents of today's child therapy should guard against forgetting Santayana's dictum about repeating the errors of the past by choosing to be ignorant of the past. How have previous ages shaped attitudes toward children through their institutions? What modes of child care were used to clarify the child's place in the society or to inculcate adaptive behavior? Over time, the family, the school, the church, and the healers have served in different capacities in the socialization of the young—or in promoting their deviant development.

PRETWENTIETH CENTURY

In Western culture prior to the nineteenth century, families lived close together and society was organized communally. Little distinction was made between children and adults when one considers that in most respects the child was admitted to the adult world by the time he was 7 years old (Ariès, 1962). Whatever he was taught, if at all, came informally in the expectation that he carry his fair share of the work in the family. Its objective was clearly the fostering of preservation and the survival of the community. Only for the few of wealth and nobility did education become somewhat more formal toward the end of the fourteenth century, centering around the needs of the church. Therefore, education was almost exclusively religiously oriented (Ariès, 1962).

The healing arts of that time were primitive by today's standards and were intertwined with religion (Zilboorg and Henry, 1941). Many practices were based on notions rooted in magic or mysticism. Deviancy was suspect as the work of Satan. The young child was considered simple and innocent, a source of amusement to the adults, but also invulnerable to evil. A coddling attitude characterized the adult posture to children up to age seven.

Following the Reformation and with the Age of Enlightenment in the eighteenth century, some changes in attitudes evolved. The child was more and more viewed as a "fragile creature of God" who required special nurturance. On the one hand he had to be cared for, and on the other, strengthened for independent growth. The family was becoming a considerably stronger and also a more private entity. Parents felt themselves to be more responsible for the training and education of their children. Their objective still remained oriented toward replication of parental modes and, whatever formal education prevailed emphasized religious teaching, largely in the hands of parish priests. Higher education for the sons of the well-to-do revolved around religion, canon law, or medicine (Ariès, 1962).

Toward the end of the seventeenth century, childhood began to be extended to what would now be called the preadolescent period. This, for the most part, occurred as a function of the greater formalization of education. Changes in society's views of childhood were influenced by the emerging humanism which implied causal connections between experience and attitudes. An awareness that the child is father of the man slowly dawned. Gradually, educational institutions where the training of teachers could proceed spread over Europe. This necessitated the development of a frame of reference toward an expectation of childhood tasks and goals. In defining a base line for expectations of childhood the groundwork was laid for considering deviance from normal in a new light. A coexisting phenomena, the emphasis on corrective and more punitive measures for the control of children's cooperation in their socialization for the Puritan ethic, also emerged (Lowrey, 1939).

The major philosophies that were to govern future perceptions of childhood were laid down during this period (Crutcher, 1943). Of these, the two polar points of view of Hobbes and of Rousseau continue to dominate our thinking today. The Hobbesonian sees the child as basically amoral and uncivilized and needing to be controlled by society. If the child is to take his place in adult society, he must be raised properly for this task. Rousseau's view holds that adult society corrupts the child whose impulses are basically pure and innocent of wrongdoings. All adults need to do, according to this belief, is to provide an interest in children and offer sufficient experiential stimulation for them to thrive. In these formulations the seeds of conflict were sown over the benefits of structural and progressive education, of guided versus permissive child-rearing practices, and of behavior modification contrasting with psychotherapy.

This essentially philosophic controversy did not stand in the way of technologic forces that would eventually have a profound influence on the place of children in society. Strides were beginning to be made in the physical sciences —in chemistry, physics, physiology, biology, and medicine—that would alter people's social and personal environment. The displacement of a spiritual disease theory by a physical disease concept eventually became the foundation for the application of the medical model to the control of physical and mental illness in adults and children.

The idea that abnormal behavior was a nuisance to be hidden emerged during the latter part of the seventeenth century. Out of this change in outlook arose the practice of locking up adults in asylums and of sequestering children in attics or other make-shift cells. Thus, the stage was set for later reactions that would provide more satisfactory solutions for controlled out-of-home care to disturbed children.

The eighteenth century was a time of ideas whereas the nineteenth century ushered in the application of these ideas to society (Crutcher, 1943). Childhood as a developmental stage was now firmly established but, except for the well-to-do, little formal education was provided. Prevailing at that time was the practice of rigid indoctrination as carried over from the church-oriented educational practices. A pioneer educator, Pestalozzi, who knew of Rousseau's view about the nature of children, proposed that children should learn by doing, by observing, and by discovering the world about them. His method opened the door for schooling greater masses of children more meaningfully, and he defined in a clear way some of the tasks of childhood.

Another person who fought the dominant view of his time, that children can only learn if forced into accepting the ideas of their elders, was Froebel (1903) who believed that early training would be helpful in developing "good habits" (Crutcher, 1943). He introduced preschool education in the form of kindergarten in 1836. In such a school the child's play was organized and controlled, so as to stimulate and guide his physical, mental, and spiritual development. His work led Elizabeth Peabody to establish the first kindergarten in the United States in 1860 in Boston. Thirteen years later in St. Louis, Missouri, the first public school kindergarten was opened.

Once the genetic concept of development took hold and pedagogy became more formalized, the emphasis of the educational enterprise shifted to curriculum content. In the mid-1800s texts and programs on how to teach appeared. Herbart (1901), one of the most influential educators of that era, stressed that the child assimilates new knowledge on the basis of past experiences and that the curriculum must be adjusted to help him move from earlier and familiar material to new and unfamiliar knowledge.

From these early writers are derived two major principles of modern education: (1) a child's spontaneous and natural activities are tools for learning; (2) each child's passage through definite developmental stages requires proper sequencing of activities. These principles galvanized a shift in the appreciation of children as the carriers of civilization's future. Now, children became worthy of attention, study, and care for their own sakes. What unique features did children possess that made it possible for them to learn environmental mastery? And again, what conditions fostered this tendency? What impeded or distorted it?

The early stress in the study of children was on education, i.e. on methods of imparting environmental mastery. However, beginning observations of their biological, physiological, and psychological nature were stirring. In 1787 Dietrich was probably the first to keep a detailed careful record of a child's growth. Darwin, the noted evolutionist, published a biographical sketch of an infant in 1877, which was followed a year later by Preyer's two-volume work on the mind of the child (Crutcher, 1943).

These early writings led to a more and more scientific interest in childhood behavior. Thus in 1895 Sulley published his studies of children, which placed importance on their play activities. Among other things, he believed that a better understanding of children's play would increase knowledge of childhood and that free play should be viewed as communication akin to talking in adults. These observations also laid the groundwork for a therapeutic philosophy from which came play therapy as currently practiced.

Yet, for a more comprehensive study of children to occur, the dynamics and potentials of growth had to be measured. During the 1890s, studies were undertaken at the University of California to detail the development of early infant motor coordination and of speech (Shinn, 1893). The groundwork for delineating deviation from normal, begun two centuries earlier, was finally taking hold. Debates over the inheritability of abilities heated up as education of the young became more widespread. There was a need to recognize and classify children who had poor academic prospects so that they would receive the benefit of special training—if such could be formulated.

Already in 1800, Itard (1932) made a pioneering training attempt with a boy, presumably mentally retarded, who had been found wandering in the woods near Aveyron, France. Itard's contention that knowledge is acquired through the senses was to be tested by a program of patient speech training and socialization. Although he did not reach the standard of transforming the "wild boy" into a normal civilized person, his work showed that even damaged children can profit from careful and laborious training. One of his students, Sequin, opened a private school in Paris and later introduced the first school for the feebleminded in the United States. Massachusetts led the way in 1848, quickly followed by New York in 1851, in opening up state training schools (Kanner, 1964). These early institutions began as temporary experiments in the education of the feebleminded, and not as asylums. The hope was that after a period of training, the pupil could return to home and community. Schools for the deaf and blind soon followed these efforts for the feebleminded.

As a result of educating the retarded or handicapped child, there arose the need to measure progress. Consequently, an emphasis on learning about individual differences and a practical necessity for measuring abilities combined to give impetus to an interest in intelligence testing. Binet's (1916) monumental work in this field was published as a series of tests in 1905. The door was opened for improving the diagnosis of learning disabilities and for techniques of educational rehabilitation.

If children were impaired, what causes could be considered? Arguments that surrounded the nature/nurture controversy of the time gave rise to a rational method of infant observation out of which evolved the developmental point of view. Only by a definition of norms could deviation be classified and investigated. Perhaps, by knowing more about the ontogenetic stages of child growth, the unfolding of inherited attributes would guide a life education philosophy eugenically, habilitatively, and therapeutically. Both in Europe and in the United States, child study associations were founded. Cattell (1890), G. Stanley Hall (1904, 1923), and Gesell (1928) were early developmentalists who left a profound impact on child-rearing attitudes based on a rational and phenomenologic point of view. Their work spurred a variety of investigations of children in the context of the family, school, and community, eventually coming to flower in the epigenetic model of human development (Erikson, 1950).

Cultural, social, economic, religious, and political moods have always markedly influenced people's perceptions of children. When children were valued as servants, they were pressed into service early in life. As members of the worker pool, following the industrial revolution, the young labored side by side with their elders. Indigent children found their way into wretched alms houses, were indentured, or became thieving street urchins. In the period just before the end of the nineteenth century social reform affecting children emerged, hesitantly at first, but then cascaded into a virtual crusade for children's rights. Charitable institutions came into existence, often under church auspices, that literally took homeless and needy children off the streets; these were soon supplanted by the foster home idea. The beginnings of modern social work can be traced to attempts to deal with homeless immigrant children who wandered the streets of New York and were placed in free foster homes (Children's Aid Society, 1928).

Programming for parent education gradually evolved before the turn of the century, moving away from the excessive concern expressed by James Parkinson in 1807 about the effect of indulgence on child behavior (Hunter and Macalpine, 1963). The newspapers of the nineteenth century offered parents a liberal sprinkling of advice columns on obedience training. As this attitude became outdated with the discovery of the child as a subject of investigation, organizations were formed, like the Child Study Association of America and comparable clubs in Europe, with the assumption that the parent role, to be performed properly, required intelligent comprehension of children's ways (Lowrey, 1939).

TWENTIETH CENTURY

An unprecedented interest in children and their development has come to dominate the twentieth century. The rise of the affluent middle class, of urbanization, of longevity, of technology, and of leisure are among factors that converged to give the child a new status in society. Preparation for the adult role became a paramount concern. Little wonder that quite suddenly, at the turn of the century, special attention was being focused on learning-disabled children and on nonhandicapped children who were behaviorally deviant (Reisman, 1966). If it were possible to understand such children, or to at least fathom the causes of their deviance, it might be possible to offer prevention and alter aberrant courses in development. The psychologist Lightner Witmer started a clinic for the detection and remediation of children's learning difficulties in Pennsylvania in 1896, and the psychiatrist William Healy founded a clinic for delinquents in Chicago in 1909. The latter became the forerunner of the child-guidance movement that at first sought to develop diagnostic and therapeutic insight into delinquency and behavior disorders. Gradually broadening its scope to include the whole range of mental disorders of childhood, it gave a more scientific basis to working with children and families (Glueck, 1947; Glueck and Salmon, 1929; Healy, 1934; Stevenson and Smith, 1934; Witmer, 1940).

At the same time a number of American psychologists under the leadership of G. Stanley Hall brought a scientific bent into developmental child psychology. In 1909 Henry Goddard (1914), as a result of his interest in the influence of heredity on mental deficiency, introduced the first usable intelligence test to America and established the Vineland Training School for defective children.

The pioneering efforts of these early years spawned Gesell's (1928) eventual mammoth cataloguing of child behavior and growth, based on the assumption that intelligence is relatively fixed and controlled by the process of maturation. For the most part psychological assessment and intervention centered on discovering the level of a child's development and determining whether learning lags related to intellectual and/or skill deficits. These early workers were interested in plotting the different stages of motor, language, social, and intellectual development and, in doing so, added further refinements in defining the expectations of childhood tasks and goals. They also firmed up the description of adolescence as an important developmental stage.

Since most children have to be taught, psychological understanding of their social and cognitive development became a crucial educational issue. William James' "Talks to Teachers on Psychology," published in 1899, represented an early attempt to bring education and psychology into closer harmony. His pupil, John Dewey (1916), extended this view and laid the foundation for the progressive education movement. Dewey held that children should be taught to cooperate with one another on socially useful tasks. Frustrations ought to be minimized and the child freed from inhibiting or repressive constraints. It was a functionally oriented philosophy which had as its main thrust a problem-solving approach to learning social intercourse.

While James and Dewey were striving to emphasize the child as a person in the educational process, several other phenomena emerged that did not immediately appear to have a bearing on child study and child therapy. Freud had begun to publish his views on psychosexual development starting in 1896. His theories were derived from retrospective adult analyses of remembered childhood experiences. "The analysis of a phobia in a 5-year-old boy" (1909), although carried out through correspondence with the child's father and without benefit of direct observation, became Freud's seminal contribution to child therapy. The importance of paying attention to unconscious factors in behavior, to bring about symptom abatement, was now introduced. Once one grasped the psychodynamics and manipulation of symbolic communication of the disturbed child, interpretation or clarification of the connection between act, thought, and distorted perceptions would relieve anxiety and symptoms. Therefore, psychodiagnostic and psychotherapeutic efforts could be encompassed within a primarily cognitive-verbal method.

Although Healy's work with juvenile offenders, first in Chicago and later in Boston, was influenced by Freud's findings, he became aware also of the social determinants of behavior and included the social worker in his assessment procedures (Healy, 1934). Many youths had growing-up experiences sufficiently deviant to explain the etiology of their maladaptive behavior. This model of team work among several disciplines eventually became standard procedure in child guidance clinics. Once the bases for personal motivation, for multicausal determinants, and for their interplay could be fathomed, then programs for the reeducation of delinquents and for the therapy of neurotics followed easily. It must be remembered that up to the early decades of the twentieth century, Lombroso's views on the primacy of heredity in criminality was still shared by many psychiatrists (Zilboorg and Henry, 1941).

By way of contrast to the pedagogic and therapeutic models, the concept of man-as-system took on considerable viability with the work of Pavlov (1928) who described the conditioned reflex in 1901. Man learned by the effects that his behavior produced for him. Building on Pavlov's work and utilizing Thorndike's law of effect, John B. Watson (1925) articulated a theory of behavior demonstrating that childhood behavior, including deviance, could be learned (conditioned) and inhibited (counter-conditioned). However, it was not until the 1950s and later that his work and that of his pupils regained popularity as behavior modification.

The place of the individual in the large social system brought the issue of adjustment and maladjustment into a wider context. If a child is to live among people and learn with them, the group or milieu can be used for habilitative and maturational ends. In Vienna during the early decades of the 1900s Alfred Adler trained teachers in a classroom procedure that became an early model for group treatment (Reisman, 1966). Later, he experimented with interviewing entire families in front of audiences, a precursor of family group therapy. Aichhorn (1925), also in Vienna, applied psychoanalytic principles to the study and treatment of delinquents and to structuring their interpersonal milieu.

Experimental pedagogy (Claparède, 1913), although in its infancy in the 1910s and 1920s, eventually would have much impact on developmental psychology and special education. Studies on higher thought processes of young children (Piaget, 1928), of perceptual distortions upon learning (Orton, 1937), and of social deprivation on underachievement (Montessori, 1912) lay dormant many years before their significance was recognized and applied on a wider scale.

During the 1920s and 1930s, education and treatment were mostly influenced by psychoanalytic-psychodynamic theories. Pedagogy was moving away from its exclusive emphasis on academic learning. Schools were beginning to be recognized as places where children learn social and personal adjustment in addition to academic subject matter. Deviance and deficiency were now thought of in terms of a child's being blocked in his development, and symptoms were likely to be an expression of internal or interpersonal problems (Lowrey, 1939).

Like its adult counterpart, child therapy in midtwentieth century came to be dominated by psychoanalysis and its variants. One of the most astute contributors was Anna Freud (1928) who advocated cooperative work with parents and teachers and advanced the adaptive and educational value of play therapy. These views were to be modified and extended by others who used play in lieu of the adult's free association (Klein, 1932), who suggested controlled play situations for working out problems (Levy, 1933), and who guided the child to play out present dilemmas in the relationship with the therapist (Allen, 1934). Slavson, in 1934, began applying some psychoanalytic concepts to working with children in groups that offered corrective emotional experiences for them.

Large numbers of children with special problems remained relatively impervious to the psychodynamic treatment methods. Bender (1952) and others (Despert, 1938; Kanner, 1943; Mahler, 1952) investigated the nature of childhood psychosis and viewed the disorder in terms of a profound developmental dysfunction for which medical treatment was not to be overlooked. Hyperactive, behavior disordered, and learning-disabled children required other than psychological methods—often responding to environmental change such as residential care, to medication, or to specific training and behavior modification techniques.

Longitudinal studies of children helped to delineate differences in temperament and coping styles (Escalona and Heider, 1959; Kagan, 1971; Murphy, 1956; Thomas et al., 1968). This was applied to further refine parental guidance and child-rearing tactics. Cross-cultural and anthropologic studies threw light on social and ethnic dimensions of personality and child-raising practices (Mead, 1928, 1930, 1935). A dawning awareness of the social-class variable alerted therapists to the special needs of minority group children (Knobloch and Pasamanick, 1958). Finally, communication as a process in daily encounters between parent and child—as popularized in best selling paperbacks and magazines—was a culmination of the sweeping changes that characterized the growth in social sensitivity toward the child over the last century (Ginott, 1965, 1969).

CROSSROADS

The present day abundance of therapeutic strategies, which has its roots in a rich and divergent past, is by no means an unalloyed blessing. How easy it is for the practitioner to feel lost among myriad roadsigns pointing haphazardly in all directions! Modern man already has to contend with an overabundance of choice making, evocative of a "choice shock," which Walter Kaufman (1973) refers to as "decidophobia." Most significantly for the clinician, the inability to make decisions in the face of apparently too many therapy options may be quickly succeeded by the tendency to embrace one method exclusively over others in order to sidestep the complexity of choosing. This may prove to be an unfortunate evasion of responsibility, for while ignorance of history fosters the repetition of error, ignorance of choice enhances infatuation with one's mistake.

What are some questions that the clinician faces in deciding on intervention techniques when confronted by the child in need of his services—no matter whether the child's problems are within himself, in the matrix of family relationships, at school, or among peers? Is the child to be treated alone or in a group? Should the family be seen collaterally or as a unit? Is quick symptom removal preferred or should more extensive relationship therapy be tried? What are the indications for environmental maneuvers? For pharmacotherapy? What conditions make parent education primary? When do school programs become important treatment modalities in their own right? Obviously, the answers to questions such as these must remain tentative when presented as generalities. Among the welter of child psychiatric case material, relatively few conditions lend themselves to *ex cathedra* pronouncements about their precise management.

Yet, as a tour guide acquaints the interested traveler with the available routes to his objectives, so may a mapping of the terrain on child therapies and resources similarly orient the clinician. Only when the divergent choices are available, can one try to answer the question as to "what type of intervention works best with what kind of problem under which set of circumstances."

This book is a beginning attempt in bringing together an array of intervention strategies most often utilized with children who show maladaptive or deviant behavior. Individual chapters describe major categories of treatment and their derivatives, and, when possible, discuss those indicators that serve to discriminate among them. Admittedly, much overlap exists when application of techniques is discussed since no single method needs to preempt all others or to abrogate the right of personal preference for clinicians. Nonetheless, the authors are of the opinion that knowledge of existing diversity does not have to be a burden and even may offer hope for continued scientific progress by improving the child practitioner's discernment and skills.

REFERENCES

Aichhorn, A. *Wayward Youth*, New York: Viking, 1925.

Allen, F. H. Therapeutic work with children. *American Journal of Orthopsychiatry*, **4**, 193–202, 1934.

American Association of Psychiatric Services for Children, *Directory of Member Services*, New York, 1972.

Ariès, P. *Centuries of Childhood: A Social History of Family Life*. New York: Knopf, 1962.

Bender, L. Childhood schizophrenia. *Psychiatric Quarterly*, **27**, 1–19, 1953.

Binet, A. & Binet, S. *The Development of Intelligence in Children*. Baltimore: Williams and Wilkins, 1916.

Cattell, J. McK. Mental tests and measurements. *Mind*, **15**, 373–381, 1890.

Children's Aid Society. *The Crusade for Children*. New York: Children's Aid Society of the City of New York, 1928.

Claparède, E. *Experimental Pedagogy*. London: Edward Arnold, 1913.

Crutcher, R. Child psychiatry: A history of its development. *Psychiatry*, **6**, 191–201, 1943.

Darwin, C. A biographical sketch of an infant. *Mind*, **2**, 285–294, 1877.

Despert, J. L. Schizophrenia in children. *Psychiatric Quarterly*, **12**, 366–371, 1938.

Dewey, J. *Democracy and Education*. New York: Macmillan, 1916.

Erikson, E. H. *Childhood and Society*. New York: Norton, 1950.

Escalona, S. & Heider, G. *Prediction and Outcome: A Study in Child Development*. Menninger Clinic Monograph No. 14, New York: Basic Books, 1959.

Freud, A. *Introduction to the Technique of Child Analysis*. New York: Nervous and Mental Disease Publishing Co., 1928.

Freud, S. The analysis of a phobia in a five year old boy (1909). *Collected Papers*, London: Hogarth Press, 1933.

Froebel, F. *The Education of Man*. New York: Appleton, 1903.

Gesell, A. L. *Infancy and Human Growth*. New York: Macmillan, 1928.

Gesell, A. L., Thompson, H. & Armatruda, C. S. *The Psychology of Early Growth*, New York: Macmillan, 1938.

Ginott, H. G. *Between Parent and Child*. New York: Macmillan, 1965.

Ginott, H. G. *Between Parent and Teenager*. New York: Macmillan, 1969.

Glueck, B. & Salmon, W. T. The child guidance movement. *Journal of Juvenile Research*, **13**, 79–89, 1929.

Goddard, H. H. *Feeblemindedness: Its Causes and Consequences*. New York: Macmillan, 1914.

Hall, G. S. *Adolescence*. New York: Appleton, 1904.

Hall, G. S. *Life and Confessions of a Psychologist*. New York: Appleton, 1923.

Healy, W. *Twenty-Five Years of Child Guidance*. Chicago: Institute for Juvenile Research, 1934.

Herbart, J. F. *Outlines of Educational Doctrine*. New York: Macmillan, 1901.

Hunter, R. & Macalpine, I. *Three Hundred Years of Psychiatry: 1535–1860. A History Presented in Selected English Texts*. London: Oxford University Press, 1963.

Itard, J. M. G. *The Wild Boy of Aveyron*. New York: Century Company, 1932.

James, W. *Talks to Teachers on Psychology*. New York: Henry Holt, 1899.

Kagan, J. *Change and Continuity in Infancy*. New York: Wiley, 1971.

Kanner, L. Autistic disturbances of affective contact. *Nervous Child*, **2**, 217–250, 1943.

Kanner, L. The thirty-third Maudsley lecture: Trends in child psychiatry. *Journal of Mental Science*, **105**, 581–593, 1959.

Kanner, L. *A History of the Care and Treatment of the Mentally Retarded*. Springfield, Ill.: Charles C. Thomas, 1964.

Kaufmann, W. *Without Guilt and Justice: From Decidophobia to Autonomy*. New York: Peter H. Wyden, 1973.

Klein, M. *Psychoanalysis of Children*. New York: Norton, 1932.

Knobloch, H. & Pasamanick, B. The relationship of race and socio-economic status to the development of motor behavior patterns in infancy. *Psychiatric Research Reports*, **10**, 123–133, 1958.

Levy, D. M. Use of play techniques as experimental procedure. *American Journal of Orthopsychiatry*, **3**, 266–277, 1933.

Lowrey, L. G. Trends in therapy: The evolution and present status of treatment approaches to behavior and personality problems. *American Journal of Orthopsychiatry*, **9**, 669–706, 1939.

Mahler, M. S. On child psychosis and schizophrenia: Autistic and symbiotic infantile psychoses. *The Psychoanalytic Study of the Child*, **7**, 286–305, 1952.

Mead, M. *Coming of Age in Samoa*. New York: William Morrow, 1928.

Mead, M. *Growing Up in New Guinea*. New York: William Morrow, 1930.

Mead, M. *Sex and Temperament in Three Primitive Societies*. New York: William Morrow, 1935.

Montessori, M. *The Montessori Method*. New York: Schocken Books, 1964, (Berlin, 1912).

Murphy, L. B. *Personality in Young Children*. New York: Basic Books, 1956.

National Institute of Mental Health. *Mental Health Statistics: Utilization of Psychiatric Facilities by Children*, Series B., No. 1. Washington, D.C.: U.S. Government Printing Office, 1968.

Orton, S. T. *Reading, Writing and Speech Problems in Children: A Presentation of Certain Types of Disorders in the Development of the Language Faculty*. New York: Norton, 1937.

Parkinson, J. *Observations on the Excessive Indulgence of Children.* London: Symonds et al., 1807, pp. 1–5.

Pavlov, I. V. (Tr. by Gannt, W. H.). *Lectures on Conditioned Reflexes.* New York: International Publishing Co., Vol. 1, 1928.

Pestalozzi, J. H. *Leonard and Gertrude.* Boston: D. C. Health, 1895.

Piaget, J. *Judgement and Reasoning in the Child.* New York: Harcourt Brace, 1928.

Preyer, W. *The Mind of the Child.* New York: Appleton, 1888.

Reisman, J. M. *The Development of Clinical Psychology.* New York: Appleton-Century-Crofts, 1966.

Rousseau, J. J. *Emile.* London: Dent and Sons, 1911.

Seguin, E. *Idiocy and its Treatment.* New York: William Wood, 1866 (first publ. 1846).

Shinn, M. W. *Notes on the Development of a Child.* Berkeley: University of California Studies, 1893.

Stevenson, G. S. & Smith, G. *Child Guidance Clinics.* New York: Commonwealth Fund, 1934.

Stone, M. H. Child psychiatry before the twentieth century. *International Journal of Child Psychotherapy*, **2**, 264–308, 1973.

Sully, J. *Studies of Childhood.* London: Longmans Green, 1903.

Thomas, A., Chess, S. & Birch, H. G. *Temperament and Behavior Disorders in Children.* New York: New York University Press, 1968.

U.S. Statistical Abstract. Washington, D.C.: U.S. Government Printing Office, 1972, p. 80.

Watson, J. B. *Behaviorism.* New York: Norton, 1925.

Witmer, H. L. *Psychiatric Clinics for Children.* New York: Oxford University Press, Commonwealth Fund, 1940.

Zilboorg, G. & Henry, G. W. *A History of Medical Psychology.* New York: Norton, 1941.

CHAPTER 2

Environmental Change as a Corrective Measure

When children become sufficiently troublesome to adults, they often are literally "sent packing." One of the earliest means for bringing about change in child behavior was their removal from home. There were periods when it was fashionable to send children to live with relatives, to prescribe rest cures in the country, or to apprentice the young to craftsmen and tradesmen. Presumably such placements were arranged in connection with incipient developmental crises as well as to sidestep the tensions generated in the caretaking adults. Separation was used as a device for strengthening the coping potential of the child. How often the discontinuity engendered in the children must have left emotional scars can be inferred from more recent studies of grief reactions in juveniles (Yarrow, 1964).

In contemporary times the summer period still serves as an opportunity for parents to place children in extrafamilial environments. Parents hope for a maturational spurt in their offspring while being momentarily separated from them. That this occurs under the guise of providing vacation fun, peer camaraderie, and experiential enrichment need not blind us to the underlying parental search for relief from, and resolution of, developmental problems. Upon his return to the family the child often has acquired additional skills that do indeed make him less dependent on the emotional resourcefulness of parents and, therefore, he becomes less threatening to them. By the same token, with a demanding child out of the way for a brief period, parents usually achieve sufficient respite to pick up their caretaker roles again more effectively later on.

A totally different situation pertains to children who are homeless or who are forced by circumstances or design to leave behind their normal attachments. Here the distinction and correlation between the protective function of the society and its therapeutic concerns come into play. If children are not properly cared for they may not survive. Therefore, the society has a mandate to guarantee survival of unwanted children as long as social values dictate adherence to a belief in the preservation of human life. Society is also concerned with fulfilling the self-development of its citizens, and thus applies therapeutic influences to its more damaged or disturbed members. If the latter are children who are unattached to families of their own, the commitment of a community is measured by the efforts it can muster in providing the most supportive and growth-promoting environment for them.

Placement Choices

Although foundlings, feral children, and juvenile paupers have been known since ancient times, they appeared in larger numbers as a result of the social changes associated with the Industrial Revolution (Thurston, 1930). They were early housed in congregate living quarters which were administered by untrained personnel and, for the most part, were unsuited to the needs of homeless youth. The behavioral problems spawned by these conditions were formidable and discouraged the custodians from promoting reform measures for young outcasts until nineteenth century social consciousness crystallized into social work, and the professional entered the field of group care. Only then did it become possible to consider out-of-home placement for problem children as a potential option short of imposing a hopeless sentencing to custodial care.

Defective or organically damaged children were particularly vulnerable to a consignment to an institutional existence without hope. As habilitative techniques came to be developed in more recent times, many more children were capable of returning to family and community or were saved from institutional placements (Eisenberg, 1969; Fernald, 1917).

It should not come as a surprise that, over time, out-of-home group care of children acquired a mystique of its own. On the one hand the public was relieved that there were places to put unwanted, damaged, and difficult children while, on the other, it clung to the belief that institutional care at best was static and more often than not led to deterioration.

Several developments allowed for some revision of this thinking. Pioneering efforts in the care of the institutionalized retardate demonstrated that sufficient social and habit training can bring about a return of many individuals into the community (Boggs and Jervis, 1966). When better environmental conditions were substituted for inadequate home care, sickly children convalesced with greater speed and better results. Moreover the type and quality of nurturance by surrogate parents determined the effectiveness of placement rather than nutrients, cleanliness, or routines per se. The better the opportunities for a warm and continuing relationship with a significant caretaker, the more likely was the child's chance of approximating healthy growth under conditions of group care (Bowlby, 1953; Spitz, 1965).

Since an institution is not as "natural" a caretaker unit as the family, other placement modalities were bound to come into vogue. With the realization—buttressed by scientific study—that a continuing attachment is the foundation of the child's emotional well-being, the family was perceived to be the best vehicle for providing this relationship. Child placement in families, wherever such transmigration had to occur, upheld the principle that optimal socialization is rooted in the exclusiveness of firm mutual attachments between parental adults and the dependent young. The earlier the child begins this relationship the tighter the bond. In multiple placements the risk of less than adequate emotional involvement with others increases. For this reason adoption is now believed to be most desirable at birth, or even before birth. In short-term placements where parents are temporarily incapable of carrying out their child care role, foster family care is offered. Here special arrangements are made to cultivate the ties to the family of origin to the fullest extent possible. Should the child's own family be incapable of reconstituting itself for longer periods, then the foster home is expected to pick up the functions of the primary caregiver.

In time the impetus to keep children out of institutions and in families resulted in the virtual disappearance of foundling homes and orphanages in the Western World. However, in their place emerged different types of residential group facilities for those children who were unsuited for foster care, who could not adjust to foster-family life, and who seemed to gain more from living in a social environment less emotionally demanding than the family. Most of these centers accommodated problem children from broken homes, either because the parents resisted foster-family care for their children or because there had been already one or more failures in adjustment to life in foster families. Some of these homes, centers, and hospitals specialized in working with handicapped and disturbed children for whom they organized rehabilitative and therapeutic programs. Custodial care in hospitals or schools was limited to the most mentally disabled children who could not live at home (Hylton, 1964).

For delinquent and incorrigible youth the responsibility has been vested principally in state schools which, in addition to affording protection to the child and to the community from the consequences of antisocial behavior, may provide some educational and therapeutic assistance to its residents. Usually, the juveniles are placed under Court aegis and ordinarily experience the placement as punishment for their misdeeds. Rather than to maintain large groups of children in one place, the trend has been for decentralizing care in clusters of cottages or in scattered small-group homes, thus minimizing the penal aspect of their segregation.

Economic necessity and equality of the sexes, that is both parents working and seeking substitute supervision for their children, led to the development of additional resources. Partial rather than total removal of a child from his family came to be practiced through the device of communal group care (Rabin, 1965), day care centers (Caldwell and Richmond, 1965), day foster homes (Edwards, 1968), and day treatment (LaVietes et al., 1960). Under the conditions of such programming, the compensatory and remedial impact of the experience on troubled children can be made significant without necessitating the disruption of family life. Often the family can be worked with also to modify itself in collaboration with changes occurring in the child. Moreover, the community's resources and its commitment to the spectrum of childhood problems are more likely to grow to an optimal effort if the children remain a visible part of the social landscape.

What are the indications, clinical and otherwise, for rearranging the physical life space of children? Sometimes necessity dictates the decision, e.g. in adoption, whereas at other times there is considerable latitude in decision making. It is possible to categorize three rationales for therapeutic environmental intervention. The child is placed essentially for one or more of the following purposes: (1) He is in need of protection; (2) he requires emotionally corrective experience; (3) he can benefit from training not available to him in his home or community.

PROTECTING THE CHILD

Most custodial arrangements, legal commitments, detentions, and correctional remands are protective in that they serve to keep the child and the community from harm. Unwanted, neglected, and abused children usually require foster care, at least during a crisis. Runaway children need shelter. Aggressive and destructive children may benefit from the security of a detention center. Delinquents often do better if removed from a seductive or socially bankrupt environment. In all such instances a more suitable setting is substituted for one considered insufficient to carry out certain essential requirements of care, particularly supervision, over varying time periods. However, little if any attention may be paid in such settings to the psychological and interpersonal problems of the child. The hope is that the new experience will also prove to be corrective because the children have been removed from the offending factors.

Adoption

Of all placements the adoptive one stands as the paradigm of the protective impulse toward the unattached young. A child born into circumstances that do not give him legitimacy or the security of being wanted becomes a prime candidate for adoption—a legal, social, and psychological process of transferring the right of possession of the child. Parents may choose to relinquish their claim upon a child or may be found unsuitable to exercise their rights in relation to the child. About 1% of all children in the United States are thought to be adopted by nonrelatives (Madison, 1966).

Adoption is the legal means to assure that the illegitimate and unwanted children have an opportunity to be members of a family where they can learn the tasks of living and of maturation toward a self-sustaining adulthood. The child's psychological need for continuity of a relationship with loving parents is hereby protected. Most adopted children are not dislodged from a primary emotional tie since the majority of cases occur with legitimization of placements with relatives or by acquiring a stepfather.

"Common-law adoptive parent-child relationship" (Goldstein et al., 1973) designates those experiential ties that arise out of casual, nonlegal or foster care arrangements that have become long term. Children left with relatives, friends, or foster parents may find themselves in mutual attachments to surrogate parents indistinguishable from relationships characterizing bonds to biological parents.

In *Beyond the Best Interests of the Child*, Goldstein et al. (1973) offer several broad guidelines for adoptive placements. The authors believe that the preadoptive waiting period should be held to a minimum and that the legal sanctions become operative the moment the child is placed with the family. Thus the placement is considered as "final" so that revocation of the adoption could be initiated only by abuse, neglect, or abandonment.

Since the placement of older children presents more problems, adoption often arouses turmoil in both child and parents. The older child, aware of his history, must contend with feelings of split loyalties, name change, and shifting identifications. For the parents, there is self-doubt as the older, and therefore more ambivalent child, is less likely to confirm their adequacy than is the responsive infant or toddler. With older children the chances are greater that they experienced early deprivation, are handicapped, are multiracial, and are "hard to place" for behavioral reasons, further compounding the psychological hardship of the participants. As fewer babies are born, the adoption of older children with problems gains new importance.

Case A

The adoption of an 8-month old boy, born out of wedlock and surrendered by his mother, had been delayed because he had experienced marked neonatal distress. At the time of birth spontaneous respiration was absent as a result of cord compression and was associated with meconium stained placental fluid. The infant was incubated for purposes of artificial respiration. At 8 minutes after birth he was still flaccid but then gained good color and heart tones within the hour. Several seizures were observed shortly after birth, presumably related to hypoglycemia. A small left pneumothorax was noted. The child's hypoactivity, hypotonia, and weak reflexes persisted through the neonatal period. He was placed on phenobarbital in appropriate doses to protect against convulsions and, after 16 days, was discharged from the hospital's special care nursery to a foster home as a normal newborn child. There had been a weight gain of 11 ounces from a birth weight of 5.5 pounds.

Despite his early difficulties, he developed adequately. At his 1-month follow up examination, he was found to be active and alert. Phenobarbital was gradually discontinued. However, because of the atypical birth history, a cautious prognostic statement was included in the physician's report which postponed the search for an adoptive home. When the child continued to make progress without further evidence of central nervous system damage, an adoptive placement was deemed feasible with parents who could accept the potential for future risk such as a learning disability or epilepsy.

Case B

For the first 5 years of this boy's life, several moves in foster care had to be arranged because he was very demanding of attention and would punch, bite, or scratch if thwarted. At 16 months the removal of an eye for a suspected malignancy had resulted in considerable alarm in his caretakers about the potential loss of vision in the remaining eye. He had reacted with behavior problems to these events. Since he had been released for adoption, a permanent home was sought for him. Before this was accomplished he had to be fitted for a prosthesis, which delayed the adoption process. After a year of visiting with his prospective adoptive parents, the adoption was finalized when he was 6 years old. He soon exhibited serious behavior problems necessitating several years of therapy with the family in a child guidance clinic.

Foster Homes

When the state, county, or local private social agency places a child in a family for bed and board, the status of foster care attaches to the child. The terms of foster care generally are contractual and relate to financial payment to foster parents as well as to the services required. The child is to be cared for physically, emotionally, educationally, and morally. Various day-by-day arrangements concerning visits from biological parents, allowance, recreational activities, health, and counseling are supervised by social agency representatives. The assumption remains that the child is not released for adoption by his biological parents and that he may be returned to them if conditions warrant a restoration of the presumably primary relationship. This may occur if the situational, psychological, or legal reasons for placement have moderated or have been corrected. Foster care is arranged by governmental or private agencies when parents request such a service for sufficient reason, e.g. the breakup of the family due to lack of living space, illness, separation, emotional inadequacy, or death of a parent; and when intervention is called for if parental action or inaction endangers the well-being of children, e.g. abuse, neglect, and abandonment. Wherever possible siblings are placed together in order to protect the familiarity of existing emotional ties. Since most children return to their homes, the continuity of the relationship to parents is safeguarded by encouraging visits with a regularity that allows the child to remember his parents while simultaneously accommodating to a foster family. That this is fraught with many problems is self-evident. On the one hand the parents question whether they can retain an emotional beachhead with their child while, on the other, the foster parents withhold from making a deep emotional penetration with the foster child who, more often than not, finds himself in a psychological no-man's land. To minimize the problems social workers in the placement agencies try to help both sets of parents and the child to recognize some of the conflictual predicaments of their positions. Their fondest aim is to be able to work out with them a routine that is least damaging to the child and is acceptable to all adult parties involved.

From time to time such routines need to be modified as conditions change. In transient foster home placements the tenuousness of the relationship requires the participants to maintain a measured distance from each other, although the adults must remain open to the child's concerns. Concurrently, the involvement with parents or with a worker is expected to be more intense in order to keep the child aware of and tied to his previous attachments.

By contrast, in long-term placements the child should have an opportunity to develop ties to foster parents that will allow the latter to become his "psychological parents."

Case C

A young woman requested foster care for her newborn daughter because she could not bring another out-of-wedlock child into her parents' home. She refused to release the child for adoption. As soon as the baby gave evidence of making a good adjustment to the foster family, the mother asked for her return. Counseling with the mother attempted to prepare her for the difficulties encountered in the transfer of affection at this stage in the child's life. Planned visits were arranged for a 3-month period to strengthen mutual attachments between the girl and her mother.

Case D

A 7-year-old boy had been in a foster home since age 3 because his mother frequently had behaved abusively toward him. During episodes of agitation and depression she screamed at the child, struck him without provocation, pulled his hair, or alternately lavished profuse affection upon him. Although she was vehemently opposed to adoption, she consented to have him placed in care. Psychiatric treatment of the mother, including hospitalization, did not appreciably alter her tendency to create crisis situations, but it supported her sufficiently to enable her to strive for vocational self-improvement. After placement of the boy she acquired a high school certificate, was employed, and enrolled in secretarial courses during evenings. A year later she married, only to start up a hostile relationship with her new husband. Because she was afraid that she would resume her assaultive behavior on the child if he were to return into her household, she asked that he continue to be maintained in the foster home.

Case E

When she was 3 years of age, this 15 year old's mother, sister, and brother succumbed in a fire. The father deserted her some 3 years later. She was passed from one relative to another as behavior problems arose. In her early teens she was placed in a juvenile detention facility for repeated running away from the home of an aunt. Subsequently she was placed in a foster home since the relatives, not having established legal guardianship, felt free to withdraw from exercising responsibility for this girl. The felt rejection made it difficult for her to accept a foster family so that a group placement loomed most attractive as an alternative. In the long run, supportive treatment strengthened her capacity for trust in the foster parents who showed much warmth and understanding.

Special foster homes are considered for those children who as a result of behavioral or physical problems require more personalized attention, compensatory care, or close supervision. For some the fact of being the only child or having a small sibship is salutory. When early deprivation was pronounced, or when organic factors such as minimal brain damage are present, the ensuing handicaps demand more than the usual habilitative effort from adults. For the neglected child much nurturance is necessary if he is to develop trust in the adult's capacity for caring. Defective and unsocialized children need to be taught routines that train them for a more effective and reasonable interaction with their world. Aggressive and destructive children look to control agents who are nonpunitive yet firm, are authoritative yet available. In its essentials, the special foster home is a child-centered, habilitative family.

Case F

This infant girl was placed temporarily in foster care at birth because the mother did not wish to bring her second out-of-wedlock child home to the grandmother. The placement lasted 6 months, when the mother requested her return. When the child was 16 months the mother asked a child care agency to put the daughter into a foster home because she feared she might harm the girl.

In the foster home, the child appeared to be functioning on a regressed level. She refused to walk or to use her hands for purposive action. She constantly pulled at her fingers, opened and closed cupboards, dug into her skin until she drew blood, and knocked over chairs. Moreover, she was demanding of the foster mother's attention and cried incessantly if denied physical contact. After awhile the foster mother, who had to care for several children, could not cope with the demands of this child and asked for her immediate removal. A special home was found where the pressure of competition for the mother was minimized. The problem behavior gradually waned in this home.

As more mothers have entered the work force and as one-parent families are on the rise, it has become necessary to consider partial placements of children, that is day or night care. In order to approximate the family life style for infants and toddlers or for those with special problems, selected foster homes are used on a day basis while the biological parents pursue vocational or other objectives.

Most children in these circumstances are placed in day care centers (or night centers) rather than day homes, as these are more readily available and also give the older preschool child a group experience. For older children the day care center must augment school before and after regular classroom hours through supervision of social activities. In selected cases such arrangements may be carried out for reasons quite different from economic ones, such as offering relief to immature or overwhelmed parents and enriching the experiences of disadvantaged children.

Case G

An 18-month-old boy was placed into a day care family at the request of his parents so that the mother could work to support them while her husband attended school. As a consequence of the mother's overanxious and ambivalent attitude toward her son he was manifestly immature and slow in his development. For example, she was still feeding him as if he were an infant so that he made no attempt to put food into his mouth. In the day care home the child made immediate behavioral gains but would regress after spending the weekend with his parents. Efforts to assist the mother in taking a more realistic attitude toward the boy were rebuffed, although the father acquired more confidence in his role vis-a-vis his son.

Group care of children who maintain affective ties to parents was developed in the farm collectives (kibbutz movement) of Israel as a means of maximizing the participation of its members in the economic life of the community. In isolated instances, some communal arrangements of this type have sprung up recently in the United States, indicative of the continuing modification in child care methods (Eiduson et al., 1973).

Group Homes

If fostering children family-style fails or if it is considered inappropriate, placement in a variety of group settings becomes an alternative. Children's homes, boarding schools, and admixtures of both dot the landscape to attest to the fallibility of home care for some children. The majority of these residential facilities are designed for older children and adolescents who are in one or more of several categories. For example, some parents may prefer a group over a family placement for their children. They argue that if they were unable to succeed with a child in the family setting, no other like method is suitable. Then again, there seem to be children who, because of a low tolerance for intimacy, benefit from the dilution of cathexis more prevalent in group care. Others need geographic distancing from family and friends as a form of social control when they cannot defend themselves in any other way against provocative influences. Among them may be those children who have already exhausted several foster homes before arriving in a residential children's home. Finally, for the specially handicapped who can receive the unique educational and social rehabilitation they require only in distant boarding schools, leaving family is a hardship that they must bear in order to cope better with their defects, e.g. blindness, deafness, retardation, and brain damage.

The majority of these facilities are privately run and are therefore in a position to screen out candidates whom they deem unsuitable for their programs. Some are open settings, in that their residents use community resources such as public schools, whereas others are self-contained in most respects. The choice of setting depends on many factors, the most central being the child's adaptability to a more or less structured and protected environment. Obviously, tolerance of the open setting, although not the only criterion, is the most relevant factor in selecting such a setting. Additional considerations are the age of the child, the availability of resources, the cost, and the nature of the child's problems. Private institutions are loath to admit those with a history of firesetting, repeated running away, sexual deviance, or significant behavior difficulties. By decentralizing large settings into small group homes, it has become possible to broaden the admission criteria while offering a more personal and less institutional mode of living for these children. Some communities have set up centers exclusively for runaways in order to offer a protective environment that will also mediate the youngster's return home (Butler et al., 1974).

Case H

For the first 12 years of his life, this asthmatic boy was closely attached to his mother. The youngest of four children whose only brother was in the Marine Corps, he started to exhibit negative leadership qualities among peers at school and in his neighborhood for which the family became involved in out-patient therapy. When the parents learned of their son's participation in several predelinquent episodes of trespassing, vandalism, school absenteeism, and petty thievery, they asked that a residential placement be considered. The boy, too, believed that he needed time away from home in order to prove himself capable of maturing more independently. His thirteenth year was spent in a private children's home at a distance from his community which still allowed for weekend commuting. He attended public school there and did not show any of the problem behaviors that led to his separation from home. During his absence the mother continued to be counseled so that, on the youth's return, the previous overprotectiveness might be ameliorated. That the mother had been able to let the child go in the first place demonstrated her genuine concern for his well-being.

For youth who come into conflict with the law either through nonconforming or delinquent behavior, the courts may consider placement if other alternatives have foundered or if removal from home becomes necessary for protective reasons. Juvenile or Family Courts can utilize both private and public facilities for young offenders. Among the public resources are correctional institutions or state training schools, youth homes, camps, and vocational training centers. A decision for placement by a judge is based on the probation officer's investigation of the complaint against the child and of the several options open for disposition. In this situation, too, the Court's bias favors retention of the child in his family and in his community. An unfavorable home environment that is not subject to modification, and/or behavior problems in the child that would be criminal acts if in an adult, together represent the prime reasons for judicially sanctioned placements.

Case I

A 15-year-old youth of average intelligence, the adopted and only child of a suburban family, came to the court's attention for arson. Already at age 5, his affinity for playing with fire and for stealing had led to a psychiatric referral. He had to be removed from kindergarten because he was immature and lacked self-control. Hospitalization had occurred at age 6 months under conditions of relative isolation while he was treated for whooping cough over a period of 3 months. His parents had never informed him of his adoptive status.

The mother had suffered from an unhappy childhood with an alcoholic father and a harsh mother. Upon leaving home at age 18 she never returned to see her parents. In turn she was punitive, rigid, and controlling with this son. The father played a negligible role in his life. After being placed on probation, the boy again set a fire and was ordered to a state training facility for delinquent youth.

Case J

After repeated episodes of truanting and running away from home, during which this 15-year-old girl of normal intellectual capacity was picked up for public intoxication and shoplifting, court intervention was sought. Counseling with the family had failed to have an impact on the girl's actions. A younger brother also gave evidence of behavior problems. Both parents were plagued by a history of alcoholism. The father's employment record was most uneven. As a result of the maternal grandmother's promiscuity and drinking, the mother had spent many years in foster care. Paternal grandparents separated after much discord when the father was an adolescent. With the parents' agreement the girl was court committed to a private residential facility for predelinquent juveniles.

Case K

When this 15-year-old girl, the youngest of six children, resorted to a physical assault on the mother, the latter turned to the court for help in placement. Prior to this request there had been longstanding difficulty in the mother's relationship to this daughter as well as to her other children. She had been unable to supervise them effectively subsequent to the father's death from a heart attack some 7 years previously. Poor school attendance, association with undesirable companions, unauthorized absences from home, and delinquent behavior such as trespass and shoplifting had already led to prior court petitions on behalf of the girl. Because the family history offered little assurance that meaningful parental control would be forthcoming, even with counseling which had been tried over a 2-year span, she was placed in a structured-community group residence for girls.

A small number of youth find their way into state hospitals through involuntary commitment when the nature of their behavior suggests endangerment of self or others. Presumably the security of a closed setting where personnel is also accustomed to dealing with aberrant behavior, prompts such a step for poorly controlled children who require therapy.

Case L

A 13-year-old boy came to the Court's attention for repeated fire setting at home or in its vicinity. On psychiatric examination he spoke of a compelling need to set a fire each time he had a dream of burying his mother. This dream had become a nightly occurrence. The mother was in the habit of taking him frequently to the cemetery to tend the gravesites of two sons who had died in infancy. Moreover, the household of parents and six children was disorganized and in constant conflict with neighbors. Because the boy was disturbed and posed a real threat to his family and to himself, he was admitted to the adolescent unit of the local state hospital for protection and treatment.

HEALING THE CHILD

The great majority of placements under psychiatric aegis take place for reasons other than protective custody. Children are referred for inpatient care to hospital mental health services or to residential treatment centers in the hope of better resolving their difficulties in a controlled therapeutic milieu (Reid and Hagan, 1952; Robinson, 1957). Removal from home of the disturbed child must be sanctioned by parents or parent surrogates. Recently children's rights in these and other matters have come under increasing scrutiny (Joint Commission on Mental Health of Children, 1969).

Residential Care

Young children are referred for residential care if the nature of their disturbance precludes outpatient treatment and if the family's tolerance for the problematic behavior has been stretched beyond endurance. Severe conduct disorders and psychotic manifestations are the prime indicators for considering this placement alternative. In adolescence suicide attempts and serious drug abuse are additional cause for hospitalization.

One prominent treatment orientation in residential children's centers has been based on psychoanalytic principles. If the assumption is held that childhood conflict arises because the child is unable to fend off successfully noxious parenting or to defend appropriately against threats from within, then an environment that is nurturant and permissive could be expected to assuage hurt as well as permit an understanding of his behavior (Bettelheim, 1950). This method encouraged children to regress behaviorally in surroundings deemed safe and accepting of them, no matter what emerged, so that corrective emotional experiences could be introduced into the treatment regimen. Thus the treatment unit becomes "the safe center of their lives, to whose security they can return from excursions into the outside world, and within whose walls they have the feeling that nothing really bad can happen" (Bettelheim, 1955). Parents and relatives are excluded in some places. Here, the belief is strong about the bad effect of their intrusiveness and about the importance of the institution for developing the child's capacity to withstand future stresses. The Sonia Shankman Orthogenic School of the University of Chicago has been in the forefront of those institutions that consider the management of the children's emotional life as of paramount importance: ". . . tolerance and even temporary encouragement of asocial or regressive tendencies often take preference over the encouragement of academic progress. In respect to sex behavior, verbal expressions, orderliness and cleanliness, polite conventions yield to emotional honesty. Protection of property takes second place to emotional needs" (Bettelheim, 1955). Nonetheless, the ultimate aim is to improve socialization where a well-organized program hopes "to strengthen the child to such a degree that he is able, by himself, to master adverse circumstances with relative success" (Bettelheim, 1955). Most treatment units incorporate aspects of this philosophy but see the therapeutic needs of the child in a somewhat broader perspective. For example, counseling with parents or even treating them as members of a disturbed psychosocial unit is standard procedure in all but a few instances (Goldfarb, 1961).

Hospitalization

Bender (1952) writes about a multicausal etiology contributing to the hospitalization of children. Commonly found are one or several of the following factors:

1. Early inadequate or distorted child-parent relationship.
2. Early emotional-social deprivation and discontinuities in relation to mother or mother surrogate.
3. Early environmental stresses due to hazards of minority status such as economic insecurity, conflicts in identification with family and group, lack of privileges, and problems with language.

4. Special deficits of intellect and communication.

5. Organic and pathologic states such as encephalopathies and schizophrenias.

Because the children are considered afflicted by environmental deficits, personal impairments, or both, their therapeutic needs ought to be met with reparative and constructive techniques. A child-adult relationship on some realistic basis is the rockbed upon which are built opportunities for further growth. Group experiences with contemporaries under the guiding direction of trusted adults keep children attuned to a larger world in which they must share. At the same time they need opportunities for the projection, formulation, or living out of the inner fantasy life by means of projective or play techniques and to experiment "by trial and error with new formulations of personality mechanisms and conflicts" (Bender, 1952). In order to build up the child's intellectual, motor, and language patterns, he must be taught techniques of acting, feeling, thinking and living. Bender believes that a well-established daily pattern of routines based on the child's biological rhythms and those of his surroundings serves to harness the scattered energies of troubled children into a more cohesive adaptive response system. In order to achieve these objectives, she states that it is necessary to have a well-organized unit where the entire program is arranged as a model of realistic expectations with school, recreation, ward routine, and housekeeping activities an integral part of the treatment milieu. The presence of a sensitive staff, adequate in numbers and in training, is mandatory for implementation of a program that should include group discussions and other group interactions; all types of play outlets in graphic and plastic arts; and participation in music, puppetry, and drama. Individual play therapy, utilizing the range of available techniques, may add significantly to the child's awareness of himself and of others. Medical therapies, particularly chemotherapy, when judiciously applied, make the anxious or disorganized child more accessible to environmental treatment, individual therapy, remedial tutoring, language training, and other modalities that impinge on him.

Case M

After two years of psychiatric outpatient care, including day treatment, for this 7-year-old boy and his parents, a residential program was considered to be a necessary condition of his care. The boy was impulsive, verbally and physically assaultive, excessively distractible, and only minimally responsive to the range of therapeutic efforts used in his behalf.

He had been adopted by this elderly couple who had been childless, after their niece abandoned him to their care. They were ineffectual and superstitious people, afraid to set limits for fear of overreacting with rage to the provocative behavior of this child. Only a removal from the ambivalent nature of the family environment and the substitution of a more ordered experience for the inconsistent one seemed to offer hope that the boy would eventually learn to internalize some controls.

Ultimately the children are expected to return home. Those services located in general hospitals seek to expedite the young patient's reunion with his family as quickly as possible. If the likelihood of a more normal life setting cannot be so readily achieved, a longer stay in public or private children's facilities may be arranged. Of these, units in state hospitals tend to receive the more damaged children who require extensive habilitation. Private psychiatric hospitals and residential schools are more likely to select for intensive treatment programs those disturbed youngsters who have a better prognosis. The cost of hospital and residential school have made this avenue of help a choice of last resort, even when out-of-home placement is thought to be desirable.

TRAINING THE CHILD

Some residential settings give a different emphasis to their program in that they define the rehabilitative efforts almost exclusively in educational and social rather than in exclusively psychotherapeutic terms. They propose to train or retrain children who have been subjected to deficient or faulty learning. This reconstructionist strategy is one which in the briefest time necessary works toward specific, concrete goals. It engages the child's energies toward task orientation, teaches him skills, and modifies his native system to which he must return. Educational programming, behavior management at the symptomatic level, and structured social systems are designed to bring learning and organization into the child's life. Sequential learning experiences are introduced in a systematized manner with the goal of teaching problem-solving skills and acceptable role performance. Discrete handicaps in reading or language are remediated with the use of appropriate conditioning methods, e.g. rewards of food or by means of a token economy system. Presumably, as the child's coping capacity enlarges he will have less need of maladaptive behaviors. Moreover, the structured milieu can be manipulated to help children explore and learn from the consequences of behavior in a fairly predictable social setting.

Case N

Despite good intelligence, this 12-year-old boy had not learned to read. A number of remedial efforts, such as special classes, tutoring, and family counseling had failed to have an impact on this symptom, which was at least partially ascribable to a perceptual handicap. Unable to satisfy himself or his parents, he was on bad terms with both teachers and parents. He began to smoke and drink, stayed out late at night, and quickly threatened to be beyond parental control. A residential school that specializes in working with learning disabled children who have associated behavior problems was believed to be the most appropriate resource for the boy, both for interfering with a deteriorating situation and for offering reeducational procedures.

Residential Programs

Project Re-ED (Lewis, 1967) was established to test the feasibility of a brief, high-impact residential treatment program for emotionally disturbed children by providing an engaging goal-oriented education climate during all of a child's waking hours and keeping him related to his natural environment both by weekends at home and by careful liaison with that environment. After an average stay of 6 to 7 months the way would be prepared for the child to return home. While at the Re-ED school a group of eight children between ages 6 to 12 and two teachers trained in teaching, recreation, camping, physical education and crafts use the brief stay "to get into reasonably functioning order the circumscribed social system of which the child is an essential part" (Hobbs, 1964). The teacher-counselors are backed by psychiatrists, psychologists, social workers, pediatricians, and curriculum specialists who function in a consultant role. When the system reaches a level of functioning where possibility of success outweighs the probability of a bad outcome, the child is returned home. There may be a little improvement across the board or a singular advance on one front. In either case if the change has made the system operational for the child he is considered to have benefited sufficiently to warrant reintegration in mainstream education.

Analogous residential programming exists in several European countries where professional youth workers known as educateurs, orthopedagogues or psychagogues utilize crafts, vocational, and recreational activities to gain a close personal relationship with a group of 10 to 12 troubled children. All of the daily time outside of formal school hours is utilized by the educateur and is carefully planned for in terms of the child's needs and interests. The educateur involves himself totally with his group of children, finds jobs for them, contacts their teachers, and follows through in most respects like a parent surrogate (Linton, 1969). Therefore he serves in a deliberate and trained manner as an object for identification and often is the central and dominant figure in the child's life. As such he is the key in the reeducation and resocialization of the maladjusted child.

Some treatment units have been designed particularly for special categories of disorders, e.g. childhood autism, learning disabilities, or delinquency. What they have in common is a well-organized life space where the ordinary daily activities and routines bring order into the child's existence, where overstimulation is avoided, and where constructive channeling of energies is advocated (May and May, 1959).

Although the previous ideologies have dominated the environmental usages for corrective intervention with troubled children, there is considerable overlap in program execution. Children removed from home, for whatever reason or amount of time, offer some respite to parents. Therapeutic group treatment includes some use of social process and schooling as a rehabilitative tool. Even the most routinized systems approaches must include opportunities for relationships with surrogate parents to be meaningful. It is the special mix of the clinical ingredients, often irrespective of the prevailing philosophy propounded, that gives each program its particular character. Nonetheless, there is good reason to consider differences in program for the special needs of youth so that effectiveness and cost can be compared for various categories of problems. Out-of-home placement, by its very nature, is an expensive undertaking requiring sound justification for its utility and relevance to special youngsters.

Day Programs

For reason of cost, but also for quite sound clinical purposes, the partial removal of the child from the home has grown into an important treatment adjunct in recent years. Communities, having learned that extrafamilial institutions could function as surrogate child caretakers, have developed day programs for those youngsters who can not be managed in the usual manner or whose handicaps require special care. Moreover, parents often function better if a troubled child is not totally their responsibility and burden. Pre-school children from impoverished families needed enriching experiences on a systematic basis, such as offered by Project Head Start, in order to slow down the consequences of the depriving or disorganizing environment and, with luck, instill an interest in school.

Child Development Services

The Project Head Start Child Development Center, as a community facility, emphasizes that the family is fundamental to the child's development. Therefore it encourages parents to play a role formulating Center policies and to participate in its programs. In addition to widening the education horizon, the aims of the Center emphasize therapeutic elements in its acculturation goals, e.g. that the child "grow in ability to channel inner, destructive impulses—to turn aggression into hard work, talk instead of hit, understand the difference between feeling angry and acting angry, feel sympathy for the troubles of others" (Office of Economic Opportunity, 1967).

Case 0

A 4-year-old girl, the youngest of six children of a poor inner city family living in a three-bedroom apartment, was an unusually somber child. The parents' expectation for their children was that they play quietly at home. Much time was spent watching television without verbal interaction between parents and children. Their lives were structured in a way to limit interaction and imaginative play.

A visit from a public health nurse led to a discussion of the parents' wishes for their children. One step taken in helping to bring about a less stultifying climate was to have them enroll the little girl in a nearby Head Start Nursery where she gradually learned to talk and play more freely with the other children.

Day Treatment Services

While residential care was less and less considered a necessity for some of the most disturbed children and child guidance treatment insufficient for others, the hole in the spectrum of services became identifiable as day treatment. The 1950s saw the introduction of day programs for schizophrenic and other seriously disturbed children (Fenichel and Freedman, 1960; LaVietes et al., 1960). LaVietes and co-workers (1965), in describing their experiences with a psychiatric day treatment center and school for young children excluded from school, made five assumptions for justifying the substitution of partial modification of the environment for total removal from home:

1. On the whole, keeping the child at home is the lesser of two difficult and costly routes.

2. Early intervention prevents or at least ameliorates later problems.

3. Only when parents are interested and sufficiently cooperative can children profit from day treatment.

4. Rehabilitation must include treatment of the child, treatment of the parents, and therapeutic education.

5. For the psychiatrically ill child, the clinical teacher is the principal change agent on the mental health team.

Hospitalization or other group placements have disadvantages such as the traumatization of separation, the alienation of the child from his family, the danger of institutional accommodation, the inconvenience of placement at great distances from home, and the large cost of maintenance. The principal objectives of transitional services, of which day treatment is one type, are one of maintenance in the community and of improvement of functioning.

An example of such a service can be found in the Day Treatment Unit of the Rochester Mental Health Center, Children and Youth Division (Gold and Reisman, 1970; Halpern, 1970), where school-excluded, disturbed children ages 3 to 12 are enrolled in an intensive psychoeducational program. The child's return to mainstream education is the ultimate aim. Broadly speaking, the unit admits those children for whom all resources in the home school districts have been exhausted, whose upper limit for intellectual development is potentially above the moderately retarded category, and whose parents will involve themselves with the program on at least a nominal level. Structuring of the "school day" is the primary tool for introducing a predictable order into the lives of these children who, in the main, come from disorganized environments or who do not possess the integrative mechanisms important to normal processing of sensory inputs. The severity of their disturbances can be judged by the observation that the majority of this population would have been considered good candidates for long-term residential care two decades ago.

Case P

A 3-year-old boy with strabismus was referred to a pediatric neurologist for medical treatment of hyperactivity associated with minimal brain dysfunction. Clinical examination and psychological testing revealed that the child was of possibly average intellectual potential but that his behavioral and language difficulties allowed him to function only on a borderline defective level. In addition, he had a sufficient degree of mixed hearing losses to warrant a hearing aid.

In order to help the mother care for this multihandicapped child she was included in a treatment group of mothers whose children were enrolled in a special nursery. Once the boy reached kindergarten age he was accepted in the all-day school program of a day treatment service in a community mental health center because he remained too distractible and impulsive to be manageable in the special classes of the public school system.

Case Q

The mother of a 7-year-old girl who had been born out of wedlock applied for treatment because the daughter engaged in lying, stealing, and sexual activities with boys. Much of the time the mother did not know the child's whereabouts.

Between the second and fifth year of life the girl had been reared by the maternal grandmother who could no longer cope with her soon after entry into school. At this time primary care was returned to the mother who previously had discharged her parental duties only on weekends. A brother 1 year younger than herself had remained with their working mother and a babysitter. The latter soon tired of looking after both children, particularly when the girl was suspended from school for behavior problems. Although the mother enjoyed working she had to give it up in order to provide supervision to the daughter. Increasingly, the mother vented her frustrations on the child, often by striking out physically.

When the school referred the family to a community mental health center the child was deemed appropriate for inclusion in the school program of its day treatment unit.

Although based on the engineered classroom model (Hewett, 1967), the Day Treatment Unit has broadened the concept of learning for severely disturbed children to include language training for small groups of autistic children (Halpern, 1970) as well as for individual children (Halpern et al., 1973). The curriculum includes the whole gamut of teaching modalities and socializing tactics that can be fit into the available timetable in a controlled fashion. Trust in the adults is nurtured by a conscious adherence to regularity, clarity, safety, order, and predictability. Close collaboration with parents is arranged through regular contacts in groups and individually. Exclusion of parents from direct participation in the day treatment of their children rests on the premise that the environment would be more difficult to control in their presence. However, they are invited to observe the classroom activities regularly through one-way viewing screens as part of the parent guidance program. They gain a great deal from the mutual support they can give to each other in groups as well as receive respite from their disturbed children who are in the program for a great part of the day. Some programs report benefits from including parents as auxillary staff (Doernberg et al., 1969; Halpern et al., 1971).

In a few decades the recognition that environmental influences have a significant role to play in the appearance of pathologic childhood behavior has been supplanted by the belief that environmental modifiers can also be potent, preventive, and therapeutic agents if carefully applied. In an overview of environmental intervention models a rich spectrum of methodologies is discernible. On the one hand the basic family unit is substituted by surrogate care systems including adoption, foster care, group homes, and residential centers. On the other the family is altered through augmenting the child's experiences or through partial replacement of unfavorable with favorable experiences. These two care categories match the demands for services of problems and types of disorders not susceptible to the usual outpatient treatment methods. In all likelihood this area will continue to undergo changes in philosophy as community psychiatry comes into its own, as newer techniques emerge, and as cost accounting effects the nature of the mental health delivery system. Institutional or residential treatment of children along traditional lines may well be increasingly deemphasized while costs increase and other alternatives emerge.

REFERENCES

Bender, L. *Child Psychiatric Techniques: Diagnostic and Therapeutic Approach to Normal and Abnormal Development Through Patterned, Expressive, and Group Behavior*. Springfield, Ill.: Charles C. Thomas, 1952.

Bettelheim, B. *Love is Not Enough: The Treatment of Emotionally Disturbed Children*. Glencoe, Ill.: The Free Press, 1950.

Bettelheim, B. *Truants From Life: The Rehabilitation of Emotionally Disturbed Children*. Glencoe, Ill.: The Free Press, 1955.

Boggs, E. M. & Jervis, G. A. Care and management of the retarded. In S. Arieti (Ed.), *American Handbook of Psychiatry*, Vol. 3, New York: Basic Books, 1966.

Bowlby, J. *Maternal Care and Mental Health*. Geneva: WHO Technical Monograph Series, No. 2, 1951.

Butler, D., Reiner, J. & Treanor, B. *Runaway House: A Youth-Run Service Project*. National Institute of Mental Health, Washington, D.C.: U.S. Government Printing Office, 1974.

Caldwell, B. M. & Richmond, J. B. Programmed day care for the very young child. *Child Welfare*, **44**, 134–142, 1965.

Doernberg, N., Rosen, B. & Walker, T. T. *A Home Training Program for Young Mentally Ill Children*. Brooklyn, N. Y.: League School for Seriously Disturbed Children, 1969.

Edwards, E. Family day care in a community action program. *Children*, **15**, 55–58, 1968.

Eiduson, B. R., Cohen, J. & Alexander, J. Alternatives in child rearing in the 1970's. *American Journal of Orthopsychiatry*, **43**, 720–731, 1973.

Eisenberg, L. Child psychiatry: The past quarter century. *American Journal of Orthopsychiatry*, **39**, 389–401, 1969.

Fenichel, C., Freedman, A. M. & Klapper, Z. A day school for schizophrenic children. *American Journal of Orthopsychiatry*, **30**, 130–143, 1960.

Fernald, W. E. Growth of the provision for the feeble-minded in the U.S., *Mental Hygiene*, **1**, 34–59, 1917.

Gold, J. & Reisman, J. M. An outcome study of a day treatment unit school in a community mental health center (Abstract). *American Journal of Orthopsychiatry*, **40**, 286–287, 1970.

Goldfarb, W. The mutual impact of mother and child in childhood schizophrenia. *American Journal of Orthopsychiatry*, **31**, 738–747, 1961.

Goldstein, J., Freud, A. & Solnit, A. J. *Beyond the Best Interests of the Child*. New York: The Free Press, 1973.

Halpern, W. I. The schooling of autistic children: Preliminary findings. *American Journal of Orthopsychiatry*, **40**, 665–671, 1970.

Halpern, W. I., Arkins, V., Hammond, J. & Gold, J. Working with parents of psychotic children. *Bulletin of the Rochester Mental Health Center*, **3**, 35–42, 1971.

Halpern, W. I., Cipolla, C. & Gold, J. Children with communication disorders: Some observations of an adjunctive program to their schooling, (Abstract). *American Journal of Orthopsychiatry*, **43**, 233, 1973.

Hewett, F. M. Educational engineering with emotionally disturbed children. *Exceptional Children*, **33**, 459–467, 1967.

Hobbs, N. Mental health's third revolution. *American Journal of Orthopsychiatry* **34**, 822–833, 1964.

Hylton, L. F. *The Residential Treatment Center: Children, Programs, and Costs*. New York: Child Welfare League of America, 1964.

Joint Commission on Mental Health of Children. *Digest of Crisis in Child Mental Health: Challenge for the 1970's*. Washington, D.C.: Joint Commission on Mental Health of Children, 1969.

LaVietes, R., Hulse, W. & Blau, A. A psychiatric day treatment center and school for young children and their parents. *American Journal of Orthopsychiatry*, **30**, 368–482, 1960.

LaVietes, R., Cohen, R., Reens, R. & Ronall, R. Day treatment center and school: Seven years experience. *American Journal of Orthopsychiatry*, **35**, 160–169, 1965.

Lewis, W. W. Project Re-Ed: Educational intervention in discordant child rearing systems. In E. L. Cowen, E. A. Gardner, and M. Zax (Eds.), *Emergent Approaches to Mental Health Problems*. New York: Appleton-Century-Crofts, 1967.

Linton, T. E. The European educateur program for disturbed children. *American Journal of Orthopsychiatry*, **39**, 125–133, 1969.

May, J. & May, M. The treatment and education of the atypical, autistic child in a residential school situation. *American Journal of Mental Deficiency*, **64**, 435–443, 1959.

Madison, B. Q. Adoption: Yesterday, today, and tomorrow. *Child Welfare*, Part I, **45**, 253–258, 1966.

Madison, B. Q. Adoption: Yesterday, today, and tomorrow. *Child Welfare*, Part II, **45**, 341–348, 1966.

Office of Economic Opportunity. *Community Action Program, Project Head Start, I. Daily Program for a Child Development Center*. Washington, D.C.: U.S. Government Printing Office, 1967.

Rabin, A. I. *Growing Up in the Kibbutz*. New York: Springer, 1965.

Reid, J. H. & Hagan, H. R. *Residential Treatment of Emotionally Disturbed Children: A Descriptive Study*. New York: Child Welfare League of America, 1952.

Robinson, J. F. (Ed.) *Psychiatric Inpatient Treatment of Children*. Washington, D.C.: American Psychiatric Association, 1957.

Spitz, R. A. *The First Year of Life: A Psychoanalytic Study of Normal and Deviant Development of Object Relations*. New York: International Universities Press, 1965.

Thurston, H. W. *The Dependent Child*. New York: Columbia University Press, 1930.

Yarrow, L. J. Separation from parents during early childhood. In M. L. Hoffman and L. W. Hoffman (Eds.), *Review of Child Development Research*, Vol. I. New York: Russell Sage Foundation, 1964.

CHAPTER 3

Programs for Learning Problems

Children who are exhibiting serious problems in learning have variously been referred to as underachievers, perceptually handicapped, behavior disordered, neurotic, minimally brain damaged, slow learners, learning disabled, or hyperkinetic (Bateman, 1964; Hewett, 1968; Lerner, 1971). Teachers, guidance counselors, and school psychologists often refer children to mental health services when learning problems are the chief complaint. The actual incidence of children with learning problems is hard to arrive at. Due to such factors as the unreliability of the classification system—be it psychiatric or educational—and the confusion between learning difficulty as a primary or as a secondary reaction, much disagreement exists about the accuracy of the estimates available. In a report prepared for the Joint Commission on Mental Illness and Health of Children (1969), it was suggested that approximately 30% of all school-age children have maladaptive school problems (Glidwell and Swallow, 1969). A more conservative estimate, that approximately 7% of the school-age population exhibit severe learning problems, has also been cited by authorities (Hewett, 1968; Lerner, 1971). Even if we use the conservative estimate of 7%, a significant number of children, in excess of 3 million, are showing problems in learning and are not successfully coping with the primary socializing agency of our society. These failures can have dire consequences for the preservation and advancement of the social structure.

The child's preschool experiences have been overemphasized, at times at the expense of later developmental stages (John, 1963). That early deprivation, rejection, abandonment, lack of infant stimulation and overprotection affects later development is not being challenged. Nonetheless, classical psychosexual theory of development placed great emphasis on the preschool years, slighting the contributions and importance of the school years (Blanchard, 1954; Silberstein, 1967). The focus on object relationships and personality development—how the child approached, reacted to, and internalized other people—and the belief that childhood development was "set" during these preschool years led many early practitioners to characterize children's learning difficulties as derivatives of unconscious impulses or to relate them to the complex process of impulse and defense.

In association with the influences of temperament and constitutional factors, the preschool years provide children with experiences that can either foster or hinder formal learning in the school years. The development of positive attitudes towards learning, the ability to tolerate anxiety and frustration, the expectation that new situations will be rewarding and the ability to conform to routine are necessary precursors for a child to succeed in school. In short, the preschool years provide interpersonal and readiness skills that are the foundation of a positive spiral. However, the resolution of the critical tasks facing a child during the 13 years that he spends in school will, to an even greater extent than his preschool experience, determine his destiny. The inability to develop appropriate skills during these years will take its toll not only during the child's early development but also in his later life.

Schooling, as we know it, is a product of the twentieth century and only recently have schools emerged as the primary agency for training, teaching, and socializing children. Initially the society at large permitted considerable student deviancy, although children who were feebleminded or physically impaired were trained in special schools. However, those children who today would be considered learning disabled, whether as a result of emotional turmoil, perceptual limitations, or brain damage, were not considered atypical, and special educational services were therefore unavailable to them.

The expectations and demands placed on school-age children by rapid urbanization and by the knowledge explosion—coupled with advances in medicine, education, and psychology—brought a new awareness to the job of educating children unable to conform to the regular curriculum. Children with learning handicaps are viewed as having the capacity to learn; they are not mentally deficient but unable to cope with the stresses and strains of the regular school, or to respond to the usual teaching methods, or to yield to the demands of teachers and classmates. Failure, frustration, insecurity, and inadequacy stem from the fruitless attempts made to educate such children with the usual tools. Two early attempts to cope with the problems resulted in the development of special schools and of self-contained classes within regular schools.

Special School Approach

Towns and villages, areas with relatively small districts but large educational problems, discovered that by joining forces they could meet their combined needs, which would otherwise be economically unfeasible. Throughout the country school districts in related regions have formed Boards of Cooperative Educational Services (BOCES) which operate facilities and classes for children who have exceptional learning needs.

The special school approach to the education and remediation of children troubled in learning offers a curriculum adapted to the student's needs from kindergarten through high school. It is guided by a philosophy that emphasizes the individuality of the student and the freedom to deviate from usual education practices and procedures. One such school declares, "By daring to fit education to the student, we expect to provide him with success. Success brings satisfaction and feelings of security. Feelings of security enhance one's self-concept" (Monroe County Association for Children With Learning Disabilities Newsletter, 1972). Such schools have the freedom and the resources to diagnose educational needs and learning disabilities and to develop and provide suitable programs. These programs can be made to measure for individuals and small groups. They can utilize unique and unconventional methods and combinations of methods: "All this is expected to be the rule rather than the exception in special education" (Monroe County Association for Children With Learning Disabilities Newsletter, 1972). While a program's philosophy addresses itself to aspirations and goals, its implementation is more pragmatic and person oriented.

The teacher-student ratio is approximately 1:10 in most learning centers. Distinctions are not made between children disabled by emotional difficulties, neurological handicaps, or perceptual limitations; nor are children grouped by I.Q. above the retarded level. In general the essential criterion for entry is a home school's inability to meet the learning needs of a child. As such, no specific level of disability or criteria for admission can be specified, for example, the number of grade levels lagging behind. Children usually enter the world of the self-contained special school through a thorough and well-organized intake procedure. The home school teacher or guidance counselor initiates a referral. If the child is considered appropriate, based on behavioral, neurological, and psychological evaluations, a conference is held by members of the special school's intake team and by the school district's personnel. This is followed by a visit of the child and parents to the school. The orientation period can involve several trips to the special school. Guidance and teaching specialists, as well as the child's prospective homeroom teacher, meet with the family to arrange schedules, discuss the implications of the school and begin to map out an individualized program.

Intervention in this approach focuses on the learning process, which is highlighted by a discrepancy between expected and actual achievement, and stresses educational techniques for remediation. Behavioral difficulties are conceived of as resulting from, rather than causing a child's inability to learn. The school thus provides a four-pronged approach: (1) educationally oriented diagnosis; (2) classroom management; (3) academic and social growth and development; and (4) parental involvement. Although the education of children is mandatory, direct involvement of their parents is not. Therefore, considerable flexibility and variability accompany the involvement of parents. While rehabilitation and an occasional return to regular school occur, habilitation and learning for living within the self-contained school setting— whether social, personal, or economic—is stressed. Approximately 25% of children referred to a typical self-contained school system return to their home school around 2 years after entering.

Case A

Frank, a 10 year old, was at an educational standstill. After a year filled with frustration and failure in a parochial elementary school, his parents transferred him to a middle-class, suburban public school setting. Another year of failure followed with the suggestion that he be sent to a special school catering to children who have trouble with the regular curriculum.

Despite the recommendations Frank continued to attend a regular class in addition to weekly visits to a reading clinic.

The school psychologist and Frank's pediatrician concurred that Frank was a learning disabled youngster whose inability to accurately perceive information was making it impossible for him to learn in the usual manner. Additionally, 3 years of school failure and frustration led him to become belligerent towards schoolmates, tune out his teacher, and generally give up on learning.

Rather reluctantly his parents permitted the special school placement. Initially the belated placement exacerbated his behavior problem, which led to a mental health center referral.

The psychiatric team concluded that the placement was appropriate. He was retarded in reading and arithmetic, and his writing was illegible. He evidenced an extremely poor self-concept. His inability to relate to authority figures made it most difficult for him to cooperate with teachers. In addition to his school placement, individual psychotherapy was instituted with the aim of helping Frank recognize and accept his limitation in order for him to be more accessible to the special program.

After a few months of special school and weekly therapy sessions, teachers reported that he had begun to take part in activities and seemed more ready to learn. Therapy terminated after 6 months. A year later he was still in special school, far behind his age mates, but making progress. Indeed, in the 1 year in the school, he had progressed farther than in the previous years in regular school. His parents had accepted the fact that Frank would probably not return to regular school, but complete his education (elementary and high school) in the special setting.

The value of placing a child outside of his natural environment, whether his home or school environment, is a serious action and can be the beginning of a journey into a cul-de-sac. An alternative to placement outside a child's normal educational system is to practice containment in his home school, where instruction is provided in a special class. Open-closed, structured-flexible, and humanistic-controlled are some axes influencing the orientation of a self-contained classroom. In practice, the day-to-day administration of such programs incorporates many of the features of the engineered classroom designed by Hewett (1968, 1972).

Self-Contained Classrooms

The engineered classroom combines the rigid methodologic emphasis of behavior modification and of developmental education to provide the troubled student a structured classroom environment. Each child is assessed developmentally according to the following seven educational areas, which are viewed as hierarchically ordered: attention, response, order, exploration, socialization mastery, and achievement. Thus, the behavior disordered child is viewed as failing to achieve one or more of the stated educational goals.

Such an assessment assists the teacher in answering such questions as "Who is the child with a behavior disorder?" and "What does he need in order to achieve success in learning at school?" But it fails to answer a most critical and often neglected question: "How can I do something about his problem in the classroom?" It is at this point that the behavior modification strategy is extremely useful. The teacher must select some object or goal most basic to the child's problem in school (e.g. on the lowest level of the developmental sequence where he is having difficulty), relate it to a specific curriculum task or class assignment, present it to the child making clear what is expected and then guarantee a meaningful reward will be provided if the child successfully accomplishes it. When the child is not successful, the teacher reflects on the nature of the task assigned (stimuli) and the available rewards (consequences). . . . Such reflections are based on the teacher assuming responsibility for the child's inability to be successful (Hewitt, 1972, p. 404).

In this particular program, 9 or 10 students meet with a teacher and teacher aide in a classroom divided in three major sections: (1) an attention-response center which features such devices as puzzles and games for aiding attention, following directions, and promoting participation; (2) a social-exploratory center which provides experimental materials and opportunities for students to participate in projects together; and (3) a mastery-achievement center which emphasizes different academic accomplishments. Throughout the day the child's behaviors are monitored and acknowledged in the form of points which act as rewards. He is always aware of the number of points he has accumulated. At times, however, the structure of the classroom and the resourcefulness of the teacher are not sufficient to bring a child's behavior under control. When this occurs the teacher is encouraged to send the child outside the room where he must wait quietly 5, 10, or 15 minutes without earning check points. If this intervention is not successful, "the teacher may consider sending him home . . . the child was unable to 'be a student' and since only students stay in school, 'it will be necessary for him to leave' " (Hewitt, 1972, p. 406).

It is clear that this approach is educationally based although the educationally handicapped child is conceptualized as a child who suffers from a behavior disorder. Intervention is thus aimed at the behavioral level, with little concern regarding the degree of learning disability stressed in medically or psychologically oriented strategies.

Case B

Tom, a 9-year-old third grader, was the third child in a family of four. His father left high school at 18 to become a house painter. A series of dissatisfying work experiences led to heavy drinking. Fighting and arguments prevailed in the home. Tom's mother complained of being tired, tense, and under considerable pressure.

Tom was promoted into third grade despite his second grade teacher's opinion that he should repeat second grade. She felt he was beginning to catch on to second grade work and was beginning to settle down behaviorally. A highly uneven performance on the Stanford-Binet Intelligence Test resulted in a functioning I.Q. of 91, although the tester concluded that the performance was a minimal estimate of Tom's intelligence. It was felt that Tom was unable to use his ability effectively or efficiently, and this was borne out by his teacher who found him to be achieving in reading and arithmetic at a late first grade early second grade level. She characterized his behavior as often chaotic, disruptive, and, at times, uncontrollable. Previous teachers had commented that he showed good leadership potential and could be a likable child. According to the mother, his teachers did not dislike him despite all his upsetting school behavior.

After a stormy 3-week period, at the beginning of the school year, he was transferred to a self-contained class designed to provide structure and direction for behaviorally disturbed, learning handicapped children.

Whether the major interest is with educating children who have special needs or, as some have suggested, with protecting the normal school child (Christopolos and Renz, 1969), the segregated approach of special learning programs minimizes the familiarity the educationally handicapped have with the normal world while making it difficult for normal children to gain some understanding of the handicapped. The resource room attempts to maintain children not only in regular schools but also in regular classes, while recognizing the limitations and special needs of the child.

Resource Room Programs

The school administration defines the philosophy of resource rooms, although the nature of such programs can be as broad as attempting to change an entire school or as narrow as providing individual tutoring. Resource rooms are directed to the mild to moderately disabled child whose learning problems do not stem from severe underlying emotional turmoil, whose poor self-concept is the result of chronic frustration and failure, and whose limited attention span interferes with the reception or expression of information but whose mental abilities are intact. Knowledge regarding the child's strengths and weaknesses is used by resource room teachers in two ways—first, designing methods of remediation and, second, by incorporating such information into the school day to guide the interaction between able and learning disabled children. Gym, art, math, reading, lunch, social studies, or history may find the competent and the disabled rubbing shoulders (Reger, 1973).

The more disabled a child academically, socially, or emotionally, the more important becomes the resource room teacher's support of and feedback to the regular teacher. In this program homeroom teacher and resource room teacher share responsibility for the education of a child. As such the resource room teacher can (1) provide special material to the homeroom teacher, (2) instruct homeroom teachers in the use of new and special approaches, and (3) alter attitudes and methods of teaching by specific examples. While these services are directed towards the homeroom teacher, the learning disabled child receives the benefits as he is maintained within the mainstream of public school education without the unfortunate but real stigma attached to attending a special program.

This approach implies that the learning disabled child is not seriously emotionally disturbed, i.e. psychotic or showing severe behavior disturbance, and that he has some islands of strengths, either academic or social.

Case C

Billy, 8 years old, was referred to a private neurologist because of his extremely immature and emotionally labile behavior at school. Although his teacher described him as a likable child, she stated he had few friends in class. Academically he was functioning as might a dull child, although an intellectual evaluation showed him capable of achieving within the bright normal range (Verbal I.Q.—134; Performance I.Q.—99; Full Scale I.Q.—118).

The neurologist concluded that Billy was an organically impaired youngster with hyperkinetic behavior and perceptual disturbances. The anxious and attention-seeking school behaviors were thought to be associated with his feelings of insecurity, which were a direct result of poor academic accomplishments.

An educational evaluation by the learning disability specialist revealed Billy to be approximately 1 year behind in arithmetic and 1.5 years retarded in reading. Word attack skills were very poor. He showed good ability to relate to an adult in a one-to-one relationship, and as his attention-seeking behavior was ignored he was able to focus on tasks. Although Billy's visual perception and visual-motor skills were poor, he showed strength in the auditory area. Additionally, he had a positive reaction to medication in that there was a lessening of hyperkinetic behavior.

A team conference with the teacher, neurologist, principal, learning disability specialist, and school psychologist concluded that Billy should be seen for daily 30-minute individual sessions in the resource room. In addition his homeroom teacher began emphasizing auditory communication in the classroom, i.e. he was shifted from a visually orienting reading method to a linguistically orienting system.

The resource room teacher reported that Billy had difficulty involving himself in the program until he was helped to understand his school problems as a result of "the tricks his eyes play on him." His homeroom teacher reported him to appear more grown-up and involved with other children in the class.

Mental Health in the Schools

The mental health orientation to the education and socialization of children who are unable to learn or adjust to the rigors of regular school differs from the previously discussed educationally based stratagems. Educational approaches emphasize the need for cognitive or perceptual training. Skill deficiencies are viewed as the major problem and are considered the bases of emotional turmoil and interpersonal dissonance.

The mental health orientation emphasizes interpersonal relationships, attitudes toward and methods of learning, at times at the expense of content and curriculum. Emotional difficulties are viewed as the primary component in the child's inability to learn, and as such, the mental health approach places a greater premium on parental involvement in the remedial program, especially as the child is seen in clinics and mental health centers located away from school.

Implementation of the mental health orientation within schools has been strongly influenced by the primary prevention philosophy (Zax and Cowen, 1967), whereas services provided to children in clinical settings are rooted in the child guidance movement and have come to be known as day treatment units (LaVietes et al., 1960). These are often part of comprehensive mental health centers (Gold and Reisman, 1970). Some of the mental health prevention programs have attempted to change the orientation of entire school systems by suggesting alterations in the curriculum and the type of content taught to students (Ojemann, 1961). Others have placed emphasis on altering the manner in which children are taught and suggest that psychodynamic principles and mental health concepts be applied to the way teachers transmit knowledge to their students (Biber, 1961). Some mental health programs place greater emphasis on secondary prevention and stress the importance of early detection of school problems. One of the more ambitious of such programs is the Primary Mental Health Project of Cowen and his associates (Cowen et al., 1963). Basically, this project is a two-phase operation. The first phase focuses on early detection and uses a combination of group personality tests (Goodenough Draw-A-Man, California Test of Mental Maturity), social work interviews with mothers, teachers' rating scale, and classroom observations. The screening procedures identify children who in first grade have a high probability of becoming troubled. Intervention is the second phase of the program. Housewives, intensively trained for 5 weeks, meet with identified children to establish a warm, positive, and meaningful relationship. The aide works with the child individually for a few sessions a week. The number of weekly sessions, as well as the duration of each session, vary according to the problem of the child and the specific aims of his program.

Case D

Susan was described by her teacher as a colorless, "mousey-looking," thin girl who always appeared ill, although not known to be a sickly child. She evidenced little spontaneity and seldom participated with her first grade classmates. Yet, Susan did not refuse to cooperate. When she was asked to work with other children she obeyed, but by the end of the assignment she usually managed to be excluded from the group.

The mother also described her child as a shy, quiet girl who was obedient at home and in the neighborhood. She was said to be more comfortable in play when older children were present. Early development was considered normal, and she did not show evidence of phobias or peculiarities.

At school, it was difficult for Susan's teacher to know how much she was learning. She seemed unable to perform, especially in group oriented tasks. Written work was seldom completed, and it was "like pulling teeth" to get Susan to answer a question during class discussion. However, when she was quizzed in a one-to-one situation Susan demonstrated reading and arithmetic skills appropriate to her grade placement.

The school psychologist reported her to be an anxious child with average intelligence but with an inability to express herself. He did not find evidence of a neurotic personality structure but felt she was excessively worried about being made fun of by the other children. According to mother, Susan's two older sisters often teased her or did things for her because it took her so long to do anything for herself.

Susan was seen twice a week for 30 minutes by a case aide. Initially she chose activities that were restrictive, required little verbal involvement, and seemed to minimize failure, for example, coloring and connecting dots. However, after a few meetings Susan began talking a little more, asked the case aide for help, and carried out manual activities such as making a change purse and jewelry, which were of interest but where the outcome was uncertain. Susan's next marking period showed an increase in self-confidence and comments that Susan was trying much harder to participate with her classmates.

Day Treatment

Over the last 15 years educational programs have been developing for children exempt from school on psychiatric grounds and who could not be accommodated in regular, modified, or special classes in public schools (Fenichel et al., 1960; Gold, 1967; LaVietes et al., 1960). Although these programs differ from each other in their methods, some utilizing behavior orientations and others psychodynamic approaches, they all stress as a major goal the provision of security and stability; and they all share a common philosophy. Accordingly, a day treatment service will be described as a composite of these programs where eligible children are viewed "within a context of understanding the individual child's problems and the social matrix in which he develops. The philosophical basis for this understanding rests on two assumptions, viz. that the majority of severely emotionally handicapped children would be served best by remaining with their families, rather than becoming insulated from them by institutionalization and that most parents in concurring with this belief would choose to participate in a demanding task of rehabilitation" (Halpern, 1970). Institutionalization of a child, in addition to making family participation difficult, often stimulates the family to reorganize itself so that it is not able to accept the child back when he is rehabilitated. Parents, as can be seen, are an integral part of the educational and therapeutic program. In addition to casework, when indicated, parents participate in groups that not only discuss the interrelationships between child and parent but also yield opportunities for parents to observe their children in the classroom and to learn new techniques of relating. This is in marked contrast to mental health programs for children in school that involve parents minimally. The contrast can be attributed to the different mandates of the programs as well as to the type of children involved.

For the most part, children who are referred to day treatment units are atypical, developmentally primitive, or seriously undersocialized. Children attend classes in groups ranging from three to six with a teacher and a teacher assistant. Generally children are of at least kindergarten age to be enrolled in day treatment and are not usually held beyond their twelfth birthday. However, some programs are designed to accommodate the preschooler. The age limits and location define the service as a transitional one: "Children are selected whose treatability (and whose parents' treatability) holds promise of their being able to return to a regular school within 3 years of their admission to the program" (LaVietes et al., 1960). Chronological age, maturational level, and ego-functioning determine the group in which a child will be placed. Children attend school for 6 hours a day and "living-playing-learning" is the crux of the curriculum (Fenichel et al., 1960).

In one of the programs (Fenichel et al., 1960), where children are all diagnosed schizophrenic, they relate to the same teacher 6 hours a day 5 days a week; in another unit (Gold and Reisman, 1970), where there is a greater heterogeneity of pathology, children are rotated among the entire teaching staff so that each 30-minute period brings a different subject and teacher to the child, although teachers tend to teach the same subjects each day. Individual relatedness, readiness skills, impulse controls, and responsiveness are the primary learning tasks during the child's early phase. Greater emphases on academic demands are made as anxiety associated with learning and relating is diminished.

Near the end of their stay in day treatment plans are made for children to reenter school. This usually entails a series of conferences, observation of the child in the day treatment facility by the regular receiving school faculty, and preparatory visits by the child to his new school.

Case E

Bruce, a 6-year-old first grader, was excluded from continuing at a private school because he was uncontrollable. He ran all over the school, attacked both teachers and classmates, and was unable to handle the academic requirements of his grade.

An educational and psychiatric evaluation of Bruce found him to be a child of high average intelligence, whose extreme diffuse anxiety made it difficult for him to function effectively or efficiently. Surface behavior of overactivity, aggression, and counterphobic maneuvers were viewed as expressions of anxiety which resulted from a poor self-image. Social work interviews with the parents revealed that this self-concept was being reinforced at home. His mother felt quite fearful, helpless, and highly unsure of her ability to control her son. On several occasions, Bruce physically hurt his mother.

During the diagnostic evaluation Bruce seemed to respond well to the predictable and benign relationship provided him by adults who responded to his aggressive and counterphobic maneuvers in a nonretaliatory but protective manner. Day treatment was recommended as the intervention of choice in light of the boy's need for a therapeutically oriented educational program and his parents' need for casework. Psychotherapy was not instituted until the middle of Bruce's second year in the program to help solidify his gains and help him with the transition from a highly structured, secure and safe environment to the newness of the regular school setting that was being considered for him.

In addition to learning to verbalize his feelings more accurately, less intensely, and more directly, Bruce was achieving at a late second grade level in reading and in arithmetic and exhibited good ability to work independently at tasks once he understood what was required.

In the fall of the academic year he entered a regular second grade in a middle class suburban school system. After a few weeks of school he was moved ahead to a third grade class as a result of school personnel's belief that he was initially misplaced. At a 2-year follow-up, he continued to be achieving at grade level with no problems relating to peers or teachers.

All these educationally based interventions, of course, make use of ancillary therapeutic services. Bruce, who received his schooling in the day treatment unit of a comprehensive mental health center, also was in individual psychotherapy during his last year. Frank found it extremely difficult to benefit from his placement in a special school until he was helped to recognize his limitations and to accept himself. Chemotherapy was used to help Billy with his hyperactivity while he was being provided an appropriate program of instruction. Certainly the positive teacher-student relationship, which attempts to maximize acceptance and understanding while minimizing frustration and anxiety, has psychotherapeutic implications. Moreover, the educationally based aim is the watermark of all the programs described. Regardless of whether stress is placed on curriculum variables (e.g., perceptual training, linguistic approach to reading, attenuating motor disabilities), interpersonal skills (e.g., expression of feelings, developing a better self-concept, cooperation with other students), or distractibility (e.g., focusing attention and minimizing confusion) the educational milieu is the major change agent with the enhancement of present achievement or future learning potential as the goal. To the degree that programs such as these are successful, children will be given skills that decrease the probability of their becoming maladapted adults.

These strategies all stress (1) a reduction of class size with a minimization of internal or external distraction; (2) a focusing of the child's attention by emphasizing novelty and high student interest; (3) establishing a positive relationship with the student; (4) controlling and limiting destructive behavior; and (5) enhancement of learning by providing a high degree of success. All programs for the learning handicapped child emphasize the three Rs—routine, regularity, and reward. The severity of the child's classroom behavior, the degree of his emotional turmoil, the generalness of his learning handicaps, and the philosophy of his school administration enter into the determination of what type of intervention will be provided.

As a rule of thumb, however, the greater the developmental primitiveness of the child, that is, the more areas of functioning adversely affected, then the more stringent the method of intervention required. Resource rooms and day treatment programs can be conceptualized as two ends of the educationally oriented continuum with self-contained classes within a regular school and special schools falling in the middle.

REFERENCES

Bateman, B. Learning disabilities, yesterday, today and tomorrow. *Exceptional Children*, **31**, 167–177, 1964.

Biber, B. Integration of mental health principles in a school setting. In G. Caplan (Ed.), *Prevention of Mental Disorders in Children*. New York: Basic Books, 1961.

Blanchard, P. Psychoanalytic contributions to the problems of reading disabilities. *The Psychoanalytic Study of the Child*, **2**, 163–187, 1946.

Christopolos, F. & Renz, P. Critical examination of special education programs. *Journal of Special Education*, **3**, 371–381, 1969.

Cowen, E. L., Izzo, L. D., Miles, H., Telschow, E. T., Trost, M. A. & Zax, M. A preventive mental health program in the school setting: Description and evaluation. *Journal of General Psychology*, **56**, 307–356, 1963.

Fenichel, D., Freedman, A. M. & Klapper, Z. A day school for schizophrenic children. *American Journal of Orthopsychiatry*, **30**, 130–143, 1960.

Glidwell, J. C. & Swallow, S. The prevalence of maladjustment in elementary schools. Report prepared for Joint Commission on Mental Illness and Health of Children. Chicago: University of Chicago Press, 1969.

A study of the Foreman Center programs available for junior and senior high school students with learning disabilities. *Newsletter*, Rochester, N. Y.: Monroe County Association for Children with Learning Disabilities, March, 1972.

Gold, J. Child guidance day treatment and the schools. Washington D.C.: American Orthopsychiatric Association, 1967.

Gold, J. & Reisman, J. M. An outcome study of a day treatment unit school in a community mental health center (Abstract). *American Journal of Orthopsychiatry*, **40**, 286–287, 1970.

Halpern, W. I. The schooling of autistic children: Preliminary findings. *American Journal of Orthopsychiatry*, **40**, 665–671, 1970.

Hewett, F. M. *The Emotionally Disturbed Child in the Classroom: A Developmental Strategy for Educating Children with Maladaptive Behavior*. Boston: Allyn and Bacon, 1968.

Hewett, F. M. Educational programming for the behaviorally deviant child. In H. C. Quay & J. S. Werry (Eds.), *Psychopathological Disorders of Childhood*. New York: Wiley, 1972.

John, V. P. The intellectual development of slum children: Some preliminary findings. *American Journal of Orthopsychiatry*, **33**, 813–822, 1963.

Joint Commission on Mental Health of Children. *Digest of Crisis in Child Mental Health: Challenge for the 1970's*. Washington, D.C.: The Joint Commission of Mental Health of Children, 1969.

LaVietes, R., Hulse, W. & Blau, A. A psychiatric day treatment center and school for young children and their parents. *American Journal of Orthopsychiatry*, **30**, 468–482, 1960.

Lerner, J. *Children with Learning Disabilities: Theories, Diagnosis and Teaching*. Boston: Houghton-Mifflin, 1971.

Ojemann, H. Investigation of the effects of teaching an understanding and appreciation of behavior dynamics. In G. Caplan (Ed.), *Prevention of Mental Disorders in Children*, New York: Basic Books, 1961.

Reger, R. What is a resource room program? *Journal of Learning Disabilities*, **6**, 609–615, 1973.

Silberstein, R. Treatment of learning difficulties. In M. Hammer & A. Kaplan (Eds.), *The Practice of Psychotherapy with Children*. Homewood, Ill.: Dorsey, 1967.

Zax, M. & Cowen, E. Early identification and prevention of emotional disturbance in a public school. In E. L. Cowen, E. A. Gardner & M. Zax (Eds.), *Emergent Approaches to Mental Health Problems*. New York: Appleton-Century-Crofts, 1967.

CHAPTER 4

Parent Education

Conventional wisdom affirms that education begins at home. Scientific confirmation of this observation and of its importance in human development has generated a host of enterprises that aim to strengthen parenting roles (Brim, 1961; Tavormina, 1974). Parents have found themselves increasingly isolated from transgenerational support at a time when the diversity and complexity of life seemed to mushroom ominously, and they have had to learn a new reliance on professional advice givers (Mead, 1957).

Two groups in the forefront of traditional parent education are the Child Study Association of America and the Parent-Teacher Association. Whereas the first, which had its origins in 1888 as an education organization, tries to strengthen the parent-child relationship by promoting parental understanding of children's growth and development, the latter came into being as a cooperative venture between parents and the public schools to strive for the betterment of the child as student. The Child Study Association and comparable groups have poured forth an avalanche of child development guides to cover multiple facets of parenting. These materials frequently have served as talking points in discussion groups common to both organizations.

Ordinarily a local Parent-Teacher Association chapter consists of parents, teachers, and administrators who are affiliated with a particular school building. Through periodically scheduled informational and discussion meetings the parent acquires some knowledge about the teaching and learning processes applied to his child. If he so chooses he has the opportunity for dialogue with teachers about the needs of the student and about home-school relations, an early practice promoted by Alfred Adler (1930).

Recognition came gradually, however, that the informational and instructional methods did not allay parents' anxieties about responsibility for their young. By the very fact that child expertise was becoming lodged in persons and institutions outside of the family, and not within the immediate circle of kinsmen, a shift of authority had occurred that left parents uncertain and confused. Indeed, consistency among advice givers was more likely to be the exception rather than the rule. As a result the search for the expert parent-consultant intensified. The expectation arose that an authority would eventually write a codified rule book of child-rearing practices, forever banishing doubt. Perhaps the most popular of this genre has been Spock's *Baby and Child Care* (1946). The backlash that this book and the author received a generation after its initial appearance suggests that people blamed a perceived authority external to themselves as having failed in achieving the implied promise of infallibility. Although the popular writings about modern child care must be considered significant culture change agents, spreading enlightenment by the book evidently had its limits. Nonetheless, this has not dimmed the stress on educational efforts through the written word.

The publication of literature on child rearing has become a thriving business. Pamphlets and books exist for virtually every phase and problem of childhood. The assumption is made that parents who have available to them a compendium of guidelines about raising children are likely to be more secure in their role than those who must do without such backstoppers. How much prevention of trouble in the child and parent is achieved by this broad spectrum of interventions is hard to know. Sometimes specific bibliotherapy is recommended as an educational adjunct to a personal counseling process when those with responsibility for children require a more thoroughgoing understanding of growth, development, and constructive child management techniques than can be conveyed in a face-to-face encounter. Moreover, publications are used in parent discussion groups as a means of focusing thinking about their youngsters (Brim, 1961).

Reaching Out to Parents

With the awareness of shortcomings in impersonal mass education, a deepening interest evolved in methods that might better prepare people for the parenting role through a direct commitment to the learning process itself (Group for the Advancement of Psychiatry, 1973; Auerbach, 1968). Given enough skills to carry out their roles with greater confidence, would parents feel more secure with their children? Would they thus regain their former sense of authority—that is, consider themselves effective caregivers (Ginott, 1957; Shapiro, 1956)?

Early attempts in this direction, e.g. in nursery school programs, were tentative and fragmentary (Ruben, 1960). One of the more conspicuous attempts came out of the cooperative nursery school movement following World War II when mothers of enrolled children regularly contributed time to the program under the guidance of a teacher or early childhood specialist (Boulding, 1955). In this manner young mothers retained a sense of participation in the care of their children while gaining first-hand observations of adult-child and peer interactions against which they could evaluate their own activities.

Another development occurred in connection with the public schools where some systems offered guided observation programs for prekindergarten children and their mothers (Klein, 1964). While the children spent a couple of hours or more each week with a teacher, the mothers gathered together in discussion groups with a professional trained in early childhood education. Similar efforts have been carried out by public health district nurses who organize Parent-Child Conference Groups (Sculti, 1974) and in child guidance clinics (Cary and Reveal, 1967).

Case A

A young mother in her early twenties, who had been reared in a punitive fashion, harbored high hopes of bringing up her children more tolerantly. When she found herself feeling strong anger with her only child, a 3-year-old boy, she believed she was a failure as an empathic parent.

By enrolling in a Guided Observation Program she hoped to learn greater tolerance for the child who was already on the verge of controlling her. Instead she discovered a group of mothers struggling with the question of balancing personal needs and those of their children. The shared experience permitted her to reexamine the previous method of working out a problem from her own childhood in a more realistic fashion. In addition to learning about adequate limit setting for the child, she softened in her self-criticism and thereby averted more serious pathology from emerging.

Case B

The mother of three children was unhappy with the youngest, a 3-year-old girl who was shy, clinging, and easily given to tears. Neither of the older children had presented similar behaviors so that the mother looked upon this daughter as a thorn in her side.

In choosing a Guided Observation Program, the mother hoped that the separation would be of benefit to both of them. In the process, she became aware of other children with similar temperaments to that of her daughter, which made it easier for her to be more empathic and helpful to the child. She began to understand the importance of individualizing all her children.

Laudable though these attempts have been, they fell short of a revitalization of parenthood and did not prevent rising adaptive disabilities among the young. Speculations about the many vitiating influences on the modern family are legion. First of all is the relative isolation of the nuclear family as a social system. Today's family requires of its members a degree of solidarity that will permit it to carry out its basic functions satisfactorily and without relying on substitutes to provide relief. Each member has certain formal and informal sanctions, obligations, responsibilities, and rewards that must be negotiated if the family is to coalesce. Stress and strain occur if these are not properly balanced or are improperly conveyed. Furthermore, family cohesiveness is burdened by the modern life expectation of the inculcation of considerable independence at an early age. This contributes to role and goal confusion in families, with a high potential for emotional insecurity and behavioral dissonance among its members.

The high incidence of family disintegration, although attributable to multiple factors, derives in part from the failure of families to deal with difficult, constantly changing, and often paradoxic group tasks. Although it is considered to be a versatile social unit, the nuclear family has its limits of adaptability (Miller and Swanson, 1958). For example, high rates of divorce and remarriage introduce discontinuity in child care which calls for a more sensitive responsiveness to children caught up in such experiences. Another concern is the effect of the working mother on children since it is estimated that by the mid-seventies nearly 50% of mothers will be employed (Howell, 1973a; 1973b).

The more dire the predictions about the modern family have become, the more prolific the outpouring of family life education materials and of family counselors. One of the wide-spread side effects of such a programmatic mass education effort has been the introduction of child-rearing standards and systems that tend to level differences arising out of a highly individualistic social structure as represented by the nuclear family (Bower, 1972). Whether the women's consciousness movement will turn out to be more individualizing or more homogenizing in its effect on the parenting ethos, must still be ascertained over time (Eiduson et al., 1973; Klapper, 1971). This century has already witnessed the growing expectation that with explorations into mind and behavior the individual will be capable of improving or even changing his characteristic methods of dealing with life.

The psychoanalytic uncovering of dynamic mental forces operative in each human being led to a way of thinking about an individual's personal struggle with his destiny in terms of self-actualization. It was conjectured that if a person could gain a rational understanding of himself and of the forces that shape him, he should be in a good position to choose a course of action for himself that is optimally adaptive and productive. However, personal analysis as a preparation for parenthood is hardly practical, given the necessary motivation and investment of resources, even if there were proof about the validity of this claim. Other means have had to be found that are both more economical and efficient and that could reach potentially large numbers who aspire to parenthood.

Although there has long been an awareness that the individual also exists within an external field of forces, the emphasis has shifted only slowly to the structures that are their carriers. Because the family has served as the primary unit for child rearing, the idea has begun to loom large in the conceptualization of parenting that it is the best medium for large-scale life education programs. Despite its shifting boundaries it must still be considered the functional unit which needs strengthening. Indeed, for its survival the family depends very strongly on support it receives from the community surrounding it. The response to this need has been the introduction of new methods and modification of old ones to augment or even supercede the traditional supportive therapies.

Preparation for Parenthood

Basic attitudes and coping styles are acquired in the process of individual growth, primarily in the formative years through the interaction with significant persons such as parents and teachers. The competencies necessary for rearing children are only incompletely formed when called into play—quite simply from lack of practice. Many parents form the opinion that by the time they have learned what works on a trial and error basis, they find themselves at the end of their careers as growth enablers for their children. Even peer consensus with regard to agreed upon expectations and proper child-rearing tactics, whether operative through the influence of television and other mass media or through casual neighborliness, falters in the nitty-gritty practice of daily living. The lack of on-site problem brokers who can give prompt emotional first aid, advice, and relief tends to work a particular hardship on young parents.

As a result a multilayered support system has sprung up, which more and more assumes that explicit methods for imparting specific parenting skills are preferred to vague formulations about tender loving care and discipline. Whether viewed as coping strategy (Adler, 1930), as game playing (Berne, 1964), or as contingency management (Skinner, 1953) parent-child exchanges are considered fitting material for stylized course work and training manuals to be applied in the education of novice and journeymen parents (Becker, 1971; Dreikurs and Grey, 1970; Gordon, 1970; Patterson and Gullion, 1968).

One way of categorizing the stratification of educational opportunities for improving parenthood can be schematized on an intervention continuum. At one end of the spectrum are those methods offering general information about child rearing through mass media; at the other are social engineering projects where a prescriptive life style determines most aspects of relationships within the family or its extended connections within a commune. The intermediate methods between these extremes have gained most in popularity recently. Six types can be identified.

1. Parent education: informal
2. Parent education: formal
3. Parent advocacy
4. Parent training
5. Parent habilitation
6. Parent systematization

Although these representative philosophies of education for parenthood may overlap in practice, their quintessential qualities as exhibited in prototypical formats allow for sufficient distinctions to be made to guide the reader through a maze of good intentions.

Parent Education: Informal

Probably the most widely used publications for gleaning helpful hints about child rearing are newspapers and women's magazines. Professional advice givers and columnists abound in this medium. Ann Landers and Abigail ("Dear Abby") VanBuren are household names in this respect.

Radio and television bring their messages to the public differently. Portrayal of family communication and behavior styles during prime time television programming undoubtedly has a powerful influence on the viewing audience but one that remains beyond self-awareness. For example, the situation comedy, the principal entertainment staple for many people, holds up to ridicule outmoded behavior and thinking, thereby promoting a more rapid acceptance of current ideologies in all areas of human relations, including the parent-child axis.

Along traditional lines are publications targeted for parents. Both public and private sector vie for the attention of the parent as consumers of reading matter. Preferences for one or another pamphlet, brochure, and book are related to cost, special interest areas, ages of children and easy readability. A selected annotated bibliography is included as a sampling of well-received texts and is not meant to be a comprehensive listing.

Films: Listings available by writing to

National Medical Audiovisual Center Annex
Station K
Atlanta, Ga. 30324

Publications

Arnstein, Helene S. *What to Tell your Child about Birth, Illness, Death, Divorce, and other Family Crises.* New York: Pocket Books, 1964. The book addresses itself to parental concerns with managing children's emotional reactions to traumatic events.

Arnstein, Helene S. *Your Growing Child and Sex.* Indianapolis, Ind.: Bobbs-Merrill, 1967. The subtitle of this book is "A Parent's Guide to the Sexual Development, Education, Attitudes and Behavior of the Child—From Infancy through Adolescence."

Baruch, Dorothy W. *New Ways in Discipline.* New York: McGraw-Hill Book Co., 1949. The author offers principles of handling aggression based on psychodynamic understanding of feelings in the child and in the parents.

Chess, Stella, Alexander, Thomas, and Birch, Herbert. *Your Child is a Person.* New York: Viking Press, 1965. The authors describe categories of temperament and offer suggestions for guiding development from the perspective of individual differences.

The Child Study Association of America, Inc. 9 East 89th Street, New York, N.Y. 10028. Their publication program includes an annual annotated booklist of recommended readings for parents.

Children's Bureau Publications. U.S. Department of Health, Education and Welfare. Superintendent of Documents, Government Printing Office, Washington, D.C. 20402. The bibliography order form is entitled "Your Child—A MUST List for Parents" and contains all currently available publications.

Dreikurs, R. and Grey, L. *A Parents' Guide to Child Discipline.* New York: Hawthorn Books, 1970.

Fraiberg, Selma. *The Magic Years*. New York: Charles Scribner's Sons, 1959. Easy readability, sensitivity, and practical suggestions for handling many aspects of problems in early childhood are the hallmark of this classic.

Gardner, Richard A. *The Boys and Girls Book about Divorce. With an Introduction for Parents*. New York: Jason Aronson, 1970.

Gardner, Richard A. *The Family Book about Minimal Brain Dysfunction*. New York: Jason Aronson, 1973.

Ginott, Haim G. *Between Parent and Child*. New York: The Macmillan Co., 1965. The book offers a code for conversing with children through the use of constructive praise and the avoidance of self-defeating patterns.

Ginott, Haim G. *Between Parent and Teenager*. New York: The Macmillan Co., 1969. The author extends his dialogue as healing art to the conflicts of the emancipatory period. Many vignettes illustrate the talking technique.

Gruenberg, Sidonie M. *The Parents' Guide to Everyday Problems of Boys and Girls: Helping your Child from 5 to 12*. New York: Random House, 1958. This book encourages parents to enjoy their children and gives helpful hints in how they might obtain this objective.

LeShan, Eda T. *How to Survive Parenthood*. New York: Random House, 1965. The emphasis is on creative, genuine relationships which allow children and parents to be opened up to life.

Minde, K. *A Parent Guide to Hyperactivity in Children*. Montreal, Que.: Quebec Association for Children with Learning Disabilities, 1971.

Patterson, Gerald R. and Gullion, M. Elizabeth. *Living with Children: New Methods for Parents and Teachers*. Champaign, Ill.: Research Press, 1968. This is a simplified manual for acquiring social learning principles.

Pilkington, T. L. *World Mental Health Films: International Catalogue of Mental Health Films*. New York: World Federation for Mental Health, 1960.

Rees, E. L. *A Doctor Looks at Toys*. Springfield, Ill.: Charles C. Thomas, 1961.

Public Affairs Committee. *Public Affairs Pamphlets*. 381 Park Avenue South, New York, N.Y. 10016. These pamphlets cover every conceivable childhood topic. A complete listing is available from the above address.

Spock, Benjamin. *Dr. Spock Talks with Mothers: Growth and Guidance*. Boston: Houghton Mifflin Co., 1961. A Book-of-the-Month Club selection in 1962 that elucidates the nature of emotional attachment and autonomy in the process of normal development.

Spock, Benjamin. *Problems of Parents*. Boston: Houghton Mifflin Co., 1962. The author examines the dark side of parenthood in sympathetic terms.

Spock, Benjamin. *Raising Children in a Difficult Time: A Philosophy of Parental Leadership and High Ideals*. New York: W. W. Norton and Co., 1974. This is a review and a defense of the author's belief about fostering good attitudes in children.

Steinzer, B. *When Parents Divorce*. New York: Pantheon, 1969.

Parent Education: Formal

When parents choose to go through a formal teaching program about inter-personal skills in family living, they are utilizing a format generally dubbed "Family Life Education." Small group discussions of parenting issues in child development are meant to give a rational basis for communication between the generations (Shoemaker, 1966). So-called sex education is often at the core of the curriculum content. Psychodynamic formulations generally form the theoretical basis for much of this approach. Reaching vulnerable members of the community, for example teenage mothers (Weigle, 1974), has high priority.

Guided group discussions are led by trained leaders who may assign some of the aforementioned pamphlets and books for home reading, may show slides and films depicting common life situations, and may utilize guest speakers for more specialized topics. The method assumes that people can be helped to tap their inherent strengths and apply them constructively in daily routines if they have an intellectual grasp of the known facts and of expertly derived opinions about human issues. It plays down the potential for inter-ference from unconscious sources, ambivalence, or cultural differences.

Ultimately, the formal educational methodology has been concretized by accrediting parents who enroll in officially recognized course work and human service programs in community colleges (Guerney, 1969). The expectation is that the student-parent master the material outlined in a course syllabus. Such courses are most likely to attract those who desire to be professional parents for presumably ulterior motives, e.g. providing expert foster care. Although field trips to childcare agencies or even brief field placements may be included in some programs, the usual emphasis is on bookwork, house-work and teacher-led discussions.

Parent Advocacy

A growing number of parents are aligning themselves with special interest groups that have as their specific mission the improvement if not the eradica-tion of a particular childhood disorder. The ordinary reason for parental affiliation with such groups is attributed to concern for a child suffering from the affliction with which the organization is identified. In the course of their politicization through the advocacy function of their cohorts, many parents also become involved in an educational process in relation to their children. They come to realize that, in no small measure, their attitudes and behaviors toward the handicapped child can become important determinants in the successful outcome of habilitation efforts (Katz, 1961; Lance and Koch, 1973).

For this reason many self-help organizations maintain a strong educational component in their programs for parent membership. The format, although highly variable, relies heavily on those strategies that bring people together for purposes of mutual support and for advancing their cause. Town hall meetings and addresses by invited speakers are often used because they serve both purposes. In addition, workshops and small group discussions become incorporated into the program as a means of tackling the practical issues of care raised by parents who must deal with the exceptional child. Some groups may even sponsor socialization programs with parent assistance (Kysar, 1968).

Without question, parent organizations have been instrumental in promoting a range of necessary services for children in special categories. In the process the parents gain a broader understanding of children's needs and of their own roles. Most of the local organizations are members of national associations which publish newsletters and other informational material, such as directories of facilities, as a guide to parents. Not only can such groupings of people acquire the tools for behavior change but they can also help each other in the relief of guilt and of inadequacy or inferiority in struggling with a difficult task. Moreover, such self-help groups as Parents Anonymous, which seeks to enroll potential or actual child beaters, can serve an important preventive function as perhaps no other method currently achieves. On the practical side such associations can also introduce respite service through the use of homemakers, babysitters or co-parenting (Page, 1973).

Some of the following groups are among the principal parent membership and advocacy associations:

Al-Anon and Alateen (alcoholic parent)
Association for Children with Learning Disabilities, Inc.
Child Welfare League of America, Inc.
Council for Exceptional Children
LaLeche League International (promote breastfeeding)
Momma League (single parents)
National Association for Retarded Children, Inc.
National Foundation for Sudden Infant Death
National Society of Autistic Children

Parents Anonymous
Parent Cooperative Preschools International
Parents of Large Families, Inc.
Parents Without Partners
The National Association for Mental Health, Inc.

Parent Training

Beyond the teaching and advocacy model is the parent training model which has come more and more into vogue. Three basic forms of shaping parents into change agents can be delineated: (1) parent effectiveness training, (2) child-parent training centers, and (3) parent training in behavior modification. In addition, there are also special parent training models with specific therapeutic overtones.

Parent effectiveness training (Gordon, 1970) grew out of the humanist tradition of clinical psychology. It makes the assumption that if parents can learn a nondirective but feeling-related style of communicating with their children, a more harmonious family life and a better method of conflict resolution will automatically bring out the best in the younger generation. A claim is made, and cogently so, that in our culture the proper attitude and language for fostering healthy emotional growth in both child and parent are not prevalent and therefore must be learned from knowledgeable instructors and then practiced through conscious effort. To do so parents meet in groups with a parent effectiveness training teacher who educates them in: "active listening," or feeding back the child's feelings; in "I-messages," or sending personal statements meaningful to the child; and in the "no lose" method for resolving conflicts, or negotiating a mutual agreement. The parents are encouraged to role play with the instructor those problematic encounters with their children for which they seek a better outcome. Courses cover an 8-week training period. During this time parents share their feelings and problems with each other in an informal classroom. People sit in a circle and are encouraged to talk freely with each other while the instructor listens and demonstrates understanding with his active listening. The atmosphere of the classes is designed to be noncoercive yet encourages the parents to practice the parent effectiveness training method in the classroom before it is introduced at home.

Whereas parent effectiveness training is best suited to middle-class families, being dependent on a good repertoire of preexisting skills in language for verbal empathy, it is less useful in working with poverty families or with the less culturally sophisticated parents. Moreover, for those fathers and particularly for those mothers who lack a background in basic understanding of emotional growth of the developing human being, the training program must encompass a comprehensive learning experience (Guerney et al., 1967). Such programs were sponsored by the Office of Economic Opportunity in the 1960s and became known as Parent and Child Centers (Hamilton, 1972; Johnson et al., 1974; Pechman, 1972; Work, 1972). The "staff" is recruited from mothers of the poor and is trained by professional supervisors in infant stimulation, child care, and communication with their own and other people's children. In this manner the mothers gain the self-respect necessary to consider their role as a significant influence for the sound emotional and social development of their children. By sharing in the child's success the mother is more likely to grow with the child. Some training programs for mothers are primarily home-based in that their schooling at the centers is looked upon as a model and a resource for improving their efforts in child care in their own households. They go there for courses, demonstrations, discussions, and practice in living with children. Not only do they take what they have learned home with them, but also they may borrow toys and educational materials from the center's lending library (Schreiber, 1971). In short, this method of reaching parents is an updated technique which was used by settlement houses of another era to bring immigrant or marginal families into the mainstream culture. Hamilton (1972) lists five objectives of such intervention programs: (1) comprehensive health care; (2) activities for children designed to stimulate physical, intellectual, emotional, and social development; (3) parent activities centering on child development, family management, employability, self-confidence, and family relationships; (4) social service to entire family; (5) programs to increase the family's knowledge of and participation in the neighborhood and community.

Parent training in behavior modification is thought to be applicable to nearly all circumstances (Berkowitz and Graziano, 1972). For a start, the behavior therapist teaches parents general behavioral concepts, that is basic principles of operant conditioning and contingency management. This is followed by discussion of specific techniques applied to the problem behavior of their own children. The parent then has the responsibility for carrying out an assigned home program. Instruction may be augmented by the use of program materials, by modeling (i.e. parent observing the therapist apply the technique) or by even direct coaching with the use of signals or the "bug in the ear."

In working out a program with parents it is necessary to establish specific goals and priorities (Krumboltz and Krumboltz, 1972). Once this is agreed upon, the target behavior is subjected to corrective social learning whereby unacceptable performances are ignored and desired actions are responded to with positive reinforcement such as a material reward and/or praise. Punishment and other aversive techniques are not usually preferred for shaping behavior since they encourage the parent to exploit his power role with the child (Patterson, 1974). This does not foster self-reliance in children who succumb to parental authority only because they wish to avoid pain (Wagner, 1968).

In special circumstances parents are trained to be auxiliary therapists for their autistic children (Kozloff, 1973; Schopler and Reichler, 1971) or as behavior modifiers for their retarded offspring (Freeman and Thompson, 1973; Santostefano and Stayton, 1967). This method is particularly fruitful when the parents themselves are not primarily disturbed. Short training sessions and periodic refresher courses in understanding stage-specific behavior and in management techniques support the parents' efforts and keep them abreast of changes associated with growth. Well-planned reciprocal support, and even co-parenting among families who have developmentally damaged children, has been an outgrowth of such training efforts. A more general program of converting parents into therapists, filial therapy, has been put together by Guerney and co-workers (Andronico et al., 1967; Guerney, 1964), and follows a client-centered orientation.

Parent Habilitation

For those families where considerable deviance exists, a reprogramming of the social environment may demand laboratory training or even direct home intervention (Bean, 1971). The therapist aims for training of the family by modeling methods, using videotape playback or cueing parents with remote signals, and by reinforcing parents with such rewards as a reduced fee for desired performance (Johnson and Katz, 1973).

Teaching homemakers (Williams, 1965), who live in for varying periods of time, attempt to demonstrate to parents a more proficient level of care so that the mother and father, whose lives may have been devoid of appropriate learning experiences, can observe and replicate the activities of a parent surrogate. Such interventions may have to be repetitive and linked to the developmental stages of the children as these require increasingly more complex coping strategies from the caretakers (TenBroeck, 1974).

Case C

The parents of four children, ages 1 to 7 years, were referred to a child guidance clinic by the school when their oldest, a daughter, was showing learning and behavior problems despite adequate intelligence. Moreover, the child came to school dirty, poorly dressed, and hungry. Both parents had experienced a deprived childhood.

The family was on public assistance because the father seemed unable to last on a job and preferred the company of his family. All members of the family presented themselves as grimy and inadequately groomed people with a paucity of social graces. A visit to the home revealed deplorable living conditions arising mainly from disorder associated with inept parenting. Both parents as well as the children were judged to be within the range of normal intelligence.

With the parents' consent, a live-in homemaker was dispatched to the family to bring some order into a chaotic household. After an initial cleaning up period, during which all were involved, the homemaker encouraged the parents to establish a few basic rules and routines with respect to mealtimes, bedtime, the protection of household goods, and the use of speech for communication in lieu of hand-to-hand combat. Only after a number of weeks had elapsed did the parents initiate reasonable controls without the homemaker's direct suggestions. The father eventually left the care of the home to his wife, found a job and earned a sufficient income to extricate himself from the welfare rolls.

Because of chaotic family conditions children at times have to be placed for care outside of the home. Those parents whose limitations contributed to the problem need the special kind of services that prepare them for the reintegration of the extruded member (Magnus, 1974).

Parent Systematization

In *Walden Two*, Skinner (1962) has proposed a utopian design based on behavioral engineering. The underlying philosophy propounds that since man is never free of all controls, a method whereby contingencies or reinforcements are managed for the sake of the best of all worlds is desirable for its own ends. Experimental and esoteric communities do exist that define parent roles, along with other function attributes, in a context different from that of the surrounding culture, e.g. the Bruderhof (Wardle, 1974), the Kibbutz (Spiro, 1958), and the American "corporate families" (Toffler, 1970). Some societies have forged large parts of their populace into communal groups such as the Soviet Collective (Bronfenbrenner, 1970) and the Chinese Communes (Bialestock, 1972) with obvious shifts in responsibilities for child care. In the United States voluntary communes have emerged where the assignment of parenting tasks occurs on the basis of preference and aptitude for the job (Eiduson, 1973).

Because the skills needed for raising children are not equally shared by all parents, Toffler (1970) proposes a system of "professional parents" taking on the primary child-rearing function for others who choose to give up this role. Family units whose members are found to be suitable to this occupation would compete in the marketplace for children, while biological parents who decided to forego the major aspects of this role function remain "friendly and helpful outsiders."

In summary, newer forms of parent education derive from changes introduced by social, economic, and cultural transformations. Community support, always a human necessity in child care, is developing models that must reckon with the family's mobility, isolation, and educational sophistication.

Although newspapers of the nineteenth century already devoted considerable space to problems of child care, it was not until the twentieth century that newspapers, magazines, books, films, television, and parent organizations in combination created an educational climate that made the responsibility of early child care a matter of common concern, serious interest, and highest priority. No matter how well the media and organizations have been exploited by this cause, there has remained an obvious need for a more personalized support system.

An important phenomenon to observe may be the spread of the self-help movement into more active parent groups. There are strong indications that the trend is for greater specialization and diversification of training for general and special skills in parenting and child care. At the same time, more attention is being paid to parents as human beings whose desire for self-development and personal fulfillment need not be diminished by the fact that they are mothers and fathers (Group for the Advancement of Psychiatry, 1973). For those whose problems may require something beyond an enlightened educational experience, or for those who are impervious to instructional entreaties, treatment-centered methods are introduced as a means of impacting on disturbed parental and filial patterns of functioning.

REFERENCES

Adler, A. *The Education of Children*. (Translated by E. Jensen & F. Jensen). New York: Greenberg, 1930.

Andronico, M. P., Fidler, J., Guerney, B. G. & Guerney, L. The combination of didactic and dynamic elements in filial therapy. *International Journal of Group Psychotherapy*, **17**, 10–17, 1967.

Auerback, A. B. *Parents Learn Through Discussion*. New York: Wiley, 1968.

Bean, S. L. The parents' center project: A multiservice approach to the prevention of child abuse. *Child Welfare*, **50**, 277–282, 1971.

Becker, W. C. *Parents are Teachers: A Child Management Program*. Champaign, Ill.: Research Press, 1971.

Berkowitz, B. P. & Graziano, A. M. Training parents as behavior therapists: A review. *Behavior Research Therapy*, **10**, 297–317, 1972.

Berne, E. *Games People Play*. New York: Grove Press, 1964.

Bialestock, D. Child care: China 1972. *Medical Journal of Australia*, **2**, 979–980, 1973.

Boulding, E. The cooperative nursery and the young mother's role conflict. *Marriage and Family Living*, **17**, 303–309, 1955.

Bower, E. K.I.S.S. and KIDS: A mandate for prevention. *American Journal of Orthopsychiatry*, **42**, 556–565, 1972.

Brim, O. G., Jr. Methods of educating parents and their evaluation. In G. Caplan (Ed.), *Prevention of Mental Disorders in Children*. New York: Basic Books, 1961.

Bronfenbrenner, U. *Two Worlds of Childhood*. New York: Russell Sage Foundation, 1970.

Cary, A. C. & Reveal, M. T. Prevention and detection of emotional disturbances in preschool children. *American Journal of Orthopsychiatry*, **37**, 719–724, 1967.

Dreikurs, R. & Grey, L. *A Parents' Guide to Child Discipline*. New York: Hawthorn Books, 1970.

Eiduson, B. T., Cohen, J. & Alexander, J. Alternatives in child rearing in the 1970's. *American Journal of Orthopsychiatry*, **43**, 720–731, 1973.

Freeman, S. W. & Thompson, C. L. Parent-child training for the mentally retarded. *Mental Retardation*, **1**, 8–10, 1973.

Ginott, H. G. Parent education groups in a child guidance clinic. *Mental Hygiene*, **41**, 82–86, 1957.

Gordon, T. *P.E.T.—Parent Effectiveness Training. The Tested New Way to Raise Responsible Children*. New York: Peter H. Wyden, 1970.

Group for the Advancement of Psychiatry (GAP). *The Joys and Sorrows of Parenthood*. Vol. VIII. No. 84, New York, 1973.

Guerney, B. G. Filial therapy: Description and rationale. *Journal of Consulting Psychology*, **28**, 304–310, 1964.

Guerney, B. G. (Ed.), *Psychotherapeutic Agents: New Roles for Non-professionals, Parents, and Teachers.* New York: Holt, Rinehart & Winston, 1969.

Guerney, B. G., Stover, L. & Andronico, M. P. On educating disadvantaged parents to motivate children for learning: A filial approach. *Community Mental Health Journal,* **3,** 66–72, 1967.

Hamilton, M. L. Evaluation of a parent and child center program. *Child Welfare,* **57,** 248–258, 1972.

Howell, M. C. Employed mothers and their families (I). *Pediatrics,* **52,** 252–263, 1973.

Howell, M. C. Effects of maternal employment on the child (II). *Pediatrics,* **52,** 327–343, 1973.

Johnson, C. A. & Katz, R. C. Using parents as change agents for their children: A review. *Journal of Child Psychology and Psychiatry,* **14,** 181–200, 1973.

Johnson, D. L., Leler, H., Rios, L., Brandt, L., Kahn, A. J., Mazeika, E., Frede, M. & Bisert, B. The Houston Parent-child Development Center: A parent education program for Mexican-American families. *American Journal of Orthopsychiatry,* **44,** 121–128, 1974.

Katz, A. H. *Parents of the Handicapped: Self-organized Parents' and Relatives' Groups for Treatment of Ill and Handicapped Children.* Springfield, Ill.: Charles C. Thomas, 1961.

Klapper, Z. S. The impact of the women's liberation movement on child development books. *American Journal of Orthopsychiatry,* **41,** 725–732, 1971.

Klein, D. C. An example of primary prevention activities in the schools: Working with parents of preschool and early school years children. In N. M. Lambert (Ed.), *The Protection and Promotion of Mental Health in Schools.* Bethesda, Md.: U.S. Department of Health, Education and Welfare, National Institute of Mental Health (Mental Health Monograph No. 5), 1964.

Kozloff, M. A. *Reaching the Autistic Child: A Parent Training Program.* Champaign, Ill.: Research Press, 1973.

Krumboltz, J. D. & Krumboltz, H. B. *Changing Children's Behavior.* Englewood Cliffs, N.J.: Prentice-Hall, 1972.

Kysar, J. E. Reactions of professionals to disturbed children and their parents. *Archives of General Psychiatry,* **19,** 562–570, 1968.

Lance, W. D. & Koch, A. C. Parents as teachers: Self-help for young handicapped children. *Mental Retardation,* **11,** 3–4, 1973.

Magnus, R. A. Teaching parents to parent: Parent involvement in residential treatment programs. *Children Today,* **3** (1), 25–27, 1974.

Mead, M. Changing patterns of parent-child relations in an urban culture. *International Journal of Psychoanalysis,* **38,** 369–378, 1957.

Miller, D. R. & Swanson, G. E. *The Changing American Parent.* New York: Wiley, 1958.

Page, R. Co-parenting. *Children Today,* **2,** 21, 1973.

Patterson, G. R. Retraining of aggressive boys by their parents: Review of recent literature and follow-up evaluation. *Canadian Psychiatric Association Journal*, **19**, 142–158, 1974.

Patterson, G. R. & Gullion, M. E. *Living with Children: New Methods for Parents and Teachers.* Champaign, Ill.: Research Press, 1968.

Pechman, S. M. Seven parent and child centers. *Children Today*, **1** (2), 28–31, 1972.

Ruben, M. *Parent Guidance in the Nursery School.* New York: International Universities Press, 1960.

Santostefano, S. & Stayton, S. Training the preschool retarded child in focusing attention: A program for parents. *American Journal of Orthopsychiatry*, **37**, 732–743, 1967.

Schopler E. & Reichler, R. J. Parents as cotherapists in the treatment of psychotic children. *Journal of Autism and Childhood Schizophrenia*, **1**, 87–102, 1971.

Schreiber, L. E. The HELP line for parents—a demonstrative project. *Child Welfare*, **50**, 164–167, 1971.

Sculti, K. Care of the well child: Parent discussion groups. *American Journal of Nursing*, **74**, 1480–1481, 1974.

Shapiro, I. S. Is group parent education worthwhile? A research report. *Marriage and Family Living*, **18**, 154–161, 1956.

Shoemaker, L. P. *Parent and Family Life Education for Low-income Families: A Guide for Leaders.* Washington, D.C.: U.S. Department of Health, Education and Welfare, Children's Bureau, U.S. Government Printing Office, 1966.

Skinner, B. F. *Science and Human Behavior.* New York: Macmillan, 1953.

Skinner, B. F. *Walden Two*, New York: Macmillan, 1962.

Spiro, M. *Children of the Kibbutz.* Cambridge, Mass.: Harvard Universities Press, 1958.

Spock, B. *Baby and Child Care.* New York: Pocket Books, 1946.

Tavormina, J. B. Basic models of parent counseling: A critical review. *Psychological Bulletin*, **11**, 827–835, 1974.

TenBroeck, E. The extended family center: "A home away from home" for abused children and their parents. *Children Today*, **3** (2), 2–6, 1974.

Toffler, A. *Future Shock.* New York: Random House, 1970.

Wagner, M. K. Parent therapists: An operant conditioning method. *Mental Hygiene*, **52**, 452–455, 1968.

Wardle, R. Early childhood programs in Bruderhof communities. *Child Welfare*, **53**, 360–365, 1974.

Weigle, J. W. Teaching child development to teenage mothers. *Children Today*, **3** (5), 23–24, 1974.

Williams, J. V. The caseworker—homemaker team. *Public Welfare*, **23**, 275–279 and 294–295, 1965.

Work, H. H. Parent-child centers: A working reappraisal. *American Journal of Orthopsychiatry*, **42**, 582–595, 1972.

CHAPTER 5

Parent Counseling

Children whose behavior suggests that they are troubled or who trouble others usually find their way to mental health specialists through their parents. It has been suggested that childhood disorders are a direct outgrowth of poor parenting, and that disturbed states of children correlate with ineffective, overly rejecting, or overprotective parents. Such links have not been established despite the intuitive expectation that the emotional climate generated within a family can have a decisive effect on the personality a child develops (Frank, 1965). It has recently been suggested that it is the perceived family climate that affects children and contributes to their maladaptive behavior (VanderVeen and Novak, 1974).

Whether one subscribes to the view of the pioneer analysts that specific traumata early in the life of the child warp his personality, or to the revision held by neo-Freudians, such as Horney (1950), that social interactions between parents and child result in maladaptive life styles, or to the behaviorist idea that holds that the child learns poor habits from the antecedent events and their consequences (Ullmann and Krasner, 1965), or to the humanists' philosophy that emphasizes the child's becoming (Rogers, 1961), the parents and the type of psychological nurturance they provide as perceived by the child emerge as the key ingredients for the development of childhood health and pathology (VanderVeen and Novak, 1974). It is not surprising then that considerable interest is expressed in a child's parents when consideration is given to providing help for him. However, this has not always been so (Mahler and Rabinovitz, 1956).

It was only at the turn of the twentieth century that an environmentalist point of view became popular and different aspects of society looked upon as contributing to personal unhappiness and maladjustment. According to Reisman (1966), not until the end of the 1920s had nurture supplanted nature as a key concept in the understanding of intelligence, and psychodynamic notions of psychopathology came to dominate child guidance.

Initially, however, parents were involved only minimally in the therapeutic process of helping troubled children. Meyer (1909) and his common-sense approach and Mary Richman (1917), who insisted the family be involved in diagnosing children's problems, were influential but soft voices. Healy (1934), a pioneer with delinquents and one of the founders of the child guidance movement, insisted that parents be interviewed to obtain developmental information to aid in a dynamic formulation of the delinquent's problems. The involvement of parents in the helping process created the team approach, which became a permanent fixture in child guidance by the time the American Orthopsychiatric Association was formed in 1924. At this point parents became involved as providers of information and receivers of advice. Essentially, parents were told that they had to mend their ways.

The strengthening of the caseworker's role on the psychiatric team brought a new understanding and prominence to working with parents. It became painfully clear that parents could not alter their behavior and attitudes unless they were an active part of the treatment process. An important shift from the mere giving of advice and information to the forming of a therapeutic relationship took place. Advice became supplanted by the establishment of relationships, and parents were considered *bona fide* clients (Hamilton, 1951). Indeed, some have maintained that this position has been carried to its extreme—adults have supplanted the child as the patient, while losing sight of the child's behavior (Weinberger, 1973).

Marriage, an important source of adult satisfaction and, indeed, the most enduring form of human relationship, has also been considered a major contributor to childhood psychopathology. During the last 20 years, there has been considerable change in this institution. It seems that marriages have been lasting for longer periods of time while divorce rates have almost doubled (Statistical Abstracts, 1972). This suggests that there has been an increase of exposure to strife in the children's environment. How, under these circumstances, does a therapist decide whether to give his attention to the individual parent, the couple in relationship to their child, or to the marriage itself (Rapkin, 1970)?

In this time of our history the acquisition of knowledge has unprecedented importance to people. In the previous chapter some of the varied approaches to information sharing and parent education on childhood development and child rearing were reviewed. When does the clinician, however, decide that providing information is not enough, or at best, can only be an adjunct to other forms of intervention? One answer rests with the distinction that can

be made with the primary locus of the problem. When parental atti/
based upon inner conflicts and distorted needs, rather than misinf
and misconceptions regarding the differing developmental needs of children
or of their own roles, then a more intensive relationship-based strategy is
required. Some of the key concepts that have bearing on the issue of parent
counseling revolve around the age and developmental stage of the child, the
degree of disturbance of the individual partners, and the stability of the
marriage.

The Preschooler

The preschool child who shows regressive behavior such as extreme crying or
loss of appetite associated with separation from mother, responding to the
birth of a new sibling with a return to nighttime wetting, and separating with
difficulty from mother when entering nursery school or kindergarten, exhibits
some of the problems that bring children of this age to the attention of professionals. Overactivity, extreme shyness, refusal to sleep at night, and poor
toilet habits are other examples that suggest that the infant or young child
may be under extra tension and can result in a referral to a mental health
specialist. An assessment of the family often suggests that underlying difficulties involve the interaction between parent and child. In the 1920s and 1930s
when children were viewed as the innocent victims of harsh, exploitative, or
even cruel parents, professionals would give parents peremptory advice and
attempt to alter the living conditions in the family. In the 1940s and 1950s
children were perceived as innocent victims of neurotic parents who, in place
of advice, were offered psychotherapy to help them overcome their neuroses.
When the parents' feelings were straightened out, they would become better
parents. Dissatisfaction with both approaches has resulted in child-centered
parent counseling.

In practice, advice and direction in the context of a therapeutically oriented
relationship with parents still remain commonplace when counseling them
regarding young children (Furman, 1960). Preschool children are assumed to
have a special relationship with their mothers. Mothers spend more time at
home during that stage and are the primary providers of security and trust.
It is also a period when parents must adjust to each other and work out
conflicts within themselves as well. When the child's behavior does not
suggest a severe developmental or dysfunctional problem such as found in

atypical children, and the adults are relatively intact, then child-oriented parent counseling is considered a suitable intervention method.

Case A

Mother requested an appointment because her 4 year old was having difficulty in nursery school where he was felt to be poorly coordinated, impulsive, and inattentive. The parents, who also had three teenaged children, readily admitted that they had not desired any more children but believed the youngster was not a rejected child.

The parents, both college graduates, seemed overwhelmed by their overly active, demanding 4 year old. Mr. A was more even-tempered, soft-spoken, and less tense than his wife, who by her own admission, was impulsive and easily upset. Mrs. A also believed that she had more difficulty managing her son with whom she seemed to be caught up in a battle of wills. Both parents reported some surprise over the nursery teacher's observation, because they saw their son as a well-coordinated child, who walked, talked, and trained relatively early and who was able to ride a two-wheel bike with little difficulty.

In a diagnostic interview, the child showed a high activity level but was goal-directed. He enjoyed playing with blocks which he manipulated well. In addition, he was aware of the different parts of his body, showed a good capacity for spatial relationships, was able to recognize letters and numbers, and had no difficulty with visual or auditory memory. Additionally, he was able to perform a series of difficult motor tasks, such as hopping, skipping, throwing, catching, and drawing at an age-appropriate level.

When he tested limits repeatedly during the interview he also responded to firmness and was quite amenable when alternatives and substitutes were suggested. Upon leaving the interview he wanted to play with a doll house in the waiting room. Mother had asked him to put away some blocks and evidently felt stymied in guiding him through the leave-taking process. She looked at the diagnostician with dismay, commenting "See what I mean?" as she stood by helplessly. The diagnostician moved closer to the boy and while addressing mother reminded him about the toy rule: One toy is put away before playing with another. After all three finished putting away the blocks, he moved towards the door to leave. The opportunity for ventilation of fears, coupled with the reassurance that her son was not a hyperkinetic child helped the mother to understand the relationship between her tension level and his activity level.

Case B

A 5-year-old encopretic boy had shown an exacerbation of behavioral difficulties with the birth of his sister. He was the first grandchild on either side,
and little was denied to him by grandparents. His parents described him as
being an outgoing, demanding child.

During play interviews he seemed like a dull boy, but an intellectual evaluation revealed him to be of average intelligence. He was inhibited and had
difficulty being spontaneous. Much of his play centered around the creation
of high-walled buildings and forts. At one point he built a bridge and then
commented that cars would not be able to pass on it because of the barrier
he had placed there. Projective testing revealed him to be an insecure child
who showed anxiety about expressing feelings and concern regarding closeness to people. He accurately perceived his mother to be the more dominant
parent who was in charge of the family. Additionally, he felt her to be closer
to his new sibling. Overall, the boy did not appear to be showing signs of
severe relationship problems, and much of his anxiety and maladaptive
activity was considered to be reactive to his concern over discharging hostilities, on the one hand, and manipulative for gaining attention, on the other.

The mother was an outspoken, anxious woman who was discontented
with her marriage, but felt compelled to make a go of it. It was clear that the
relationship with her son, which was a hostile-dependent one, mirrored her
marriage relationship. The more difficult she found it to express herself to her
husband, the more problems she had with the boy. She felt her son to be
unhappy and thought he might be in need of help. Her husband did not see the
boy as having a problem but believed he was acting like a "baby" who
should grow up. Much of his concern, however, was centered on his wife, who
he felt, by playing into his son's actions, kept him a baby. The boy's behavior
drove away his father and prompted his mother to continue catering to him.

Since the mother appeared to be the key member in the family, counseling
for her was suggested with the aim of exploring the relationship she had with
her son around his toileting and related activities. After the fourth meeting
mother reported that her son had been using the toilet with greater frequency
and that her husband felt he was behaving less like a baby. The next meeting
was held with both parents, and they decided to devote the remaining
meetings to their marital frictions.

The advice and suggestions provided by words and by deeds were helpful—
in one case they brought about a better and more relaxed parent-child relationship and in the other refocus on the major problem. However, it was the
context in which they were provided that made them effective.

Latency Children

The latency-age child is most often referred to mental health specialists by schools for either poor school achievement, behavior disorders, or a combination of both. The parents initiate the contact and introduce the problem. Contacts tend to be brief for children usually characterized as showing adjustment reactions of childhood. Diagnosis and treatment merge and are conducted simultaneously either by one person or in tandem by a team. The family may be seen as a unit or as collaterals. Another method is to observe the child with other children while his parents meet with other parents for a limited number of group sessions. These approaches are discussed in depth in the succeeding chapters. For the purpose of this chapter some examples and models are introduced to give special emphasis to the brief approach to parent counseling.

Case C

A $6\frac{1}{2}$-year-old boy who has three older sisters was referred to a mental health center because he refused to return to school after the initial 3 weeks of first grade. The family was able to get him to return, but he had to finish the school year by repeating kindergarten.

At the time of the evaluation he had some difficulty initially separating from his parents, but by the third meeting was able to leave them. Unsureness about being assertive was noted in his play and manner of relating. It became quite clear that he was not sure how his mother would respond to the advances he wanted to make toward growing up. A limited-goal approach was evolved in which the mother would be encouraged to permit her son to grow.

The mother was seen for seven sessions after which termination was mutually agreed upon. The mother felt that coming to the clinic had neither altered her behavior nor had it changed the family structure. However, while describing the changes that the boy was showing, such as playing with more children his own age, permitting parents to help him, and being more relaxed in demonstrating self-assertion, she observed that she felt calmer, less pressuring towards the boy, and more confident in handling any recurrence of the behavior that had brought them to seek help.

Case D

A 9-year-old boy, the third in a family of five, was referred for consultation by his pediatrician because of behavior problems. He had become antagonistic towards his mother, was having temper tantrums, was underachieving, and was belligerent at school. His mother dated her son's problems from the previous year when he was placed in a rapid-learning class, but it was not until he ran away from home that his parents were able to mobilize themselves to make an appointment.

The child was seen for two diagnostic interviews following interviews with his parents. He was found to be a mildly disturbed youngster who was quite manipulative and a skilled harasser of his parents. He had gained considerable control in the home through these methods. Because he was poorly motivated for treatment it was felt he would probably influence his parents to withdraw from involvements if he were to be included. The intake meetings with the parents indicated that the mother was the central figure in the current conflict, and counseling for her was suggested.

The impressions shared with the parents were reassuring, especially to the mother. Although they had mixed feelings regarding the recommendations, the mother agreed to come for counseling and was seen for 10 sessions. During the initial session most of the time was spent in helping her overcome her reluctance and fears about being involved in a counseling relationship. She perceived her visits as a means of getting things off her chest and learning new ways of relating to her son. When termination was agreed upon, she reported a marked diminution in his temper tantrums, less sibling rivalry, cooperative behavior at home, and a greater interest in school with improved grades. Primary, however, were the changes in activities between herself and her son which she expressed as follows: "Doing the right thing in small ways seems to lead to much bigger and more important changes."

In both instances, the parent, or the quality of parenting, was the major focus. While the emphasis was definitely on the parent-child interaction, discussion at times centered on therapist-parent relationships, past history of the parent, and the current status of the marriage. Such techniques as reflection, confrontation, and interpretation, in addition to advice giving, were used in fostering more adaptive parenting.

The most prevalent model employed in child guidance centers for involving parents and their children is the tandem approach (Pratt, 1963), consisting of initial social work interviews with parents, separately and as a couple, followed by play or talk interviews with the child, and capped by a summary or dispositional meeting of parents and professional team. Diagnosis is believed to precede therapy, and the summary conference attended by all parties to discuss an intervention program terminates the diagnostic phase.

Adolescence

Adolescent maladaptive surface behaviors, such as indifference, running away from home, vandalism, promiscuity, headaches, or gastrointestinal disorders can reflect a wide range of psychopathology and family interactions. Most frequent are the communication problems that seem best handled by one of the varieties of family-oriented approaches. However, sexual promiscuity, extreme indifference to authority, or poor socialization may reflect the life style of the sociologic delinquent or may mirror poor judgment stemming from a youth's inadequacy in testing reality associated with underlying ego weakness. Individually oriented psychotherapy, discussed in a later chapter, or the use of environmental resources such as mentioned in Chapter 2, need to be considered in such situations. Parents have to be helped to accept environmental resources that require a child to be placed out of the home for a period of time under certain circumstances.

Case E

Following a heated argument with his father, a 15-year-old boy took an overdose of sleeping pills and was immediately rushed to the emergency department of a general hospital. Psychiatric evaluation revealed him to be an angry youth who was chronically discontented, had few friends, and intensely disliked his stepmother of 9 years whom he found to be bossy and demanding. He believed she wished him out of the family. Moreover, he accused her of forcing his 16-year-old sister to leave the family and felt she was constantly trying to turn his father against him. A major complaint was that his mother nagged him about school and restricted him for bringing home failing grades. At one point, he complained he was "grounded" for 3 months. The youth believed that his father often sided with his wife to keep peace in the family and not because she was right. However, the day he attempted to commit suicide he felt "he had lost his father forever."

While finding the boy depressed, the psychiatrist did not think that there was a strong suicide risk and recommended out-of-home placement in a group-oriented facility. The father was made guilty by the recommendation, while the stepmother thought it might be beneficial for both her stepson and the family, especially for the two younger children of their marriage. Although the recommendation was experienced as another instance of his being rejected by the family, the boy acknowledged that a separation might allow them to gain a new perspective on each other. The therapist addressed himself mainly to the father's feelings of guilt as a way of laying the groundwork for a more positive rapprochement.

Manpower shortages and rising economic costs have led child guidance clinics to pursue group-oriented strategies to help parents deal with child management and child-rearing issues. While there are a number of different approaches, leadership styles, and frames of reference, similarities exist: (1) parents meet for a preselected number of sessions; (2) the sessions are relatively structured; and (3) parents are provided with didactic information in the context of an accepting, nonthreatening environment which, in part, is generated by the leader's behavior, and, in part, by the group-oriented sharing of problems. Two prevalant models, one emphasizing feelings and the other behaviors, encompass most points of view. However, both aim to increase parents' knowledge of childhood growth and development, make them more aware of their contributions to the child's adaptive and maladaptive behavior, and teach them better techniques of child management (Tavormina, 1974).

The significance and type of parental involvement parallels the developmental period of their child. During infancy and early childhood, parents become the main focus of the intervention as most difficulties center around the basic socializing process of the child and the budding psychological relationship between parent and child. Especially during infancy it is the mother who nourishes the child and, thus, it is she who is often the focus of intervention. A young child not performing up to parental expectations and the mismatching of a child's psychobiological temperament with the psychobiological nature of parents are among the major "etiological factors" scrutinized in parent-oriented counseling. The school-age child struggles with the internalization of parental attitudes and the rules and regulations of the world outside the family. In this period of a child's life parent and child are often both involved, that is both being seen separately by the same or different therapists. Parents are given an opportunity to reflect on their attitudes, feelings, and actions within the context of an understanding, accepting, and respectful relationship.

Adolescence, the time when young people are closer to and yet farther from their parents, often ushers in a breakdown in family communications. Service can usually be provided best when all members are present, although this arrangement may not be possible nor indicated. Parental consent is a minimal requirement for treatment of adolescents. Consent implies that the parents are giving their young permission to change. Often when the adolescent's difficulty signals the inability for the family to cope with psychopathology in a parent, or when it stems from severe marital conflict, then individual psychotherapy of the disturbed adult or focused treatment of the marriage is indicated. The stresses of adolescents can be the impetus for the surfacing of unspoken chronic marital discord or provide the fuel for a divorce proceeding.

Marriage Counseling

"When divorce impends the ordinary and customary styles of reacting to an appeal for help characteristic of general psychiatric practice may be inappropriate, ineffectual or, at worst, detrimental" (Whitaker and Miller, 1969, p. 57). Some professionals have attempted to carve out a special area of marital counseling, while others consider it no different from psychotherapy. Marital counseling can also be viewed as providing preventive services to childless couples. However, this discussion is confined chiefly to couples who have children or who come concerned about children.

In many instances the introduction of a troubled marital pair to a clinic or mental health specialist initially centers around the behavior of the child. Concerned that parents will be unable to "hear" their advice or that their suggestions will fall on deaf ears, professional counselors often avoid direct answers to parents' questions. Instead they question the family climate and the nature of the marital relationship. Indeed, one of the criticisms leveled at child guidance clinics has been the ease with which they shift the focus of the parents' complaints from a troubled child to that of a "poor" or "neurotic" marriage. Of course, the initial few meetings with the family—whether together or separate—are often helpful in deciding whether the marriage would be a more appropriate focus than the child or the parenting relationship. Such a decision must be reached carefully in order to avoid greater harm being done by opening up problems that cannot be modified.

Case F

A mother requested service for her 5-year-old son whom she described as very active and uncontrollable. She claimed that he often hit her, ran away from her, and refused to eat even after she prepared what he requested. The mother also commented that her husband did not pay much attention to the boy as he traveled a great deal and often left the two of them for weeks on end.

The child related in a relaxed fashion and played in a goal-directed manner. School readiness and perceptual testing revealed him to be functioning at a level commensurate with other children his age. He drew a picture where "Everyone has mud in their face," and then commented that when he plays with mud and dirt his mother becomes upset. There were also suggestions that he perceived himself as being pulled between both parents.

The diagnostic impressions were discussed with the parents. The father commented "I knew nothing was wrong with our son," while the mother interpreted both his and the diagnostician's comments to mean she was a poor mother. Furthermore, the father felt that his wife had been spoiling their son by giving in to him too easily and spending too much time with him, especially at night. The mother implied that her husband was too harsh with the youngster and spent too much time away from home. She complained that he was always tired and disinterested in her when he was home. This was a veiled comment concerning mother's worries that her husband was having an affair. She claimed to be the sexually aggressive partner, with her husband frequently pushing her away. The couple agreed to become involved in marital counseling and reported the time they were together became more pleasant. Mother was better able to control her son. Furthermore, the parents reported they were able to enjoy him more.

Interpersonal, financial, and sexual dilemmas are among the major areas that come under the professional's microscope in marital counseling. Often, financial problems mask the other two or occur as a result. Family planners and welfare workers have financial planning as a major focus although they use techniques and skills similar to marital counselors and psychotherapists. Financial grants, welfare allocations, and negotiation of bank loans are some of their tools for alleviating distress. However, we will not concern ourselves with financial matters per se but focus more on the interpersonal and sexual problems that families and marital couples bring to mental health professionals. In this realm considerable controversy exists. Although there is agreement that the two are not separate processes, in practice they are treated as if they were. Some professionals consider the conjugal relationship as basically an interpersonal one. When the couple is unable to communicate, so goes the argument, it makes no difference whether this occurs in the bedroom or kitchen (Lederer and Jackson, 1968; Fitzgerald, 1973). Others believe that when sexual dilemmas are mentioned by couples these need to be the primary focus and that altering the sexual inadequacies will be beneficial for the whole marriage (Neiger, 1973). Should the couple be seen individually, as a couple, or with a group of couples? Because the patient is the marriage itself, marital counseling must deal with the couple, with major stress given to communications with each other. Marriage counselors agree that the following principles are important for appropriate marital counseling:

1. The counselor needs to have respect for both marital partners and has to recognize that ultimately it is their choice that will determine the direction of the marriage.

2. The couple has to have motivation in order to work on their marriage with a particular counselor.

3. In order for a change to be lasting and effective, the focus has to be on feelings and attitudes that will make for more than a transient renewal of the relationship.

4. Such a relationship change, as implied in the preceding three, has to be formulated with a counselor by the marital partners. In other words, counseling is the important medium through which the change takes place.

In many ways, these principles are very similar to those put forth as the major aspects of psychotherapy, namely a wish to help, the conveyance of respect for the client, and an understanding attitude (Reisman, 1972).

The process of marital counseling is similar to other forms of relationship-oriented interventions with the exception that the focus is different, namely "A process by which a professionally trained counselor assists a person or persons to resolve the problems that trouble them in their interpersonal relationships as they move into marriage, live within it, or make a decision to terminate" (Goodwin and Mudd, 1961, p. 688).

Once it is decided to offer marital counseling, then which model will guide the practitioner? The behavioral approach to couple therapy is one prevalent model (Liberman, 1970; Knox, 1971). Essentially, this orientation utilizes behavior modification and attempts to help partners alter their usual responses or reactions to one another. Social reinforcements, contingency management, and modeling are among the major principles this approach employs. However, while it has been criticized as being mechanistic and based upon animal learning and conditioning, it must be kept in mind that the major ingredient for successful behavior-oriented therapy is the maintenance of a positive interpersonal relationship between couple and therapist. Liberman (1970) suggests "Implementing the behavioral principles of reinforcement and modeling in the context of ongoing interpersonal interactions, seem to be the sine qua non of appropriate behavior modification therapy" (p. 109). Furthermore, in this model the therapist structures his role as that of an educator or teacher. He attempts to provide the family with information and better ways to relate to one another, thus undercutting the idea that one member is sick or disturbed.

Case G

Mrs. G complained that the evening meal was a disaster. She and her husband agreed that from the moment he walked into the house until the children went to bed their family was in a state of turmoil. Mr. G complained that upon returning from work he felt assaulted by his 7- and 10-year-old daughters. As a result of this, he and his wife often argued and then went to bed angry. Mrs. G was rather unsympathetic to his comments and reminded him that he should be more understanding of her feelings because she gets that type of behavior all day long. Furthermore, she added that when her husband comes home she would like some attention from him because she often feels starved for adult stimulation. Mr. G characterized himself as an intense person who finds his work both exhilarating and taxing. Thus he felt the necessity for time to unwind when he gets home before entering "the family circus." His wife thought it was unfortunate that they were unable to afford "help."

The therapist suggested they keep a week's record of the number of incidents that they had been discussing. In addition, they were instructed to record precisely the activities that seemed to precipitate such events. At the next meeting, 1 week later, parents reported four nights of disruptions, i.e. fighting between the child and one parent or arguments between each parent prior to dinner. One night the father was not home, and, as usual, on weekends the problem did not exist.

The suggestion was made that both parents relax together for 30 minutes immediately after father comes home from work, talking with one another in the living room and having a cocktail. The girls were to be informed that they could not have mother's or father's attention at that period of time. Dinner was to follow, and the girls were told their father would talk with them about whatever they wished to discuss while dinner was being prepared by the mother.

An alternative point of view comes from the transactionally oriented family therapist whose approach encompasses a multitude of techniques, experiential tasks for the couple, and suggestions that often involve paradoxical intentions. Faulty marital interactions result from poor choices that the marital couple make vis-à-vis each other, and the task of the therapist is to help each other become aware of the dual level of their communications (Haley, 1963; Lederer and Jackson, 1968).

Case H

Mr. and Mrs. H were an unhappily married couple whose different opinions about raising their three children had helped to create considerable friction in their 12-year marriage. It was the behavior of their son, age 7, that brought them to a child therapist who recommended marital counseling.

Neither had been previously married. Both were attractive, intelligent, and highly articulate people. As a couple, however, they found it extremely difficult to agree, and often it appeared that one of their marriage vows was an agreement to disagree! Mr. H, a successful business executive, characterized himself as very logical, accused his wife of being short on patience, overly loud, and too demanding of the children. He often analyzed her behavior and would suggest she was responding to the children as her parents, especially the mother, had responded to her. Mrs. H was quick to agree that she often made idle threats and screamed a great deal but suggested that her husband was irresponsible and illogical when it came to family matters. She suggested he frequently seemed preoccupied with his work and his own interests.

When he offered to care for the children his wife felt he was criticizing her mothering; and while she agreed to such a plan, she tended to interfere with his attempts to discipline the children.

While lamenting his life to the therapist, Mr. H commented, with laughter and a broad grin, that if they could not resolve their difficulties, he was not planning to spend the rest of his life living "in hell." His wife smirked and turned away from him. The therapist commented on the discrepant message he was sending in that he smiled and laughed while talking about something that might be painful and/or upsetting. His wife quickly chimed in and commented that she felt her husband often gets pleasure out of saying things that might hurt her. Mr. H was quick to say that he did not derive satisfaction from seeing his wife upset. "Furthermore," he added, again with a smile, "if I didn't laugh about it, I would cry." The therapist suggested that Mr. H sends his wife dual messages, especially when he is anxious, and while he hopes she chooses the right one and will behave sympathetically, she responds with hurt feelings and anger.

The psychoanalytic approach to marital counseling, in distinction to the previously mentioned ones, is a relatively long-term, insight-oriented therapy aimed at resolving intraindividual tensions that spill over into the marriage

(Eisenstein, 1956; Fitzgerald, 1973). Difficulties are construed as residing in the unconscious and past history of the individuals who often distort the marital communications owing to their own refractory tendencies.

Case I

The I's, a childless couple, entered therapy during the sixth year of their marriage, presenting themselves as troubled over their inability to have children. The husband was 10 years his wife's senior, and they met while working in the same office. She was a secretary in the firm that employed her husband as an office manager. They had married 2 years after she graduated from high school. Both agreed their sex life together was good, although Mrs. I felt they did not have sex relations frequently enough, while Mr. I suggested that he was not "an animal." It appeared that the husband was a more domineering and assertive person who either minimized or dismissed his wife's suggestions about their marriage or his actions. He also drank more than he liked, although not to excess, and he had a quick temper. Furthermore, he was extremely critical of her housekeeping abilities and seemed to demand more than she felt was reasonable.

While Mrs. I did not openly admit to feeling inferior to her husband, she was constantly asking for his opinion, felt uncomfortable making decisions by herself, and readily called him at work. She leaned on him a great deal, and, thus, conformed to the role of a "pretty but helpless wife."

Mrs. I complained that in the last 2 years she had changed from a bubbling, happy-go-lucky woman to a tense, "shrieking neurotic" who often would tear up during the day and whose hands began trembling at times for no apparent reason. She no longer felt good or confident about herself. Mr. I, on the other hand, seemed to have become somewhat more rigid and compulsive in his activities but was quite content with his marriage. For example, if the paper was not waiting for him when he returned from work, or if he was interrupted before his morning shower, he would erupt in a tirade.

During one of their heated discussions during a therapy session, the therapist turned to Mrs. I and asked where she felt her husband learned to treat her the way he does. Of course, she suggested that it was in the home and the experiences he had with his parents. The rest of the session was spent in a discussion of the husband's early childhood experiences with his parents and the perceptions he had of how his father treated his mother.

Sex-oriented marriage counselors range in their views from the providing of information for undoing of misconceptions and distortions to the teaching of sexual practices. Basically, the therapist uses the counseling relationships in a manner similar to the behavior-oriented marriage counselor except that the content of the therapy centers around sexual problems rather than social or interpersonal difficulties.

Case J

A girl, 13½ years old, was seen for a diagnostic evaluation with her 16-year-old sister, 8-year-old brother, mother, and father who was a blue collar worker. Complaints about the child always returned to the fact that she lied for no apparent reason. She had told people that she was on drugs and had been staying away from home, sleeping at boys' houses. The parents expressed concern that when she got into high school, she might earn a bad reputation so that boys would take advantage of her. Both parents felt their daughter to be a sensitive child, and father was quick to comment that she was "a good girl who often helps around the house." The J family history was indicative of instability, with multiple separations and divorce threats. The father commented that for 14 of their 16 years of married life he would often go out drinking rather than come home after work. Approximately 2 years ago he believed that his wife really meant business when she threatened to divorce him. As a result he has attempted to mend his ways.

Mrs. J commented that since her husband began to spend more time at home with the family, she had gone out more and was behaving the way he had previously.

The parents agreed that it would be helpful for their daughter, who was often sad and sullen, to meet with a therapist. Many of the girl's behaviors masked a depression that resulted from her perception that the parents were oppressive, gave her little freedom, and liked their other children more than her. While parents agreed to their daughter being seen in therapy, they did not feel talking would help them.

The girl was brought by her mother for the initial appointment. Mrs. J agreed to talk with someone while her daughter was being seen. She commented that her husband happened to have the day off from work and wished for him to be included. When both were seen, mother commented that her husband had been worried that something was wrong with him. He had been unable to have an erection for the past two years, reducing their sexual life to virtually an abstinent state for that period. Mother commented that she had become progressively more frustrated and annoyed with him because he had refused to do anything about it. Mr. J, with considerable anxiety and embarrassment, admitted that he had been having such difficulty. Apparently, prior to this impotence he had had a number of sexual encounters outside of the marriage, and had suggested that his wife do the same. She, while denying any interest in this, hinted she had already been involved in extramarital sex. While both were disinterested in discussing the interpersonal aspects of their family, they seemed quite willing to pursue a discussion regarding their sexual dilemma and agreed to further visits centered around sexual counseling. After a physical examination for Mr. J proved to be noncontributory to an understanding of the problem, a program of sex counseling based upon the techniques developed by Masters and Johnson (1970) was undertaken.

The couple was informed that the problem resulted from the husband's worry about his inability to have an erection and that they had to become more interested in giving and receiving pleasure from each other than with his achieving an erection. For the first week they were instructed to talk, caress, kiss, and cuddle each other, clothed and nude, for as long and as often as they wished. Genital contact, however, was prohibited. At the next meeting, the wife said her husband had not been as affectionate to her in years, and he commented that he almost had an erection. Applying the "give to get" principle, the husband was instructed to stimulate his wife, either orally or manually, bringing her to an orgasm. She was still not permitted to touch his penis, but was instructed to continue caressing and kissing other parts of his body. They were to perform these tasks at least twice during the week. At the next meeting the husband confessed to an "uncontrollable" urge which resulted in intercourse. They were instructed to refrain from intercourse during the third week of the program but to engage in manual or oral genital manipulation. The couple failed their appointment and when called suggested they were not longer in need of help.

Problems in marriage will be addressed by the clinician according to his major theoretical predisposition and his personality. Those with a leaning to psychoanalytic teaching may deal with each partner individually in an attempt to search for idiosyncratic internal dissonance and worries that distort their perceptions, or may view the couple in a dyadic situation where each partner brings internal distortions from the past that influence the present. Insight is a major goal. The systems-oriented transactional counselor will insist on working with the couple and, at times, the family, focusing on apparent and covert communication patterns, schisms, collusions, and nonverbal messages. The behavior modifier will look to faulty habits, predisposing antecedents, and inadequate contingencies that maintain the maladaptive couple's poor interaction.

Each therapist is armed with his own bag of tricks, theoretical point of view, and style of interaction. While all can be effective, the optimal discrimination to be made in the individual case is among the types of intervention provided rather than between therapists' persuasions.

REFERENCES

Eisenstein, V. (Ed.), *Neurotic Interaction in Marriage.* New York: Basic Books, 1956.

Fitzgerald, R. V. *Co-joint Marital Therapy.* New York: Jason Aronson, 1973.

Frank, G. The role of the family in the development of psychopathology. *Psychological Bulletin,* **64,** 191–204, 1965.

Furman, E. Treatment of under fives by way of their parents. In J. Weinreb (Ed.), *Psychoanalytic Child Therapy.* New York: International Universities Press, 1960.

Goodwin, H. M. & Mudd, E. H. Marriage counseling. In A. Ellis & A. Abarbanel (Eds.), *The Encyclopedia of Sexual Behavior,* New York: Hawthorn Books, 1961.

Haley, J. Marriage therapy. *Archives of General Psychiatry,* **8,** 213–234, 1963.

Hamilton, G. *Psychotherapy in Child Guidance.* New York: Columbia University Press, 1947.

Hamilton, G. *Theory and Practice of Social Casework.* New York: Columbia University Press, 1951.

Healy, W. *Twenty-five Years of Child Guidance.* Chicago: Institute for Human Research, 1934.

Horney, K. *Neurosis and Human Growth.* New York: Norton, 1950.

Knox, D. *Marriage Happiness.* Champaign, Ill.: Research Press, 1971.

Lederer, W. J. & Jackson, D. D. *The Mirages of Marriage.* New York: Norton, 1968.

Liberman, R. Behavioral approaches to family and couple therapy. *American Journal of Orthopsychiatry,* **40,** 106–118, 1970.

Mahler, M. S. & Rabinovitz, R. The Effects of Marital Conflict on Child Development in Neurotic Interactions in Marriage. In V. Eisenstein (Ed.), *Neurotic Interaction in Marriage.* New York: Basic Books, 1956.

Masters, W. H. & Johnson, V. E. *Human Sexual Inadequacy.* Boston: Little Brown, 1970.

Meyer, A. After care and prophylaxis. *State Hospital Bulletin.* **1,** 631, 1909.

Neiger, S. *Overcoming Sexual Inadequacy.* Chicago: Human Development Institute, 1973.

Pratt, C. Some factors affecting the psychotherapeutic function of the orthopsychiatric team: Report of the AOA National Psychotherapy Committee. *American Journal of Orthopsychiatry,* **33,** 883–889, 1963.

Rapkin, L. Y. The patient's family: Research methods. In N. Ackerman (Ed.), *Family Process*. New York: Basic Books, 1970.

Reisman, J. M. *The Development of Clinical Psychology*. New York: Appleton-Century-Crofts, 1966.

Reisman, J. M. *Principles of Psychotherapy with Children*. New York: Wiley-Interscience, 1973.

Richmond, M. E. *Social Diagnosis*. New York: Russell Sage, 1917.

Rogers, C. R. *On Becoming a Person*. Boston: Houghton Mifflin, 1961.

Statistical Abstracts of the United States. Washington, D.C.: U.S. Government Printing Office, 1972, pp. 42, 63, 65.

Tavormina, J. B. Basic models of parent counseling: A critical review. *Psychological Bulletin*, **81,** 827–836, 1974.

Ullmann, L. P. & Krasner, L. *Case Studies in Behavior Modification*. New York: Holt, Rinehart & Winston, 1965.

VanderVeen, F. & Novak, A. L. The family concept of the disturbed child: A replication study. *American Journal of Orthopsychiatry*, **44,** 763–772, 1974.

Weinberger, G. Child guidance changes. Rochester Mental Health Center Grand Rounds, January 1973.

Whitaker, C. A. & Miller, M. A reevaluation of psychiatric help when divorce impends. *American Journal of Psychiatry*, **126,** 57–64, 1969.

CHAPTER 6

Approaching the Child
and His Family Collaterally

The impersonal, education-oriented approach provides information to parents and is basically preventive in nature. Knowledge concerning the vicissitudes of childhood development can reduce parental anxiety and lessen stress for children, thus deterring the development of symptoms or maladaptive behavior. The person-oriented counseling of parents strives to foster better and more sensitive handling of minor flare-ups within the parent-child relationship. A minimum amount of time and effort is required to achieve a maximum amount of benefit. Essentially both approaches are highly desirable and not mutually exclusive, especially in times of mounting staff shortages and of increasing costs. Nevertheless, when prevention fails or is too late, the need to involve multiple family members mandates more intensive intervention.

During the 1940s and 1950s the collateral treatment of troubled children and their parents was the prevalent mode of intervention. These golden years of child guidance clinics saw an outpouring of factual knowledge about children and the widespread application of team methods for assisting parents and children. While there have been numerous criticisms of the team-oriented plan, its costliness and inefficiency in time and money, above all, led to its decline and disfavor (Josselyn, 1964; Barten and Barten, 1973).

Of course, the need for collaboration is paramount when helping institutionalized children. Cottage parents, therapists, and teachers struggle to comprehend the destructive influences on the child as well as to create an environment for growth. Furthermore, the aim of residential care is to return a troubled child from the protected and therapeutically oriented milieu to a world that is realistically filled with multiple pitfalls. In order to make adequate preparations, a member of the team works with the child's parents and, of necessity, focuses on past and future interactional patterns. The child living at home struggling with his own inner turmoil, or perhaps unable to cope with the family interactional stresses, or expressing his behavioral unrest on the school grounds, or being the disruptive influence within the classroom often becomes a candidate for the team method of therapy. A collaboration between helpers of the child and environmental influences are mandatory under such conditions. The private practitioner providing service to a troubled child and his family collaboratively most often divides his time between parent and child, while clinics have traditionally provided collaborative service following a team-oriented tandem model.

Allen (1963), discussing the origin and traditional roles of social work and psychiatry, stresses that social work has traditionally focused on environmental influences of personality and behavior while psychiatry has been more concerned with the individual's response and adaptation or maladaptation to the stresses and strains of living. A collaboration between these two disciplines appears quite natural with each focusing on its unique vantage point in helping troubled children and their families.

Such a point of view thus requires a team rather than individual orientation to helping maladaptive children and their families. America's major and unique contribution to child psychiatry has been the tandem team-oriented approach to child guidance. While rooted in the European psychoanalytic tradition, child psychiatry as practiced in America has a more functionally based stance. In fact, American child guidance has gravitated more to a preoccupation with the present and with an emphasis on current accomplishments rather than with the past and its stress on tradition (Kessler, 1966). There was a movement away from traditional Freudian psychoanalysis to modified versions of Otto Rank's theories—focused more on current experiential relationships and the constructive aspects of human development (Rank, 1950; Reisman, 1966).

Psychoanalytic intervention with children whose action caused concern or alarm in their parents, strived to help the child become aware of the connections between past traumata and present maladaptive behavior (Freud, 1928; Kessler, 1966; Pearson, 1968). An intensive relationship between child and analyst was judged necessary to guarantee a flow of material and help gauge the intensity of anxiety. Thus, the child was seen three or four times a week and termination usually did not occur for years. Anna Freud (1928) suggested that the child's lack of insight into the problems, his poor motivation for change, and lack of confidence in the analyst necessitated a lengthy process.

Work with parents was either directed towards personality change via psychoanalysis or "guidance" (Freud, 1960), with the implication of something less than what the child was receiving. In the latter, analytic knowledge and skill are made available to help the parents adjust to a changing child.

In contradistinction to psychoanalytic teachings, Rank saw "will" as a major force in determining adaption to the human condition. He conceived "will" as a "positive guiding organization and integration of the self which utilizes creatively as well as inhibits and controls the instinctual drives" (Reisman, 1966; p. 202). In this light childhood disobedience was looked upon as a struggle of parent and child wills with both positive and negative characteristics. Ambivalence became a normal accompaniment of human relationships rather than necessarily a symptom of pathology. The child's resistance to the will of the parents stimulates individuality and uniqueness, while submission of his will brings security. Reisman (1966), summarizing this position, states: "This growth in autonomy is far from easy. Each advance away from the influence of others eventuates in feelings of guilt for having estranged them; feelings of loss, and perhaps a fear of being totally abandoned. Yet each act of compliance results in a sense of guilt and self-reproach for having betrayed or compromised one's self while often eliciting a fear of losing one's own individuality" (p. 202).

At about the same time that Rank's views were becoming popular, Europe was subjected to the influences of totalitarianism, further bolstering America's pursuit of more equalitarian principles in guiding troubled families. Relationship-oriented intervention thus had an unsolicited ally.

Active participation of both child and parent, it was believed, was needed if lasting change was to be accomplished. As a result of such a shift, the relationship between parent and child and between parent and therapist took on new meaning. The dual concept of separation and individuation became the driving force for the understanding of conflicts of childhood as well as the theoretical underpinning directing the therapeutic influence (Allen, 1942). Growth and adaptive development of the child was construed in terms of the constant interplay of forces in the child, family, and his culture. The child is not only acted upon, but also is a participating actor in his daily conflicts. Hence, both parents and child need to be actively involved in the process of treatment when such conflicts become unhealthy or maladaptive.

Under conditions where a child loses his feeling of spontaneity or sense of self-worth because his parents unyieldingly dictate actions and feelings, or when parental responsibility toward the child is abandoned and the child seemingly takes charge of the parent, collateral sessions are introduced to give each party a chance to abreact feelings and work out solutions in the attitudinal or behavioral arena. The therapeutic interview is thought to represent a life situation where the patient often expects change and new direction to come from the helper but is really unable to change unless he decides to do so. The duality of dependence and independence, passivity and activity, and negation and affirmation is constantly surfacing and submerging in the therapeutic encounter, and it is towards the constructive resolution of these universal conflicts that the therapeutic relationship aims (Pavenstedt and Anderson, 1953; Coleman, 1953). In working through such conflicts the direction taken will facilitate mutual respect and affirm rather than deny the unavoidability of conflict. Such relationship-based therapy provides help on two levels: one has to do with the content-related aspect of the problem, and the other is concerned with the feelings stimulated through the immediate experiences.

It is contended that help offered on the relationship level contributes to the meaningfulness of the specific content and to the solution of the problem. It is through such a relationship-based focus that the parents learn to accept their own human nature and, therefore, become more accepting of the human nature of their child, resulting in more realistic ways of transacting their interplay. Such a relationship emerges over time as the participants struggle together.

Responsibility for the self emerges as parent and child begin to experience responsibility for the solution to their dilemmas. Both parents and children need to be involved simultaneously and contrapuntally in the process (Coleman, 1953). The child is provided an opportunity to develop a new self-concept in relation to his parents and to others and is helped to shed neurotic symptoms or maladaptive behavior. When the same themes are dealt with in parallel sessions, the family is felt to be making progress in unlocking empathic channels (Dietz and Costello, 1956). Working with parents can prevent corrosion of gains the child is making in his therapy and can provide them a different orientation to their child and to child-rearing practices (Slavson, 1952). Furthermore, parents, with the aid of their therapist can encourage the child to bring whatever problems he experiences to therapy. Information about the child may be provided to his therapist, while parent interviews may be guided by the views that the child holds toward his family's contribution to the problem.

Often such a relationship sustains parents through the "intolerable" phases of treatment and helps them when things are "getting worse before they get better."

Kessler (1966) points out that in good collaborative treatment, parents feel informed and important: "They trust the understanding and good sense of the child's therapist" (p. 449). It is important for these feelings to be engendered in the parents, otherwise conflicts will ensue between the child's therapist and the parents which may be played out within the psychic life of the child. Multiple obstacles need to be overcome when collateral therapy is performed by different therapists who need to work comfortably with one another (Brody and Hayden, 1957). For example, each team member can become overly identified with his half of the treatment and see himself as an advocate for parent or child only. Moreover, status concerns regarding the importance of one's role can hinder communications between team members, thus adversely effecting work with the client. Petty angers and jealousies of the team can be displaced onto the patient. Feeling ill at ease with a co-worker and, as a result, avoiding the sharing of information or conferences that are an important component of collateral intervention may malignantly alter the therapy. At times, being fearful of failure, a team member may conceal information from his co-workers. Additionally, not mutually respecting each other's skills will also result in a minimum of sharing. "The need for confidentiality" will sometimes be used as a rationalization for not providing sufficient information to a co-worker. Such are some of the pitfalls that a team orientation must traverse in approaching the troubled family collaterally. One may wonder why such collaborative efforts manage to survive and, indeed, thrive!

The collateral treatment approach is predicated on the view that commonly a child's problems stem from difficulties in the mother-child relationship, and that the emotional involvement of this relationship is ultimately a reflection of the mother's poorly resolved identification with her own parents. Thus a disturbed child needs a therapeutic relationship with an individual unencumbered by concerns of other family members—past and present—while mother's unresolved relationship with her own mother is cleared up. Parents, of necessity, harbor considerable hostility toward disturbed children, and it is necessary to free them of these burdensome feelings and the related guilt in order to release the more positive feelings they have toward their child. Only in a relationship with an understanding, accepting, and respectful adult is it possible for the mother to understand and share attitudes, thus becoming better able to accept her child.

Team-Oriented Collateral Intervention

A good example of the tandem model in action is traditional treatment of school phobia. On the surface, the major aim of the school phobic child is to stay out of school. However, this behavior has been understood to represent unacceptable wishes that engender anxiety and progress to fears of abandonment because some danger may befall his parents, usually his mother. The worry that a parent may meet some disaster as a result of a violent mishap in the external world mirrors the child's internal angry impulses which are projected. Such impulses within the child stimulate regression and result in greater dependency upon the maternal object while the anger associated with the mother tends to be displaced and externalized to a setting such as school. Such is the analytic understanding of a school phobia. Parents are thought to contribute to the creation and maintenance of the malady. A close symbiotic or a hostile-dependent relationship between the mother and child is believed to preexist. Furthermore, mother is assumed to have had a poor relationship with her own mother and, therefore, has not learned successfully how to handle her own dependency needs. Father is thought to be competitive with his wife and inadvertently depreciates her role in attempting to elevate himself. Both parents are often overly possessive, domineering, and make it difficult for their child to grow independently (Johnson, 1957; Coolidge et al., 1962). Major treatment strategy is to quickly return the child to school while making it possible for parents to discontinue their participation in the problem and drop their reinforcing tactics. To expedite everyone's cooperation, collaborative work is of the utmost importance in helping children and their parents overcome such difficulties. Not only is it necessary for clinical resources to be deployed to both parents and child, but also often school personnel want to be enlisted to assist parents when they find themselves incapable of getting a child to the classroom and then to structure a school environment that will contain the child or alleviate his surface worries.

Usually the team-oriented approach as practiced by child guidance clinics views the child as the patient and his parents as collaborators. Children whose behavior suggests internalized conflicts, or who show evidence of physiological reactions, or who have difficulty developing an identity apart from parents are believed to require treatment in their own right (Cutter and Hallowitz, 1962). Furthermore, the disturbance of the child is viewed as resulting from a poor parent-child relationship or mirroring parents' difficulties. In essence, it is a relationship problem with the major focus on the child's difficulties, which result from neurotic tendencies in either parent or from a disturbance between the adults that fosters maladaptive responses within the child and contributes to his behavioral maladjustments. Therapeutic involvements of one or both parents are thus also required. When intervention is provided in tandem to the family, then both team members need to be clearly aware of the aims of the treatment program, which is predominately child centered.

Case A

The mother of a 6-year-old first grader called for help because she was unable to manage her child. She described him as resisting all attempts at control, often spitting at her and kicking when he did not get his way. At school his teachers spoke of him as disruptive, needing constant attention, and calling out answers in class. While describing his unpleasant ways, the mother was quick to add "he is a good child," who at times acts as if "he is an angel."

At the intake interview with the parents it became readily apparent that the child had been overprotected and indulged. The parents married when they were both in their late twenties and after six unsuccessful years of attempting to have a child, the mother had a successful pregnancy. She described her son as a fussy eater who was late to toilet train as he did not seem "interested" and was fearful of the dark. At night the parents were quick to come to his aid as they "didn't want him to be upset."

While the father attempted to minimize much of his son's present behavior as "all boy," the mother was more convinced there was a problem. However, she worried about expressing her own displeasure and disappointment with her son because it might result in the loss of his love.

The tandem approach was used where the child could learn better methods of responding to frustration and the mother would have an opportunity to explore some of the distorted views she had regarding assertion and aggression, while also being provided a relationship where she would find acceptance for some of her negative guilt-producing feelings.

Case B

The parents of a 9-year-old boy who was underachieving in school agreed to the suggestion of their family pediatrician that they become involved in a program of psychotherapy. His poor school performance could not be accounted for by intellectual limitations. While the parents agreed to undertake a program of therapy, the father avoided involvement with the excuse that his work schedule would not permit him to keep appointments.

During the fifth session, however, both parents were seen and expressed discouragement with the progress their son was making. Father was unhappy about his son's involvement and believed him to be a "nasty, willful brat who needs to have the seat of his pants warmed." While her husband spoke, the mother was teary-eyed and commented that she did not agree with her husband as she believed "punishment does not work." The parents repeatedly expressed the view that he was quite different from the other three children in the family, all of whom are younger. Each parent, however, saw him differently: the mother described him as a highly sensitive, easily hurt child who has to be handled gingerly, while her husband felt the boy had to be more responsible and be an example to the younger children because he was the oldest in the family.

The therapist informed the parents that it was not surprising that their child was insecure and unsure of himself: One of his parents fosters more childlike reactions in him and underreacts to his misdeeds whereas the other parent expects him to behave in a more grown-up fashion and overreacts to his actions. Both parents were taken aback and began a discussion of their own values regarding child rearing but, more importantly, were able to begin to express dissatisfaction with one another's involvement with their children. The father agreed to make more effort at being involved in the therapy program and came monthly while his wife and son continued to be seen for weekly tandem appointments.

Six months following this visit, the parents and the team decided that therapy was no longer indicated as the boy was doing better in school. The parents also reported considerably less tension around the house as they were able to discuss their difference of opinion more openly.

For the most part, the tandem procedure may vary in its duration but not in its format. A series of interviews with one or both parents yielding information about the problems and the relationship terminates the intake phase. It is important to assess accurately the parents' readiness for self-involvement. Information gathering has been thought to be of secondary importance in the procedure, and instead a relationship is offered to the parents that will allow them to express difficulties to their worker. This permits an easier flow of information and may alleviate the pressures on the child by releasing them in the interviews. A second major aim is to provide the parents with information regarding the service they will receive as well as help them prepare the child for his visits. Some agencies send informative pamphlets to parents prior to their first visit describing their services and often summarizing the tandem approach. A good example is the brochure sent to parents by the Rochester Mental Health Center's Children and Youth Division (1973):

Children live within a family and within a community. Just as their behavior affects us, our behavior affects them. We try to gain an understanding of your child with you. We try to understand what your child is doing, and how your child feels about his or her problems. In turn, we try to determine how you feel about your child's problem, and what you have done and are doing to help your child.

We may request your permission to contact those professional persons who know your child and who can help us better understand your child. We may ask, for instance, to get in touch with your child's physician or school. Since we consider your appointments with us to be confidential, we do not make these contacts unless we obtain your permission.

These early interviews usually occur before your child is seen at the Center. A social worker may interview you individually, or you may be asked to meet with other parents in a small group to discuss your children and ways of handling them.

These early interviews are very important to us and may increase your understanding of your child and his or her problems. You may feel you have gained enough from these early interviews to decide your child does not need to be seen. Most parents do wish appointments for their child, however, and are interested in the outcome of his or her meetings.

Although some children are seen in small groups, your child usually is seen individually by a psychiatrist or psychologist. Many parents express concern as to what to tell their child about these early interviews (of which there are often two). The most simple and honest explanation is generally best; that you have been concerned about your child because of problems he or she seems to be having (you might specify what these problems are); that you wish to help him or her; and that you are taking him or her to see someone who will try to talk things over and be of help. By the time of your child's appointments you will also be able to tell your child the name of the person he or she will be seeing.

Let us assume you and your child are in the waiting room for your child's first appointment. The person who has been seeing you will introduce you to the person who will be seeing your child. You will go to have your interview while your child goes to have his or hers. After 45 minutes you will both return. Understandably, you may be curious as to what has happened to your child during his or her interview.

Most children can tell us some of the things that bother them and whether they feel the need for help. Of course, things that bother them may not be the same things that bother us. Our main concern is to understand how your child sees his or her problems and what he or she intends to do about them.

This information may be given to us in so many words, or we may learn how your child feels through his or her use of nonverbal behavior or use of play materials. Frequently, children cannot tell us they are angry or afraid. Yet, they can show us their feelings or what bothers them by their actions—in games, with toys, with paints or clay, with puppets.

Your child's understanding of his or her problems, his or her intentions, and our impressions will be discussed with you in a conference ordinarily held the week following your child's appointments. At that time, all of us—you, the social worker, psychiatrist, or psychologist, discuss your child and consider further what might be done to help him or her.

During the early meetings with the child, a relationship between the child and therapist is formed that at times duplicates the kind of relationship he has with his parents and at other times is totally opposite to such a relationship. The sharing of this with the parents through their worker, as well as other materials from the child's interview, heightens awareness of the interactional nature of the problem without hindering the individual relationships.

At this early stage of treatment, both child and parents struggle with their unsureness regarding their involvement in the therapeutic process. Parents, especially, have many questions regarding what their child is revealing and how he is receiving benefit. At such times conferences between parents and team members are most helpful. Such conferences have multiple purposes. They provide parents with an opportunity to meet their child's therapist and to hear and discuss his views on their child's needs and conflicts. They also give parents an opportunity to see that the team members as well as themselves are working together towards the understanding of their child. Team members have an opportunity to observe and assess the parents' current involvement in their problem and in the process—especially as it compares with their previous understanding. During initial parent conferences parental anxiety is heightened by meeting with the child's therapist who is often perceived as a personification of their guilt for having a disturbed child, and by the total impact of meeting with both therapists, reviving memories of good and bad parent figures. However, by focusing such conferences on the psychological problems and needs of the child, that is by keeping them child-centered, the parents' cooperation can be enlisted without engendering excess anxiety or mobilizing rigid defense mechanisms.

Case C

A 6-year-old boy was referred because he was having difficulty relating to other children in his neighborhood. His school reported that he was doing fine academically and behaviorally, but the parents said he had only one friend and provoked fights when playing outside with a group. Furthermore, the mother described him as always wanting his own way.

The parents are well-educated, middle-class people with the father working at a local college and his wife as an elementary school teacher. The patient has a 4-year-old sister who is described as a quiet, well-disciplined, responsive child. The boy's developmental history was normal and uncomplicated. Mother said, however, that toilet training did not go well even though "I waited like the books suggest until he was between 2 and $2\frac{1}{2}$-years old." After struggling to train him, she gave up and at 3 years he spontaneously trained himself.

The mother expected considerably more from her 6-year-old son than was appropriate, and when he failed she felt disappointed in herself for not being a better mother. Her feelings were well-concealed. Furthermore, emotional involvement between the husband and wife as between parent and child was found to be minimal. Both parents, especially the mother, hid behind an intellectual facade. Father spent considerable time in quiet activities and wanted his son to be less of a disruptive influence in the family.

The boy related to the diagnostician in a pleasant, but, at times, uneasy fashion, especially when queried as to the problems he was having. He spoke freely and positively about a number of incidents that involved children in his neighborhood. He was cheerful about school and suggested that he was doing well. While the boy saw himself somewhat closer to his father than his mother, he sensed considerable distance between himself and both parents. Treatment was recommended, and the family embarked on a period of therapy.

During the third month of treatment, a parent conference was held because the parent worker had questions regarding the progress of the parents. Despite their comments that the boy had been doing better, they continued to vacillate in their appraisal of how therapy was progressing. At the conference considerable time was spent drawing out the mother's feelings of disappointment and hopelessness regarding her son. For the first time the mother was able to explore her own feelings rather than describe the boy's behavior. The father was spending more time with his son, as had been suggested, and felt this was helpful. The boy moved somewhat closer to him, and they were doing more together. At the conference the team was able to help the mother focus on the relationship with her son and recognize that her overcriticalness was related more to feelings of inadequacy than to her son's behavior.

The conference thus promoted greater parent involvement whereby the mother could begin to focus on her own feelings of dissatisfaction. This led to more productive sessions for the parents which facilitated the progress made by the boy.

Caseworkers report that during these early interviews, parents struggle with feelings of guilt and worry about revealing their inadequacies (Coleman, 1953; Pavenstedt and Anderson, 1953). Often much of their feeling of anger is displaced onto their child as they describe the child's symptoms with considerable hostility. Parents often appear to vacillate between experiencing responsibility for their child's difficulties and feeling annoyed with the burden and imposition of a disturbed youngster. During these sessions much effort is expended in creating a positive relationship with the parents, aiming to lead them to a better understanding of the child, and to redirect some of their concerns to the parental or marital role.

Case D

The mother of a 6 year old was finding contacts with her social worker extremely difficult. She and her husband had asked for service because their daughter was a clinging, whiny child who conformed and achieved in first grade, but quietly resisted her parents' wishes at home. The clinical team characterized the girl as a manipulative, passive-dependent child who was involved in a hostile-dependent relationship with her anxiety-laden, insecure but perfectionistic mother. The father was viewed as a calm pillar of strength, who, in actuality, kept out of the conflict by continually avoiding decision-making and relegated the executive role in the family to his wife. He found it difficult to understand her concerns and was satisfied with her as a wife and mother.

During the initial half-dozen sessions, the mother vacillated between deprecating the services of therapy to demanding she be given advice on how to handle her daughter when she resisted.

The mother often found it difficult to directly express her feelings of disappointment and anger with her social worker but would complain how demanding and difficult her child was, and how inadequate and angry it made her feel. The mother believed that no matter how much she did for her daughter, it was never enough.

During these sessions the mother was provided with understanding and encouragement while her anger was accepted. As the mother's continued demands for advice were not satisfied, she began expressing her views more directly to the social worker and commented that much of the responsibility for decision-making was on her shoulders and that the therapy was not a joint effort. She likened the relationship to her marriage where she felt responsible for making the major decisions. She became less demanding of advice, and the content of the meetings shifted to include more discussion of her husband and less of her daughter.

As work with the parents progresses, they usually become more involved with discussions of other children in the family, their own marriage, or stresses of life other than the child who brought them to the professional. Reports they give about the progress their child is making are interspersed with regressions or minor upsets. It is at such times that the therapeutic relationship that has been formed provides the necessary support to the parents.

In this phase of treatment further progress is made as the parents are helped to see clearly how their own hidden insecurities relate to their child's difficulty and to understand the neurotic basis of their interactions with the child. Furthermore, it is during this phase of work that the parents' request for advice can be more discriminately responded to as the worker has a clearer understanding of what their request for advice is all about.

During these phases the child is similarly struggling with the helping person. Initially, he feels overwhelmed and insecure in the presence of the adult therapist (Allen, 1942). He is not sure whether the therapist is sincere when he provides him a voice in how they will spend their time together, or whether this is just another "trap" set by an agent of his parents. The child's therapist (similar to the caseworker) aims to create a trusting relationship in which the child will feel free to act on his feelings and begin to verbalize his worries and insecurities. Often during these early sessions the child attempts to evade or avoid discussions of the problems and behaviors which brought him into therapy. As he becomes more involved in the process and more trusting of the therapist, he is able to provide clearer expression of his worries. Some children may verbalize directly concerns they have regarding their parents, be they anxieties regarding loss and abandonment or hostilities due to felt rejections, while others show these concerns more indirectly as their play becomes more expressive and involves the therapist. A cessation of symptoms at school, with peers, or in the family often signals termination of treatment.

The child's most dreaded fears are not fulfilled as he expresses himself to the therapist. His parents are provided the opportunity to express their own feelings regarding their parents without being shamed or having guilt provoked, are able to become more tolerant as parents, and are better able to accept their child. It is this parallel movement in collateral family members monitored by the team that contributes to the success of the program (Dietz and Costello, 1956).

Case E

An 11-year-old girl was referred to a children's service of a mental health center because she was unable to adjust to the children in her class. She was reported to have a poor self-image, to be an underachiever, and to come to school smelling of urine. The girl, extremely tall for her age, made an odd-looking appearance, but could be considerably more attractive if helped with her grooming and selection of clothes. She said that she believed her mother favored her older sister and younger brother, and did not think the kids in her class liked her because they never chose her for anything. She was hard pressed to think of anything positive regarding herself. The diagnostic impression was of a neurotic child who was moderately depressed.

In contrast to their daughter the parents, college graduates, were poised, articulate, and neatly dressed. The mother confessed to having a rather unhappy childhood as she grew up in a small town and had to struggle to please her adoptive parents. She commented that she was adopted in order to be a companion to the parents' own biological child.

Both parents expressed considerable guilt for having "emotionally damaged" and neglected their daughter. Both parents, but especially the father, were highly achievement oriented. Thus he considered his daughter lazy when she was not as responsive as he believed she should be and tended to pressure her even more.

The parents expressed eagerness for help and were seen for 17 tandem interviews. Mother was unable to verbally express her negative feelings, which paralleled one of her daughter's difficulties. As a child she was expected to show respect for her parents and never talk back. Hence, she grew up feeling that self-expression was a form of aggression that brought punishment and the possibility of further rejection. Mother was helped to see that many of the feelings of rejection and anger she felt towards her daughter had much to do with the feeling she had about being loved less than her sister who was the natural child of her adoptive parents. She began to lower some of the expectations she had for her daughter and was more responsive and outward in her expression of affection.

In therapy the girl was helped to feel more comfortable with her wishes and encouraged to verbally express her dissatisfactions to mother. These were met with greater receptivity as her demands became less exaggerated. Her grades improved, and mother reported she was wetting with less frequency and was making friends at school, whereupon treatment was terminated.

Case F

The father of a 7-year-old girl who has an older sister and younger brother asked for service because of his daughter's repeated episodes of stealing. At a recent school conference he was informed she was at the bottom of her class, whereas in the previous school year she was doing extremely well.

The parents had recently divorced as "mother ran off with another man." Father stressed the fact that he and his wife did not argue or expose the children to violence and "had a quiet divorce." The girl impressed the diagnostician as a quiet, inhibited child who was able to express her concerns regarding the divorce only indirectly either through dreams or in play. Feelings of loss and anger were handled by isolation. The father, during his interviews, was also unable to express much direct feeling regarding his wife's involvement with another man, but instead presented a rather factual and chronological picture of the events. Many of the objects that the girl was stealing from her father were inconsequential. Often she would hide them and afterwards seemingly forget where they were.

The child's therapist was out ill, and during the following session, their tenth together, the girl asked whether they would be meeting the next week. The therapist reflected her concerns regarding their missed session, and this led to a discussion of fears regarding separation. The play theme during that session centered around separation, with younger dolls being responsible for older ones going away.

Afterwards, when the team discussed the sessions, it was revealed that the father felt surprised in missing his visit, although he had decided not to attend when he knew his daughter's therapist would be away. The father was also able to discuss some hurt feelings he had regarding the divorce. Three sessions later the father reported that for the first time he and his daughter were able to talk about her mother's leaving and agree that they all felt bad about it.

Such clear and frequent communication between professionals is a major ingredient in successful collaborative treatment (Coleman, 1953; Dietz and Costello, 1956). Three major vehicles for communication are (1) face-to-face routine meetings, (2) frequent lengthy case conferences, and (3) chart notes. The well-respected 50-minute hour has shrunk in collaborative therapy to 45 minutes—allowing 15 minutes at the end of each session for both members to get together and discuss their respective meetings and the progress or lack thereof in each case. Periodic team conferences occur where team members discuss the aims and goals of treatment, sharpen the formulations of the problem, and assess the progress made. The use of the record serves as an on-going review vehicle for the team.

Teamless Contacts with the Family

The increased demand for service and lengthy waiting lists provided some impetus for changing collateral intervention strategies (Kissel, 1974a; McGee and Larsen, 1967). The rise of preventive and consultative service in the children's field also altered the delivery of clinical services. Brief, goal oriented, time-limited therapy with families in crisis seeing one therapist who assumed the treatment responsibility became highly desirable (Leventhal and Weinberger, 1975). Teaming, conferencing, and copious record keeping was regarded as obsolete. The observation that "the therapist proceeded slowly, cautiously, and thoroughly, obtaining mountains of information and incorporating as much of the data as possible into a highly complex, sophisticated but unwieldy formulation" (Barten and Barten, 1973, p. 2) is representative of the criticism directed at the team-oriented collateral approach. Not only were outcome studies dismal so that the value of child therapy per se was being questioned (Levitt, 1957; 1971), but also in cases where satisfaction was reported, parents recommended that they receive more advice and specific answers to their questions as well as a greater opportunity to talk with their child's therapist (Reisman and Kissel, 1968; Kissel, 1974b).

Interveners who have little tolerance to wait for solutions to emerge, who have a flair for more directive orientations, and who emphasize the importance of power oriented conflicts within the family stress readjustment to a previously functioning balance (Leventhal and Weinberger, 1975; Phillips and Johnston, 1973). That a minimum amount of aid, speedily deployed, and strategically planted would prove to have maximum effectiveness, has become their watchword.

The therapist refocused his role from emphasizing the child centeredness of the team approach to that of the family interactional pattern, and structures himself more often as a master strategist (Leventhal and Sills, 1964; Halpern et al., 1971), as an instructor in the management of children (Phillips and Johnston, 1973), or as a parent consultant (Reisman, 1973). Often a competency model, such as has been suggested by Leventhal and Weinberger (1975) where the child and family are viewed as having problems in living rather than as being "sick" or neurotic, provides direction to the unitary therapist seeing a family collaterally. While many therapists offer such collateral therapy by alternating sessions between parents and child, some see one member more frequently than others, and some divide the sessions equally between both parent and child. Whatever the mode, however, goals are often similar in that they attempt to reduce discrepancies between how members of a family view themselves in relationship to others, and to eliminate interpersonal power struggles that ultimately result in maladaptive behavior and feelings of anxiety and guilt. Smolen and Rossner (1963) suggest "that people who have had some experience with private practice in which they are used to assuming responsibility for the entire family are able to adapt themselves readily to this procedure ... once they have learned to shift the procedure from the child to the family system" (p. 352).

Children showing severe ego impairment or whose actions appear dedicated to maintaining a symbiotic relationship with "the mothering one" (Serrano et al., 1962) are felt to require a team-oriented tandem approach. However, the majority of families seen by child specialists show either adjustment reactions or behavior disturbances of childhood (Kissel, 1974a; Leventhal and Weinberger, 1975) and could be accommodated by one therapist working with the family for brief periods of time. Such intervention is felt to be more efficient and avoids the unnecessary use of team conferences and of possibly divergent goals for the family.

Case G

The mother of a 15 year old called the clinic quite upset that her daughter had run away from home. Although she had returned, her parents reported they were unsure how to act towards her and were frightened they might drive her away again. The mother described her daughter as bright and attractive. Until the current school year she was an honor student, active in school activities, and attended social functions frequently. During the previous 6 weeks, she seemed to have lost all interest in school. Mother, father, and daughter were assigned to a social worker and contacted within a week of their application. During the first visit the parents were seen in a brief joint interview, followed by a more lengthy one with their daughter.

The girl was the oldest in the family, having two younger sisters and a brother. She seemed more in control of the situation than either parent. The father was noticeably upset and expressed considerable anger with little provocation, while his wife spoke in a cracked voice, was highly hesitant, and appeared extremely unsure of herself.

In her interview with the social worker the girl revealed how lonely she felt in the family. She commented that her mother was unavailable to her and her father was too busy with work to pay much attention to the family. She revealed feeling depressed for about 6 months prior to running away and sleeping with a boyfriend. She also made known to her parents her concern she might be pregnant. Such behavior seemed calculated to return her to the center of the parents' interest. The joint meeting with the parents corroborated much of what the girl had said. A second appointment was suggested where just the parents would be seen.

During this interview the mother's unsureness and uneasiness in talking within the family was focused upon. She revealed that a previous visit to a private psychiatrist resulted in the suggestion that she get a job as there was nothing wrong with her. The mother reported she found work most enjoyable and recognized that in the period prior to her daughter's running away, she or her husband had been out almost every night, either working or socializing. The mother wondered aloud whether she was running away from her own responsibilities to the family. While her husband had been available to the family, for the most part he was involved in activities that involved the other children, especially his 8-year-old son. A third meeting was scheduled whereby both father and daughter would be seen, but separately. At this meeting the father was provided considerably more opportunity to vent his feelings of anger and disappointment that his daughter might be pregnant and how she was turning out. It was suggested that he and his wife arrange a visit to a gynecologist for their daughter.

The girl disclosed that she and her mother often argue over issues basically upsetting to the father. Furthermore, she commented that she did not like sharing a room with her 13-year-old sister whom she accused of being disruptive and messy. She was encouraged to ask her parents for her own room. Two weeks later a family meeting was held where the girl seemed more settled and commented that her parents were spending more time at home and were more available to her as well as to the rest of the family. The parents commented that they provided her a room of her own and were pleased with the new arrangements. They decided that further service would not be needed but felt free to contact the clinic should they feel in need of help again. The family has not been heard from in 3 years.

The Extended Team

When environmental change as a corrective measure is considered with the major aim of healing the child, as discussed in Chapter 2, then collaborative efforts are called into play. Aichhorn (1935), in his pioneering work with delinquents, emphasized the group-oriented nature of the training when he suggested "the education in an institution is, and must remain, a group training. . . ." (p. 144). Redl and Wineman (1957), working with children in an institutional treatment-oriented setting for acting out behavior, suggested that every person in the institution has major importance for the treatment of the child, whether that person is a cook, janitor, teacher, recreation instructor, cottage counselor, or psychotherapist. Bettelheim (1955), helping severely withdrawn children at the Orthogenic School, suggested ideas similar to those of Redl and Wineman. In addition, "every treatment or planning session is recorded and information correlated between the child and the family therapist as well as with the observation of the teaching staff," as stressed by Riese (1962, p. 447) in her educational therapy of deprived black children in a day treatment setting. Interventions such as these require considerable attention to the multiple influences that the therapeutic agents and milieu have on the child.

Case H

An unsuccessful year in a learning disabilities class for perceptually handicapped children led to the referral of a 7-year-old first grader to a day treatment unit of a children's community mental health center.

His parents were unable to accept the fact that they had a mildly brain damaged child as they believed their son bright in everyday learning and felt he was not different from his older sister or younger brother in his development.

Parents were able to accept that he had a slight auditory problem and learned differently than most children but put the onus for his difficulty on the school for not teaching him differently.

The day treatment unit found him appropriate for its program. Psychological testing revealed him to be functioning within the average range of intelligence, but with poor motor coordination and limited language development. Furthermore, he was socially immature and lacking in interpersonal skills.

Despite the best efforts of the clinical team, the parents continued to resist accepting their child as a handicapped youngster. They accused the public school of segregating him, thus limiting his experience in socialization with normal children. However, they agreed to acquiesce to the pressure of the public school and placed him in the day treatment unit.

During their son's first year in the program, the parents were involved minimally. The boy spent most of his time with one teacher developing relationship skills. Near the latter part of his first year, he was exposed to a language communication instructor, a reading tutor, and gym and craft instructors. Psychotherapy was instituted during his second year. He was working with a clinical team of six in addition to relating to his bus driver and lunchroom aides.

Although he became less disruptive, he continued to stir up his class as well as to cause trouble on the bus and in the lunchroom.

Weekly team meetings, instituted by the school director, provided a clearer understanding of the boy's problems, which formed the basis of consistent interventions from all of the helping adults.

While symptoms, maladaptive behavior, or parental anxiety bring children to the attention of child specialists, it may be more helpful to consider somewhat broader issues when deciding on whether to provide a team or a single therapist. Overt hostilities and suspiciousness within the family, vicarious parental enjoyment of the child's behavior, or severe marital discord requiring the child to be a referee are situations that undermine the child's development of a clear, separate, and secure identity. Under these conditions a collateral approach appears useful. In other circumstances, when both parent and child are unhappy with the overt symptoms and underlying communication process, team-oriented collateral therapy would not seem to be required. More often than not the discrimination boils down to the inclination of the therapist and to the philosophy of the particular clinic with which he finds himself affiliated. Nevertheless, collaterally based procedures require modification to reflect the current needs of the society in which they are attempting to heal, or else they will be discarded entirely, and unfortunately the "wheat" will be lost with the "chaff." The transition in outlook that currently affects the society and afflicts the family has stimulated some practitioners to abandon the collateral method in favor of treating the family as a unit.

REFERENCES

Aichhorn, A. *Wayward Youth*. New York: Viking Press, 1935.

Allen, F. H. *Psychotherapy with Children*. New York: Norton, 1942.

Allen, F. H. *Positive Aspects of Child Psychiatry*. New York: Norton, 1963.

Barten, H. H. & Barten, S. S. *Children and Their Parents in Brief Therapy*. New York: Behavioral Publications, 1973.

Bettelheim, B. *Truants From Life: The Rehabilitation of Emotionally Disturbed Children*. Glencoe, Ill.: Free Press, 1955.

Brody, W. M. & Hayden, M. Intrateam reactions: Their relation to the conflicts of the family in treatment. *American Journal of Orthopsychiatry*, **27**, 349–355, 1957.

Children and Youth Division. Rochester, N.Y.: Rochester Mental Health Center, 1973.

Coleman, T. V. Artie: A victim of an inconsistent parental relationship. In G. E.

Gardner (Ed.), *Case Studies in Childhood Emotional Disabilities.* New York: American Orthopsychiatric Association, 1953.

Coolidge, J. C., Hahn, P. B. & Peck, A. Patterns of aggression in school phobia. *The Psychoanalytic Study of the Child,* **17,** 319–333, 1962.

Cutter, A. V. & Hallowitz, D. Different approaches to treatment of the child and the parents. *American Journal of Orthopsychiatry,* **32,** 152–158, 1962.

Dietz, C. R. & Costello, M. E. Reciprocal interaction in the parent-child relationship during psychotherapy. *American Journal of Orthopsychiatry,* **26,** 376–393, 1956.

Freud, A. *Introduction to the Technique of Child Analysis.* New York: Nervous and Mental Disease Publishing Co., 1928.

Freud, A. The child guidance clinic as a center of prophylaxis and enlightenment. In J. Weinreb (Ed.), *Recent Developments in Psychoanalytic Child Therapy.* New York: International Universities Press, 1960.

Halpern, W. I., Hammond, J. & Cohen, R. A therapeutic approach to speech phobia: elective mutism reexamined. *Journal of the American Academy of Child Psychiatry,* **10,** 94–107, 1971.

Johnson, A. M. School phobia: Discussion. *American Journal of Orthopsychiatry,* **27,** 307–309, 1957.

Josselyn, I. M. Child psychiatric clinics quo vadimus. *Journal of the American Academy of Child Psychiatry,* **4,** 721–734, 1964.

Kessler, J. *Psychopathology of Childhood,* Englewood Cliffs, N.J.: Prentice Hall, 1966.

Kissel, S. The changing role of the child psychotherapist. American Psychological Association, New Orleans, 1974a.

Kissel, S. Mothers and therapist evaluate long-term and short-term child therapy. *Journal of Clinical Psychology,* **36,** 296–299, 1974b.

Leventhal, T. & Sills, M. Self-image in school phobia. *American Journal of Orthopsychiatry,* **34,** 688–695, 1964.

Leventhal, T. & Weinberger, G. Evaluation of a large scale brief therapy program for children. *American Journal of Orthopsychiatry,* **45,** 119–134, 1975.

Levitt, E. E. The results of psychotherapy with children: An evaluation. *Journal of Consulting Psychology,* **21,** 189–196, 1957.

Levitt, E. E. Research on psychotherapy with children. In A. E. Bergin & S. L. Garfield (Eds.), *Handbook of Psychotherapy and Behavior Change.* New York: 1971.

McGee, T. F. & Larsen, V. B. An approach to waiting list therapy groups. *American Journal of Orthopsychiatry,* **37,** 594–597, 1967.

Pavenstedt, E. & Anderson, I. N. Complementary treatment of mother and child with atypical development. In G. E. Gardner (Ed.), *Case Studies in Childhood Emotional Disabilities,* New York: American Orthopsychiatric Association, 1953.

Pearson, G. H. J. *Handbook of Child Psychoanalysis,* New York: Basic Books, 1968.

Phillips, E. L. & Johnston, M. S. H. Theoretical and clinical aspects of short-term parent-child psychotherapy. In H. H. Barten & S. S. Barten (Eds.), *Children and Their Parents in Brief Therapy*. New York: Behavioral Publications, 1973.

Rank, O. *Will Therapy and Truth and Reality*. New York: Knopf, 1950.

Redl, F. & Wineman, D. *The Aggressive Child*. Glencoe, Ill.: Free Press, 1957.

Reisman, J, M. *The Development of Clinical Psychology*. New York: Appleton-Century-Crofts, 1966.

Reisman, J. M. *Principles of Psychotherapy with Children*. New York: Wiley, 1973.

Reisman, J. M. & Kissel, S. Mothers' evaluation of long-term clinic services. *Bulletin of the Rochester Mental Health Center*, **1**, 13–17, 1968.

Riese, B. *Heal the Hurt Child*. Chicago: University of Chicago Press, 1962.

Serrano, A. C., McDanald, E. C., Goolishian, H. A., MacGregor, R. & Ritchie, A. M. Adolescent maladjustment and family dynamics. *American Journal of Psychiatry*, **118**, 897–902, 1962.

Slavson, S. R. *Child Psychotherapy*. New York: Columbia University Press, 1952.

Smolen, E. M. & Rosner, S. Observation on the use of a single therapist in a child guidance clinic. *Journal of the American Academy of Child Psychiatry*, **2**, 345–356, 1963.

CHAPTER 7

Family Therapies

The family unit as a target for therapeutic intervention gained sudden prominence shortly after World War II. The early explorers in this field believed they would be regarded as heretics by their colleagues. Well into the 1950s practically all formal teaching and training in therapy concentrated on the individual as the carrier of pathology. The belief was extant that if the therapist could amass sufficient knowledge about intrapsychic life and was sufficiently skillful in the practice of individual psychotherapy, then improvement would surely follow. What surprises is not that this orientation came to be questioned, but that interest in treating the family arose at all. Family therapy had to overcome an interdiction that amounted to a cultural taboo. The belief in the sanctity of the patriarchal family, one of the supporting pillars of Western civilization, namely that a man's house is his castle, had acted as a powerful but covert modifier of clinical perception. To attack such a phenomenon before the time was right must have been literally unthinkable.

In the postwar years several large-scale changes emerged that led to a number of apparent power shifts in the direction of greater transactional democratization. The essence of its philosophy, although couched in egalitarian terms, appeared to be a deauthorization of traditional control agents. Whether examined from the vantage point of world politics and the rise of the Third World nations, or of civil rights and the new status of minorities, or of sexism and the leveling of social roles, the entrenched holders of power have been under siege and have been making adjustments in their negotiating stance. Has the family been immune from these events, or was it flung into a maelstrom of change in which it can hardly find its bearings? If the latter, it need not come as a surprise that a form of therapeutic intervention had to be devised and specifically designed for the novel exigencies that might prove disruptive for families. The ascendancy of the "weak," so swift in the political and social arena, has had its counterpart in the primary institution of child-rearing. Not only has there been a perceived change in the status of the woman from a subordinate to "equal marriage partner," but also the children as well have acquired the distinction of possessing rights in concert with their parents (Marker and Friedman, 1973).

A breaking away from established patterns tends to loosen the previous cohesiveness of functional groups. Since this brings on anxiety in its members, who must now cast about for a renewal of homeostasis more consonant with the present needs of the group, all kinds of innovative problem-solving devices spring up to bring relief. In Chapter 4, the growth of a social and educational support system for parents is looked upon as a substitute for the extended kinship culture that once buffered the nuclear family. For many families this level of help was hardly enough so that a more intimate process of therapeutic involvement with family specialists became an inevitable development.

Often the problem afflicting these families can be found in the backwash brought on by bewildering changes in the balance of power among its members. In a tradition-bound family, where roles are relatively fixed and stable, there may be episodic power struggles but life on a day-to-day basis is conducted, if not placidly, at least in accordance with certain well-codified rules between those who dominate and those who submit. When the rules of conduct are less arbitrary, however, and those responsible for the upholding of the code are no longer held in awe, much more energy is expended in working out complementary arrangements so that both individual preferences and group goals can be recognized and satisfied. Because insecure people in families, as elsewhere, tend to fall back on familiar and simplistic methods of conflict resolution, considerable tension, incongruence, and maladaptive posturing is introduced into family transactions. Perhaps the most crucial issue family members find hard to manage is the sharing of power. All relationships must somehow settle the ordering of control between human beings who treasure their particular areas of autonomous functioning. When the domination-submission pattern looses its culturally prescribed quality, the task becomes exploratory and fraught with risks and challenges.

Chapter 5 deals with the tribulation of the conjugal pair and the attempts at remediation when the parental role is compromised by conflict between husband and wife. Adding the influence of children to the mix is often overlooked as an important source of tension to parents. Whereas a couple's adjustment can follow the romantic notion of serving an idealized partner or the pragmatic one of dividing the labor to suit gender role expectations, the arrival of children quickly taxes the balance established between the pair.

They discover that they must renegotiate a new arrangement whereby some of their personal and conjugal interests, which are almost exclusively centered on themselves, must give way to include an advocacy totally new to their experience.

Until recent times, the child was defined for parents in terms of possession. Parents had undisputed ownership of children and could deal with them as righteously as they wished. Disciplinary measures, if applied, were swift, harsh, and final. Although parental confidence in these measures may not have been universally strong, the prevailing public opinion certainly supported a child-rearing climate where all parties knew their place, and acted accordingly. Then, when a couple had children the transition into child-centered family life was outwardly less troubling than it appears today, with modern parents having to prove themselves both adequate and sensible in their caretaking roles. Increasingly the community's concern for the welfare of the child is invading the domain of absolute parental power, and society's protection is afforded those children whose homes place them in physical and mental jeopardy. As a consequence the dogmatic child-rearing principles of yesterday have become unreliable guides to new parents who must now labor for workable arrangements peculiar to their special circumstances.

In the family itself, as parents relinquish some of their unquestioned power to dominate the young, the children themselves step into the ensuing void and exert their own pressures for even greater parental submission. Today many parents and teachers feel tyrannized by the young as if the balance of power has swung too far to the other side. The complaints of the adults frequently sound like those of beleaguered vassals, seeking protection from a feudal lord who presumably has the weaponry and will to deal with the infidel. They feel that as parents they have been left prematurely to their own devices. At the same time, they bear the onus of failure and of associated guilt if their experimentation in egalitarian family living falters. They sometimes long for the old values of hierarchal order, and do fall back on them in a pinch, but are simultaneously pulled in the direction of moderation and leniency in parenting. The resulting perplexity and insecurity in the members of the household find expression in problems of communication, complementarity, and coordination. When a family seeks a remedy for these problems, which usually stem from a child's behavior, its hopes are for better ways of living together.

Into this arena of bewilderment have stepped a breed of therapists who refer to themselves variously as referees, umpires, catalysts, change agents, conductors, reactors, systems analysts, or strategists (Beels and Ferber, 1969; Ferber et al., 1972). They see themselves dealing with problems limited to the interpersonal sphere and thus concentrate on family group processes, searching for clues in maladaptive interactional or transactional patterns. Their aim is to help the family become aware of its own inner workings so that it can make adjustments in accordance with the values it chooses for itself. Despite the many divergencies in methods among family therapists (Ferber et al., 1972) there is a basic orientation which might best be described as teaching parents to be better power brokers. Through their own negotiating and mediating styles family therapists model for parents and children an alternative to both autocratic and laissez-faire approaches by the skillful use of clarification, role structuring, arbitration, discussion, bargaining, problem definition, controlled affect discharge, taking sides, compromise, and problem solving. The rockbed of good parenting, negotiating with children from a position of strength rather than from weakness, is preserved by offering the adults a sense of presence and effectiveness vis-a-vis those children who have challenged their capacity to conduct the affairs of family life.

The way each therapist goes about his business of bringing a family around to the transactional point of view depends as much on his personality as on his theoretical orientation. As a result, "therapeutic fadism" is a real danger in this field (Group for the Advancement of Psychiatry, 1970). A strong antimedical and even antichild bias has been noted in the family therapy movement (McDermott and Char, 1974).

Some tongue-in-cheek classification of entrepreneurial leaders among family therapists has been attempted by Haley (1962) and by Beels and Ferber (1969). In truth the distinction among them is ambiguous and is not built on any sound difference in conceptual or dynamic presentation. The major ideological schism, if such there be, derives from an emphasis on individual-oriented family therapy based on the psychodynamic model, on the one hand, and from a systems-oriented methodology based on the transactional model of small-group politics, on the other (Group of the Advancement of Psychiatry, 1970; Zuk, 1971). In practice, there is considerable overlap between these points of view. For the purposes of this chapter, family therapy methods will be classified on a continuum that has, at one end, simplicity of design and, at the other, a complex but not necessarily more sophisticated social network schema. Variability is introduced by a host of factors. Some practitioners have very formal ideas about who is to be seen and when (Bell, 1974). Others stress the importance of home visits (Friedman, 1962). The use of multiple therapists is considered efficacious by one group (MacGregor, 1962) while another sings the praises of total involvement of the single therapist in the family encounter (Ackerman, 1958). There are exponents of seeing families in group sessions exclusively (Zuk, 1971) and those who may start out on that basis but use various combinations of therapy thereafter (Minuchin et al., 1967). The degree of a family's social intactness or the definition of crisis may govern the application of several family approaches (Langsley et al., 1968). In view of the multiplicity of family therapy schools, the identified subtypes should not be considered all-inclusive.

Family Group Therapy

A well-defined, systematic technique based on reasonably cogent sociopsychological assumptions is encompassed in family group therapy as advocated by Bell (1961, 1974). His method proposes to bring about behavioral and attitudinal changes in a total nuclear family where a lone therapist arranges a series of conferences with the parents and their children above the age of 8 years. Although the referral is ordinarily made for the "problem" child, the therapeutic goals are family-centered. Presumably, if the functioning and structure of the family as a group can be altered, the individual members will modify themselves in due time. The child's symptoms are viewed as indicative of a disorder in intrafamilial communication or interaction rather than the outcome of intrapsychic conflicts in any of its members. If anything, psychic distress derives from disturbed interpersonal patterns within the family. What better way is there than to observe the offending pattern and to influence it but to enter into the family gestalt and consciously try to improve the means of interaction among its members?

The two primary goals of such therapy are (1) the release of inhibition about the verbal and affective expressions of feelings and desires and (2) the disciplined development of new patterns of expression in interpersonal communication so that members have greater access to conscious choice making in their involvements with each other. Although these goals appear to be incongruent, it is in the integration of divergent elements whereby families become more resilient and gain in strength. If a family can understand its functional unity and structural interdependence, despite the negative or dissonant feelings of its members, parents and children have more meaning for each other as human beings.

According to Bell, contact is first made with both parents for purposes of orientation. During the initial interview the therapist secures a statement of the problem about the child, including his developmental history, and he conveys in some detail his method of working with the family. The nuclear family, except for very young children, is to be seen weekly. In his role as a "referee," the therapist guarantees open discussion, but he also tells the parents how he will take the child's side to gain his trust and to give him the confidence to speak freely. The therapist further gives the parents the paradoxic instruction that he will not make decisions for them but that they ought to give in to some of the child's demands in the beginning, even if these may prove somewhat inconvenient to them. It is also anticipated with the parents that they should expect the child to become more hostile toward them before he waxes more loving. In other words, the parents are urged to take a backseat during the early family conferences.

During the first session with the family the children are oriented to the procedure. The therapist tells them that he had spoken with the parents who feel that the whole family could be more content than it is. The adults are then pictured as emotionally clumsy people who have trouble understanding children. The therapist points out how the therapy session is a medium for improving their relationships because he is there to see to it that each child will be heard with respect to those things that make everybody unhappy. Moreover, like the parents, the therapist affirms how he is on the side of the children, the only difference being in that he knows how to make parents more aware of their feelings and desires. He proceeds to point out to the children that the mother and father want to deal with them differently for the happiness of all and he permits the children "to have more say in how the family is to be run" (Bell, 1974). Finally, he invokes the paradoxic principle of family group therapy, namely of being only an umpire who, during the sessions, enforces the rules he makes.

Once the orientation statement is out of the way, the therapist embarks on a child-centered phase by asking the child to give his ideas about the things that make the family unhappy. In turn, the therapist asks the child for his ideas on solving the problems and hopes that the parents will accede to his initial demands. This method allows for some hedging, with comments about the trial basis for this or that particular solution to the problem and about the possibility of its reconsideration in further discussions. If the parents cannot accept the child's wishes, they are usually receptive to a compromise plan whose workability is subject to the same review. At this stage, that therapy proceeds most readily where parents are inclined to go along with the child because he will soon run out of demands.

When the child announces with some satisfaction that he is hurting less, the parents open the wound with a torrent of complaints, often relating to difficulties at school or in the community rather than at home. In this parent-centered phase, the ventilation of these hostile feelings is important, yet the therapist also takes steps to protect his rapport with the child by giving both sides the opportunity to express themselves, by quoting authorities on normative development to back up a contention that a given behavior is appropriate, and by interpreting the child's actions as having some meaningful purpose. Verbal and emotional exchanges between child and parents characterize the ensuing interaction. As the child continues to defend himself against the complaints, the family arrives at a better understanding and appreciation of the bonds that hold them together. The quarreling tends to become compartmentalized to the conferences while at home hostile outbursts may occur only sporadically.

At this point, the mother-father interaction often comes into the foreground. Presumably the children who learn something about their parents' problems will be better able to identify with them. Similarly if the focus moves to sibling interaction, the need for mutual listening as structured by the therapist offers opportunities for more active empathy.

The end stage, or family-centered phase, has all the earmarks of improvement. Many of the referral symptoms have vanished or are better tolerated. In the conferences family laughter appears, often in conjunction with reports about cooperative problem solving. Pleasurable family activities are on the increase as is a greater acceptance of independent forays by individual members. In the glow of good feeling, the children may even volunteer for chores. Finally, there are spontaneous expressions of improvement and confidence that the family can dispense with the services of the therapist.

Because the members of a group such as the family "are constantly engaged in a balancing act, juggling the self-wishes against the imposed demands from other individuals" (Bell, 1962), the therapist seeks to improve the accommodation of participants to each other so that individual aims are more complementary. If the family's goal-seeking activities are harmonious, smooth action is the rule. If its aims are not congruent, an ambiguous situation arises that leads to a tug-of-war or even cessation of action.

The role of the therapist in this method is one of verbal action. He clarifies his procedures and expectations repeatedly, anticipates problems and resistances, verbalizes the unspoken feelings of the group, points out historical parallels between the lives of the parents and their children, articulates the family's mode of communication and its consequences, recapitulates the therapeutic events of the various stages in treatment, structures his participation in ways that allow him to elaborate on the family's reaction to him, facilitates and promotes communication, and helps in the restructuring of roles. This form of intervention is best suited to families with a middle-class value orientation.

Case A

The parents of three sons who were 15, 12, and 9 years old requested help for the youngest child. He had some learning problems in school and behavior problems at home. He had voiced a strong dislike for school in contrast to an earlier fondness for it, had retreated from all academic achievement, and had resisted class attendance. His older brothers were annoyed with his complaints and protests. In order to avert quarrels with him, they avoided him as much as possible. The boy saw himself as a defenseless victim of his brothers and the target of bullies among his peers. Although he had been considered a responsive baby and a happy but slightly clumsy boy up to age 8 years, there had been an obvious change in personality which troubled the parents. The family was of moderate means and resided in an upper-middle-class suburban community.

When the parents were seen together for an initial interview they appeared to be an attractive and articulate couple. The father presented a serious demeanor and occasionally lapsed into self-blame for his son's problems. On the other hand, although a soft-spoken person, the mother obviously held sway over the family. She set the tone for the manner in which transactions were to be carried out.

This interplay between a mother who expected the family to tolerate a great deal of angry and demanding behavior from the youngest son and a father who felt guilty when he could not restrain his resentment came into sharp relief in the first family session. The youngest boy was most insistent about being heard. Despite the exasperation of the other male members in the family, the mother hung on the boy's every word as if she had to protect him from the control of his father or brothers, who were all shy persons. Outside the home, he was known not to be able to stick up for himself.

The mother had perfectionistic tendencies. In subsequent family interviews, she revealed that she had withdrawn from her husband over the past year in order to devote more time to being a good mother. The middle son had exhibited some learning problems a few years previously. When the youngest also followed his pattern, particularly being behind in reading, the mother gave her full attention to this child. The father's response to his wife's withdrawal and coolness had been to seek out an affair with another woman while his wife fretted that he did not take the boy's problems more seriously.

The therapist first helped the children to bring into the open their awareness of the parents' estrangement from each other. The youngest had seen himself most vulnerable, especially as his mother's benign indulgence toward him was isolating him from the father and the brothers. When the parents agreed to take another look at their marriage and actually move closer to each other over a 3-month period, the 9 year old grew less restive and took on a more positive attitude toward school.

Case B

A 14-year-old boy was a disciplinary problem at home and in school. He skipped classes, engaged in minor vandalism with other youth, and was apprehended as a passenger in a stolen car. There had been long standing tension between his parents and himself. A 12-year-old sister, frequently allied in trouble with the brother, was obese and aggressive while another sister, age 16 years, was considered to be a self-centered hoyden by the parents.

The whole family was seen together after a preliminary interview with the parents. All the children were subjected frequently to the father's caustic criticism of their failure to carry out routine chores or responsibilities. To please both husband and children, the mother swung back and forth from overcontrol to undue laxity. Because the children were not permitted to discharge their anger or frustration through verbal means, they did so by their unreliability and by their uncanny proclivity to embarrass their parents through a display of inadequacies and delinquencies.

Over a period of months the therapist made it possible for the children to overcome their caution in interpersonal communication. Once they could verbalize feelings more readily, they began to recognize, along with the parents, that their behavior was associated with conflicted feelings toward the parents. The father had feared that his children would side with their mother against him. By criticizing them he had hoped to prevent such an alliance and force his wife to support his stand against the children. The son in particular was a competitor who had to know his place.

Although the father never completely lost his cynicism in a period of a year's therapy, he granted the other family members their right to express personal needs and preferences and discovered with some relief that the children were not interested in rising up against him. The mother moved into a position where she became the pivotal person who could bring the interests of the various family factions to the attention of all so that these would be discussed and at least partially resolved.

Integrative Family Therapy

A less formal tack is taken by Ackerman (1958) although he too supports constructive complementarity in family role relations as the ultimate aim of integrative family therapy. Conceptually he gets at the emotional disturbance of the individual through an examination of the family experience. Furthermore, the family as the primary humanizing agent also accommodates itself to changes in the social order, which has an interest in molding the unit to its greatest usefulness. He considers the art of family healing as an ancient rite that has had considerable communal sanction. Various family gatherings for celebrating developmental milestones, rites of passage, feasts, and kindred events possess important restitutive and regenerative potential (Ackerman, 1971). Perhaps because he looks upon the family as such a pervious vessel, always in need of patching, he is not surprised by the lack of a unified theory of therapy. At best, family therapy must tackle multiple levels of conflict so that no one therapist may be temperamentally suited or professionally skilled enough to encompass them all (Ackerman, 1970). At one time disturbances in family relationships were corrected by social therapy carried out by social agencies rather than by psychotherapy (Ackerman, 1954). With the subsequent emphasis on the importance of the individual personality, the standardized reorientation of family attitudes and style fell into disrepute. The family therapist of today brings to his work an appreciation of both individual and social dynamics. Therefore he becomes the strategist who works for the preservation of the family despite conflict in the individual or in intrafamilial relationships.

The sequential involvement in therapy of multiple family members follows no predetermined course but depends on the cues received from the continuing observation of family processes. All manner of combinations of meetings with mother, father, and children are conceivable: "Of necessity, the proper sequence of diagnostic and therapeutic interviews involving individuals, family, pairs or the entire family group varies from family to family" (Ackerman, 1958, p. 306).

For example, an interview with a child and mother may be followed by an interview with the child and father, another with the parents alone and, at an appropriate point, with the total family. An alternate model may start with the parents as the relevant family pair and discriminatingly meander to individual meetings or to group sessions involving any two or more family members. In the case of an adult patient, personal psychotherapy may give way to marital counseling and/or family treatment. When tensions become high or a crisis ensues, home visits are utilized to deal with the acute threat to the family group.

Because family therapy is complex, the use of a clinical team is not discounted in the way various phases of treatment must be carried out. In order to counter the possibility of isolation that comes with treating individuals, the involved therapists congregate periodically with the entire family group to work on commonly shared conflictual material. Furthermore, the clinical team has the job of reflecting together on the effectiveness of the intervention on the ever changing family life processes. It is in the "flexible use of the primary techniques and their derivations" (Ackerman, 1958, p. 295), in addition to adequate motivation and a clear understanding of goals, that the therapy succeeds.

Case C

The parents of a 13-year-old boy, the youngest of four children, were concerned about his underachievement in school and his lack of stability at home. Although he was over 6 feet tall, they considered him immature because he cried easily and lashed out at two of his older sisters. His relationship to the father and to the oldest sister who was away at college was more reasonable. He had had problems with peers but these improved at the time of referral.

For the initial contact all family members with the exception of the oldest daughter met with the therapist. The boy cried copiously as he complained about being poorly understood by the women in the household. Whatever he did at home immediately elicited disapproval. If he played his record player, it was always too loud. Should he accidently bump into one of his sisters, he was accused of tripping her intentionally. Whatever special interests he pursued, for example working on cars, were generally believed to be too undignified for the family.

Both parents were indeed joined by their daughters in a litany of negative criticism of the boy. The father was a meticulous man who had high hopes of a professional career for his only son, yet he tried not to feel his disappointment in the boy's preference for the manual arts. The mother, too, was energetic in the pressure she exerted on all her children for good academic performance.

Over 15 sessions, the boy became better able to defend himself but still tended to vacillate between an aggressive and a defeatist attitude. The therapist then omitted the sisters from the meetings in order to better focus on the parents and the son. This served to strengthen the boy's resolve to speak more positively of his likes and special interests without lapsing into a querulous attack on his parents for haranguing him to follow their desires. Gradually the mother expressed discontent with her husband for not meeting her needs. It dawned on them that they had been scapegoating the son in order to keep their feelings about the marital relationship obscure to themselves. Subsequently the therapy moved into a collateral stage whereby the parents were seen separately from the boy, with the latter struggling now to raise his self esteem vis-à-vis peers and the former concentrating on their marriage.

Conjoint Family Therapy

In conjoint family therapy (Satir, 1967) the therapist establishes a positive relationship with each family member by first arranging individual interviews. After having listened to each side privately, the therapist meets with the family and communicates a desire about resolving unfortunate misunderstandings among them while emphasizing the good intention of all participants. This tends to undermine the family ploys of scapegoating or other defensive maneuvering.

Task-Oriented Family Therapy

The treatment of the disorganized family requires an active and directive intervention by the therapist-change agent according to the formulations of Minuchin and co-workers (1967). In working with delinquent boys from poor families, they studied the family structure and found in three-fourths of their cases there was no father or stable father figure and, where present in the remainder, he completely deferred to the mother in the matter of child rearing and education. At the same time the mother looked upon her role primarily in nurturant terms and therefore communicated ineffectualness when she needed to guide or control the children. Inevitably both parents felt themselves powerless as children took control. They even hastened the process of premature independence in children by insisting on their being autonomous, that is without need for parental guidance, or by vesting the authority in an older sibling. In this manner the source of reference for executive guidance and control became lodged in "parental children."

In the disorganized family the children learn to react to the parents' mood responses which encourages them to adopt an unfocused, nonanalytic behavior. As a result communication is noninstructive for future problem solving. The therapist concerns himself with these amorphous behavior patterns and then guides the family members "to perceive issues and problems that underly the ineffectiveness of their problem-solving attempts" (Minuchin et al., 1967). To do so he must master well-timed intervention techniques. Responses are geared to the typically motoric modality of communication and action through "the use of movement language and 'enactive' representations." Unlike the purposeless acts of the family members, the therapist uses the motoric modality in a differentiated and more focused fashion. Additionally, he attenuates the noisy and chaotic quality of verbal exchange by highlighting the rhythm and rules of communication. By repeating what a member says or by asking whether he was heard, he helps bring about a required directionality for meaningful exchanges to occur. Once he picks out certain focal themes, he enlarges upon them and clarifies the multiplicity of roles in interactional processes. This opens up the possibilities of modifying the direction of transactional pathways by means of task assignments.

Task-oriented family therapy includes a variety of techniques such as the filling out of questionaires (Drechsler and Shapiro, 1961), the conjoint drawing (Bing, 1970), family art therapy (Kwiatkowska, 1967), sculpting (Simon, 1972), discussion of playback material (Paul, 1966), role playing (Riessman, 1964), and psychodrama (Moreno, 1946). Minuchin (1965, 1974) uses the conflict-resolution model to shape a technique that will coach the members of the family in thinking out alternatives to stereotypic adaptation. For example, the members of the family caught up in a conflict situation remain in the room while the therapist commits the rest of the family to an observation through a one-way screen. As soon as the task-assigned group falls back on former patterns, the therapist coaches an observing family member to reenter the group situation and redirect the problem solving toward the pattern previously agreed upon. If this does not suffice, another member or the therapist himself returns to guide the interplay toward a correct solution (Minuchin et al., 1967).

Each meeting is divided into three stages. For the first 30 to 40 minutes, the session brings the whole family together with two therapists and the child-patient's caseworker in order to clarify the perceptions, attitudes, and feelings about a particular problem. This is immediately followed by two simultaneous collateral sessions with separate therapists and the caseworker sitting in on the children's session for another 30 to 40 minutes. The purpose of this interlude is to explore the perceptions, attitudes, feelings, and problems of individuals and subsystems. Finally, the family group meets with both therapists for 20 minutes to review the experience and foster better communication. A postsession staffing of therapists serves to debrief the clinicians for purposes of enhancing their comprehension of the family and of its coping style. To understand the dynamics of families from the disorganized sector of the population, the therapists must familiarize themselves with whatever support system of indigenous resources operates in those families' immediate environment. Without utilizing the leverage of that system for effecting improvements in the life of the family, the professional may find himself incapable of assisting in problem solving attempts. By taking an active role with regard to changing communicational patterns and by applying these skills to practical methods of interpersonal discourse and environmental manipulation, the therapist introduces a sense of order and mastery into the proceedings.

Case D

In the course of collateral therapy involving an 8-year-old boy and his parents, the mother alluded frequently to feeling dismayed by the behavior of all her children, mostly manifested by the obstreperous and boisterous interaction among five sons. The father suffered from a lung disease that did not permit him much display of energy beyond that necessary for his job. Their initial contact at the clinic stemmed from a referral by the school where their youngest child was withdrawn and mute. When the boy improved gradually in individual therapy over a period of months, the mother's complaints about all the children became increasingly more plaintive. In addition to the 8 year old, there were 10-year-old twins who were forever bickering with each other, a 13 year old who was aloof but disdainful of his younger brother's antics, and a 14 year old who attempted to be the disciplinarian in his parents' place.

When progress in collateral treatment was stymied by the mother's doubt about being able to manage the brood, the decision was made to see the family as a group. Very quickly the children replicated the tumultuous interaction of home in family therapy, which further discouraged both parents. Although the two therapists involved could guide the boys into more acceptable ways of relating to each other, it did not impress the mother or father who had no confidence in themselves.

In order to help them become more aware of the importance that a structured transactional system can provide to family life, a specific task was introduced into the therapy. It was proposed by the therapist that a board game that allowed multiple players would be a good way for all of them to deal with each other on a more co-operative basis. From his individual therapy the youngest child recalled having played the game Careers and, in part because he was the only family member with prior knowledge of the game, he suggested its use. Almost immediately, the focus on learning the rules of the game and the help that even the youngest child could offer in this regard served to stabilize the interaction on a more positive plane. Essentially all quarreling ceased among the siblings as the parents found themselves praising and otherwise approving of the children's happy participation in the game and as they too revealed a capacity for enjoying the interaction. After a few weeks of task-oriented family group treatment all members reported a general improvement in all spheres of their lives so that therapy was ended to the satisfaction of all.

Multiple-Impact Therapy

A group of clinicians in Texas faced the problem of geographic distance between their clientele and their facility by blocking off half a week whereby an orthopsychiatric team devoted all its time to one family (MacGregor, 1962). Follow-up planning was originally arranged 6 and 18 months after the initial contact, and sometimes included home visits. This procedure could also be repeated every 6 or 8 weeks. Their initial enterprise arose out of a need to treat disturbed adolescents but did not remain limited to that age group. Moreover, the reason of convenience for scheduling a concentrated if not marathon effort gave way to a therapeutic rationale analogous to that of crisis intervention (Caplan, 1956). Multiple-impact therapy holds to an interactional viewpoint rather than a child-centered one.

The start-up meeting is a team-family conference which may include the referring agent. Subsequently, as the situation dictates, different combinations and permutations of groupings are arranged. These include multiple therapist situations, individual interviews, group therapy, and staff conferences. On the last day a final team-family conference caps the experience.

In this process the family undergoes a series of "impact" and "release" situations. When the family is blocked in expressing conflictual or personal matters the team may debate the family or team-family problems in front of them. When a team member argues that a need exists at present for a particular defensive attitude of a family member, barriers to intrafamilial communication tend to weaken. This type of "cross monitoring" is held up as an effective device for repair of defective communication patterns.

Multiple-Conjoint Family Therapy

Another variation that found its principal usefulness in in-patient units constitutes a group meeting of six to eight family units with several therapists (Blinder et al., 1965). Such a forum provides opportunities for an open exchange of feelings and thinking about problem behavior that might otherwise take much longer to accomplish. However, group family therapy (Coughlin and Wimberger, 1968) seems to have a more limited role in outpatient work where the lack of a central or common point of interest for such a large gathering is missing and often proves counterproductive.

Family Crisis Therapy

The perspective presented in this model (Langsley et al., 1968), in which crisis combines both a hazardous event and its reaction, derives from stress and field theories. Overloading of coping function can occur for the individual as well as for the family. In general, of course, stress situations fall within a range of "optimal frustration" and, by eliciting an effective struggle, have a self-correcting and adaptive function. Thus most acute upsets are self-correcting and add to the repertoire of problem solving. In and of themselves they need not result in chaos or family disorganization. Only if certain conditions prevail will a maladaptive reaction set in.

Langsley and Kaplan (1968) give a factorial analysis of the decompensated family in crisis. There may have been intolerable amount of stress which overwhelmed the system, or the personal problem-solving capacities and personality deficiencies may have been inadequate to the task of dealing with stress. Since the coping struggle does not occur in a vacuum, current environmental and social field factors must also be scrutinized for the contribution made to the stress or for failure to protect the family from stress. If any one or a combination of these factors may be responsible, the intervention must address itself to all of them.

On the personal level, intervention at the time of upset helps the individual cope in his struggle with his current situation, whether by bringing about a reduction of excessive stress or by restoring inoperative coping functions imposed by the stress. When the social system is in upset and creates the crisis, the successful resolution of the problem depends on restoring a reasonable stability within the family. The family is seen as both the source of stress and as the resource for resolution of stress. As a crisis brings about family conflict, those who are susceptible to stress become clinically disturbed or, as "scapegoats," express the upset for the whole unit. For a restoration of the equilibrium, the therapist must use the family as the mediating system for stress moderation.

The salient treatment ideas are based on the experiences of psychiatrists who worked with acute emotional disturbances in front-line soldiers during World War II. By bringing about a prompt behavioral change and avoiding regression the therapist did not give the traumatized individual the chance to acquire a status of invalidism. To do this it was necessary to offer a highly supportive yet authoritative point of view that did not shrink from suggesting adaptive solutions to the problems. The intervenor in crisis situations obviously must be a skillful operator who is familiar with both interpersonal techniques and social or environmental manipulations. Moreover, he uses the client's expectations of help from an authority. By being broadly eclectic and practical in his dealings with the family he takes an active role in defining the crisis as a family problem, in having them face the tasks together, in praising successful accomplishments, in reducing tensions through the utilization of medication for selected family members, and in making maximum use of his community contacts to bring about an effective social milieu.

In a sense he assumes the executive function for the families during a period of disarray but does this in alliance with them and as their advocate. Concomitantly, he strives to strengthen the family's coping potential either as a team or by backing the specialized role functions of its members.

Family Council Therapy

Family council therapy is really a forerunner of today's emphasis on systems orientation although it has its philosophic roots in Adlerian educational psychology (Dreikurs, 1951). By insisting that all children in the family as well as other members of the household participate in a child guidance clinic, it was an easy step to focus on interpersonal dynamics: "This discussion of mutual problems in a democratic spirit of respect leads to better understanding all around. It begins the 'family council,' a technique initiated in most cases to carry on the therapeutic approach as part of daily family life"

(Dreikurs, 1951). The prime objective of this method is to change existing relationships. This is most evident when fathers, who were reluctant to remain involved, become more willing to attend meetings as children show signs of improvement.

The sequence of involvement adheres to a transition from the family group meeting to increasingly broader engagements with collateral children and parents groups, and eventually moves on into a community group. For example, after the family group discussion the children meet with their age mates from other families where "action experience supplements verbalization in counseling." An adjunctive "reorientation" of the child is coordinated with psychodrama (Moreno, 1946) and activity group therapy (Slavson, 1950). The parents meet in a group where they can share and compare problems and coping strategies with many others. This method also favors the introduction of the child into the adult group which magnanimously treats him as a person deserving of equal consideration, presumably a unique experience for him. In the community group, which may have as many as 100 people participating, most material presented by the parents is not of an intimate sort but focuses on conflicts in general interpersonal relationships.

Family Therapy in the Home

Levine (1964) described a program of home visiting on the basis of regular appointments where all members of the family are expected to be present. It was designed primarily for economically deprived people. The therapist brings arts and crafts media and games for the family to use during the session. This method promptly reveals conflicts and promotes free-wheeling responses that permit the therapist to act as catalyst, intervenor, or model in settling disputes.

Home visits for purposes of family conferences have also been espoused for treatment of families with a very disturbed or schizophrenic member (Behrens and Ackerman, 1956; Friedman, 1962).

Social Network Therapy

Deviance, as an expression of failure in communication, demands that corrections be made in the distortions of the system that support it. Speck and Rueveni (1969) define a social network as a group of persons who maintain an ongoing significance to each other's lives by fulfilling specific human needs. The team goes about its therapeutic task by assembling members of the kinship system, neighbors and friends of the family, and other significant agents who relate to the family with the identified problem person, usually a schizophrenic person. Ordinarily such community forums are held in the home and are likened, in essence, to tribal meetings (Attneave, 1969). The combined efforts of the network are presumed to have a confrontational and healing effect by restoring or improving effective communication and support patterns.

From Parent to Child to Family

According to Bell (1962) there are three ways of looking at the family, each giving a slant that is bound to determine a preferred methodology of therapy. As seen through the eyes of the child or as reconstructed by the adult patient, the family is painted by the brush of personal bias and emerges as a negative or ambivalent influence on the life of the individual. Such an understanding of the process quite naturally leads to an examination of the transmission of specific symptom clusters between the generations (Ehrenwald, 1963).

If the family is thought of as a sociologic entity governed by the rules of communication, of transactional patterns and decision making, and of group attitudes and objectives, then it follows that the model of intervention must take the form of socially sanctioned power bargaining among the disputants (Zuk, 1971). The therapist acts as the go-between or broker in conflicts, defining the issues and taking sides for or against the various family members who are at odds with each other. Zuk (1967) feels, not even facetiously, that the family improves when it foils the therapist's attempts to control the relationship. By making the expected changes, the family gets rid of him and his usurpation of power over it.

When the family is looked upon as a cultural creation or institution, it becomes chiefly the conduit for the transmission of values, norms, behavioral standards, and roles from the society to the individual. This conceptual approach introduces to the family a new transacting system that will steer it in the direction of more satisfactory rules, values, communication, and relating (Wynne, 1969). Twenty years ago Spiegel and Kluckhohn (1954) hinted at the ultimate purpose of a cultural emphasis in treatment programs when they said that "the United States is a family-minded nation, and that practically every visible group had some kind of stake in the family area." Consensually held value orientations are put to work in the promotion of the common good by subjecting the individual and his family to the powerful influence of group belief and of authoritative group leaders. Although all methods can be abused, the latter has considerable potential for causing damage because its immediate influence can extend to many people in a brief time-span.

Significant changes are occurring on the contemporary scene with the emergence of family life styles quite different from the traditional two-parent model (Constantine and Constantine, 1971; Eiduson, 1974). Living arrangements on the basis of a social rather than a legal contract have come into vogue. One may well wonder whether the problems associated with such alternative life styles will mark yet another departure for the family therapy field since "there is no right way" to do family therapy (Beels and Ferber, 1969). What seems apparent is that this form of therapy is highly adaptable to an institution that is very much caught up in the shifting identity and power struggles in an increasingly faceless world.

Yet not only within the family have children floundered in their relationships to each other, but they have also done so with their peers. For this problem the remedy that suggested itself has come into its own as group therapy.

REFERENCES

Ackerman, N. W. Interpersonal disturbances in the family: Some unsolved problems in psychotherapy. *Psychiatry*, **19**, 359–368, 1954.

Ackerman, N. W. *The Psychodynamics of Family Life: Diagnosis and Treatment of Family Relationships*. New York: Basic Books, 1958.

Ackerman, N. W. Child participation in family therapy. *Family Process*, **9**, 403–410, 1970.

Ackerman, N. W. The growing edge of family therapy. *Family Process*, **10**, 143–156, 1971.

Attneave, C. L. Therapy in tribal settings and urban network intervention. *Family Process*, **8**, 192–210, 1969.

Beels, C. C. & Ferber, A. Family therapy: A view. *Family Process*, **8**, 280–318, 1969.

Behrens, M. L. & Ackerman, N. W. The home visit as an aid in family diagnosis and therapy. *Social Casework*, **37**, 11–19, 1956.

Bell, J. E. *Family group therapy: A method for the psychological treatment of older children, adolescents, and their parents*. U.S. Department of Health, Education and Welfare, Public Health Monograph No. 64. Washington, D.C.: U.S. Government Printing Office, 1961.

Bell, J. E. Recent advances in family group therapy. *Journal of Child Psychology and Psychiatry*, **3**, 1–15, 1962.

Bell, J. E. *Family Therapy*. New York: Aronson, 1974.

Bing, E. The conjoint family drawing. *Family Process*, **9**, 173–194, 1970.

Blinder, M. G., Colman, A. D., Curry, A. E. & Kessler, D. R. MCFT: Simultaneous treatment of several families. *American Journal of Psychiatry*, **19**, 559–569, 1965.

Caplan, G. An approach to the study of family mental health. *Public Health Report*, **71**, 1027–1030, 1956.

Constantine, L. L. & Constantine, J. M. Group and multilateral marriage: Definitional notes, glossary, and annotated bibliography. *Family Process*, **10**, 157–176, 1971.

Coughlin, F. & Wimberger, W. C. Group family therapy. *Family Process*, **7**, 37–50, 1968.

Drechsler, R. J. & Shapiro, M. I. A procedure for direct observation of family interaction. *Psychiatry*, **24**, 163–170, 1961.

Dreikurs, R. Family group therapy in the Chicago Community Child Guidance Center. *Mental Hygiene*, **35**, 291–301, 1951.

Ehrenwald, J. Family diagnosis and mechanisms of psychosocial defense. *Family Process*, **2**, 121–131, 1963.

Eiduson, B. T. Looking at children in emergent family styles. *Children Today*, **3** (4), 2–6, 1974.

Ferber, A., Mendelsohn, M. & Napier, A. (Eds.), *The Book of Family Therapy*. New York: Science House, 1972.

Friedman, A. Family therapy as conducted in the home. *Family Process*, **1**, 132–140, 1962.

Group for the Advancement of Psychiatry. *The Field of Family Therapy*. Vol. 7, GAP Report No. 78, 1970.

Haley, J. Whither family therapy. *Family Process*, **1**, 69–100, 1962.

Kwiatrowska, H. Family art therapy. *Family Process*, **6**, 37–55, 1967.

Langsley, D. G. & Kaplan, D. M. with the collaboration of Pittman, F. S., Machotka, P., Flomenhaft, K. & DeYoung, C. D. *The Treatment of Families in Crisis*. New York: Grune and Stratton, 1968.

Langsley, D. G., Pittman, F. S. III, Machotka, P. & Flomenhaft, K. Family crisis therapy—results and implications. *Family Process*, **7**, 145–158, 1968.

Levine, R. A. Treatment in the home. *Social Work*, **9**, 19–28, 1964.

McDermott, J. F., Jr. & Char, W. F. The undeclared war between child and family therapy. *Journal of the American Academy of Child Psychiatry*, **13**, 422–436, 1974.

MacGregor, R. Multiple impact psychotherapy with families. *Family Process*, **1**, 15–29, 1962.

Marker, G. & Friedman, P. R. Rethinking children's rights. *Children Today*, **2**, 8–11, 1973.

Minuchin, S. Conflict-resolution family therapy. *Psychiatry*, **28**, 278–286, 1965.

Minuchin, S. *Families and Family Therapy.* Cambridge, Mass.: Harvard University Press, 1974.

Minuchin, S., Montalvo, B., Guerney, B. G., Jr., Rosman, B. L. & Schumer, F. *Families of the Slums: An Exploration of Their Structure and Treatment.* New York: Basic Books, 1967.

Moreno, J. L. *Psychodrama.* Beacon, N.Y.: Beacon House, 1946.

Paul, N. Effects of playback on family members of their own previously recorded conjoint therapy material. *Psychiatric Research Reports*, **20**, 175–187, 1966.

Riessman, F. Role-playing and lower socio-economic group. *Group Psychotherapy*, **17**, 36–48, 1964.

Satir, V. *Conjoint Family Therapy.* Palo Alto, Calif.: Science and Behavior Books, 1967.

Simon, R. M. Sculpting the family. *Family Process*, **11**, 49–57, 1972.

Slavson, S. R. *Analytic Group Psychotherapy.* New York: Columbia University Press, 1950.

Speck, R. V. & Rueveni, U. Network therapy—A developing concept. *Family Process*, **8**, 182–191, 1969.

Spiegel, J. P. & Kluckhohn, F. R. *Integration and conflict in family behavior.* Topeka, Kansas: Group for the Advancement of Psychiatry, Report No. 27, 1954.

Wynne, L. C. Some indications and contra-indications for exploratory family therapy. In I. Boszormenyi-Nagy & J. L. Framo (Eds.), *Intensive Family Therapy.* New York: Hoeber, 1969.

Zuk, G. H. Family therapy. *Archives of General Psychiatry*, **16**, 71–79, 1967.

Zuk, G. H. Family therapy during 1964–1970. *Psychotherapy: Theory, Research and Practice*, **8**, 90–97, 1971.

CHAPTER 8

Group Treatment Methods

The peer group is stressed as a major influence on childhood development, second only to parents (Hurlock, 1956). Psychotherapy for children when provided in groups is an occasion for the release of the positive forces in peer influence, and would appear to be a natural intervention strategy for troubled youngsters. However, unlike group therapy for adults which has flourished in the last 25 years, this approach has not fared well as a therapeutic method for children. Scheidlinger (1965) suggested that "despite numerous successful demonstrations of various kinds of groups in selected child guidance clinics and family service agencies, in general, out-patient group treatment for latency-age children has failed to flourish" (p. 9). In part his conclusions are based on a survey of family service agencies conducted during the 4-year period 1957–1961 in which less than 15% of 187 agencies engaged in group therapy reported children being seen in groups.

Might the origins of group psychotherapy have something to do with this puzzling state? The Emanuel Health Movement, which provided classes for the morally and nervously diseased, and Pratt's involvement with tubercular patients are generally credited as initiating the method of providing help to distressed patients in a group (Reisman, 1966). Discussion in an atmosphere of mutual support was considered to be the major therapeutic ingredient. Interest in the method waxed and waned until World War I heightened a desire for understanding how groups operate and how they contribute to the functioning of man.

It was also a result of the war that Sigmund Freud digressed from his interest in individual psychopathology and turned his attention to the influences that groups have on people (Freud, 1922). Freud focused his attention on the group leader and concluded identification to be the most central psychological process in group formation. Through the process of identifying with the leader each group member can relate one to another and thus develop a sense of empathy with each other. Furthermore, Freud believed much of what takes place in a group often occurs outside of the member's awareness. Thus for each member activity occurs on two levels—a latent and a manifest one. Considerable competition was believed to occur between the members as well, as it parallels the rivalry of children within a family. Through the mechanism of identification with each other the competitiveness becomes dissolved and leads to solidarity and cohesiveness, in part protecting against the fearfulness of the leader's retaliation and in part resulting in mutual sharing (Freud, 1922). Since this early writing on group process, divergent techniques and approaches toward group therapy have emerged ranging from Moreno's (1953) psychodrama to the encounter groups (Lieberman et al., 1973). In one form or another Freud's ideas provide the theoretical underpinnings for most of the group approaches including those directed at helping troubled children or their parents (Durkin, 1950; 1964).

Interest in group therapy waned until World War II when psychiatric care was required for large groups of disabled soldiers. Anthony (1972) credits the Northfield experiment in England with revitalizing the group movement. Ward patients were successfully treated through using group methods. Furthermore, a number of combat studies during World War II suggested that the small group was effective in sustaining its members under stress (Mandelbaum, 1952).

In prewar America, around 1934, Slavson (1940) had begun to develop a form of group therapy for children which he called "activity group therapy." In many ways his program anticipated group therapy for adults, a method that aims to ameliorate feelings of isolation and alienation resulting from changes in American society. Naturally enough, the changes were mirrored in the altered relationships between parent and child, and between family and extended family as well. The uprooted, mobile, and upward striving family enticed psychotherapists not only into the role of transactional power brokers, counseling the ABC's of compromise, but also into becoming group leaders whose ability to arrange and compose groups of disturbed individuals promised a better alternative to feelings of isolation, alienation, and estrangement. It is certainly commonplace, especially as guideposts change or become ambiguous, that people look to each other for definitions and affirmations of acceptable behavior. Under these conditions, the power of the group gains momentum to guide, habilitate, and rehabilitate individuals who are troubled from within or unable to relate interpersonally adequately or adaptively.

The history of group therapy is thus basically aimed at ameliorating the suffering of adults. A precursor of group methods with children can be found in the early work of Alfred Adler with child guidance clinics (Ansbacher and Ansbacher, 1956) where he would interview parent and child in front of an audience of adults and enlist cooperation in helping the family solve its dilemma. Children spend considerable time congregating in groups: street groups and gangs are common urban sights; children are educated in groups; and numerous recreational groups, such as scouts, are available to children. Thus, it was only a matter of time before the benefits of bringing children together in groups for therapeutic aims was given serious recognition.

Group Therapy for Latency Age

Unlike the diversity of family therapy where the style and personality of the family therapist count more than his approach or theory, group therapists working with children follow rather specific points of view. Slavson (1950) has had the most significant influence on therapy for children in groups. According to him, during group therapy "free play and unrestricted acting out without restraints or interpretation is the sole treatment process" (p. 12). Children are believed to develop largely through their experience and associations and to a lesser degree via knowledge and ideas. Hence "action, realistic impediments, external control, and affectionate guidance affect intrapsychic change more than do concepts and ideas" (p. 12). From this point of view, changing the individual child is the major aim so that group projects and goals are kept to a minimum. The therapist pays attention to each individual child rather than focusing on the group process and attempts to understand the latent content of the child's actions.

The approach was felt to be most appropriate for latency-age children as "acting out and the consequent reactions of others are more natural for these children than is talking out" (Slavson, 1950). However, latency-age children thought to be schizophrenic, brain damaged, in a world of autistic fantasy, or delinquent were believed inappropriate for such treatment. Subsequently, these early ideas were altered as a number of successful modifications of activity group therapy resulted in providing benefits to such children (Scheidlinger, 1960; Lifton and Smolen, 1966; Speers and Lansing, 1965). The special nature and functioning of schizophrenic and atypical children was taken into account to make group therapy an effective treatment modality for them.

For example, such materials as mirrors, wooden mannequins, and coloring books were chosen to be consistent with the idea of increasing reality testing and social interaction (Lifton and Smolen, 1966). For the most part, fantasy producing materials, such as puppets and finger paints, were eliminated or kept to a minimum. Group size was also reduced, and often free play was abandoned for more structured activities. Fantasy expression was discouraged, and the therapist shifted from his usual neutral position in traditional activity therapy to a more active, intrusive, and directing one.

Group Therapy for Adolescents

Franklin and Nottage (1969), in working with juvenile delinquents evidencing severe characterological problems, found them to accept group therapy as the lesser of two evils, the other being going to jail. They noted that such youngsters responded successfully to a highly intensive approach. The members were required to attend group sessions five times a week, and a constant focus on self-understanding was maintained. Considerably more effort was spent in verbalizing thoughts and feelings and not just experiencing and acting upon them. In place of acting out, which for such youngsters is often a way of life, the therapist attempted to substitute words and thought.

In general, disturbed adolescents have proven to be a formidable group with whom to carry out effective psychotherapy (Blimes, 1966; Josselyn, 1959; Serrano et al., 1962) for they are not old enough for self-motivated and self-conscious adult psychotherapy and yet too old for play therapy with its blatant reminders of the stages they have "transcended." Several modifications have been suggested for adapting group psychotherapy for adolescents. Slavson (1950, 1964) has commented on the need for the therapist to be more verbal and to respond to his adolescent group in ways similar to those used with his adult patients, especially as they approach late adolescence. Confrontative and interpretative techniques, especially as they are directed to group involvement and the "here and now" are considered appropriate. Kissel (1968) has suggested, for those children in early adolescence, that the group session be divided between social activity and talk activity periods. The social activity provides group members a shared experience, which, in addition to alleviating anxiety, offers up considerable material for the group to discuss during the talk segment of the session.

Middle and late adolescents function best in group psychotherapy when the groups are heterosexual, whereas latency-age children and early adolescents are thought to relate better when all the members are of the same sex. The therapist is also required to be more open in sharing his opinions and thoughts. His neutral or nondirective stance not only makes him a difficult model with whom to identify but it may also convey disinterest or dislike.

Group Play Therapy

Ginott (1961, 1964) has suggested a form of group therapy for children that he calls "group play therapy." His approach rests on the psychoanalytic notion of altering intrapsychic equilibrium through relationship, catharsis, insight, reality testing, and sublimation. Influenced by Slavson (1950), as well as Axline (1947) and Rogers (1951), Ginott upholds a reflective role for the therapist whom he expects to be verbally active and limit-setting in his involvement with the group. Furthermore, the children are somewhat younger than the children in activity group therapy, and greater attention is paid to the individual interaction between child and therapist. Ginott's approach to group therapy evolved from his experiences in a child guidance clinic and was especially attractive to verbally articulate middle class families.

Activity Group Therapy

Some 25 years previously Slavson (1943) began experimenting with group therapy in the ghettos of New York City seeing children who were often experientially deprived. Frustration and deprivation of children by adults was considered to be the major etiological force behind emotional disturbances. Such differences have contributed to the way adherents of each view approach limit testing and rule breaking in the group. While discussing the manner in which limits are provided to children, Slavson emphasizes and contrasts the distinction between children who experience real rejection, that is those children who have been disliked, neglected, and deprived, and children with fantasized rejections, that is those who are oversensitive or take unintended slights to heart.

Guiding the experientially oriented group through his neutrality, the therapist helps the group to establish rules and set limits. He is always available to provide support and affection to the love-starved child who has experienced real rejection. Both approaches, to some extent, are reflective in nature, borrow heavily from psychoanalytic theory for their understanding of children, and are more concerned with the individual members than with the group interactions. Additionally, parents are considered an important part of the treatment regimen. Whether the child is in activity group therapy or group play therapy, collateral groups of parents are customarily involved.

Behavioral Orientation

An alternative point of view of working with children in groups has emerged from the behavioral orientation. Overt behavior rather than covert attitudes or feelings is the major concern of the group therapist guided by the principles of learning theory and behavior modification. The group interaction as well as the individual child is controlled and manipulated to bring about desired results (Rose, 1972). Parents are required to furnish baseline information and keep records before they are instructed in the finer points of managing children's behavior.

Certainly, chronological age, psychological maturity, and type of malady of the child all contribute to the selection of a group program most suited to him. While all forms of group therapy for children attempt to inject interpersonal elements for bringing about experiential growth, attitude change, and behavior alteration, the special emphasis on one or the other of these objectives guides the therapist's actions in the group.

Experiential Group Psychotherapy

Man, essentially a social animal, develops and matures within the context of an interactional matrix. Children who have poorly developed ego controls or are extremely inhibited as a result of overly harsh controls can benefit from experiencing a special environment. Slavson (1943) suggests that "a permissive environment in effect removes the anxiety producing superego and releases the child to act out his infantile impulses . . . since the early superego is derived through fear of punishment or of being abandoned or rejected, it must be counteracted. In its stead is built a new superego in the group which is derived from love and positive identification" (p. 7). Such is the foundation around which activity group psychotherapy, the purest form of experiential group therapy, rests. In order to achieve such ends the activity group psychotherapist brings together children who have a very high likelihood of forming a balanced group. Instigators, that is children who are active, assertive, or aggressive, are combined with withdrawn or inhibited children and with neutralizers, those who are neither overly active or inhibited but can return the group to stability when it is disrupted. Constructing the group in this manner produces a milieu that stimulates the inhibited child while providing sufficient control for the overly active. As a result, the therapist can provide unconditional acceptance for each child in the group.

In general such groups are made available to latency-age children, usually between the ages of 10 to 12 years and of the same sex (Slavson, 1943, 1950; King, 1965). Characteristically the therapy group is referred to as a club. Before each of the early sessions, which generally run $1\frac{1}{2}$ or 2 hours, the group therapist sends a letter to each child reminding him of the meeting. Children who miss sessions are also sent letters recognizing their absence.

The presence of an adult and the spacious and nonrestricting physical environment both serve as ingredients of the treatment. The sameness and nondistractibility of the room lend stability to the experience of the children. The therapist neither initiates discussion, analyzes activity, nor sanctions behavior in this approach. It is through the child's experiencing situations in action with other children that he learns to shed his habitual maladaptive behaviors and express his pent up feelings. Activity catharsis, the equivalent of the free association of adult psychoanalysis and the play of the young child in play psychotherapy, is the major medium through which the child reveals the meaning of his inappropriate actions and permits his social encapsulation to dissolve (Slavson, 1950). The atmosphere created provides "a benign regression and reliving of the earliest life experiences in a nonrelatiatory, stable, consistent environment. The ultimate effect is to put the child on firmer footing to tackle the next phase in his psychosexual development because he has been enabled to more constructively reexperience some aspect from those stages at which he was traumatized and his growth, in consequence, arrested" (King, 1965, p. 1).

While the unblocking of pent up emotions is a primary aim of experiential group therapy, the importance and effectiveness of ego growth, active mastery, and socialization on a reality basis within the group experience is also recognized. The therapist, who does a minimum amount of talking, whenever possible, encourages group decisions and suggests that members rely on each other for help in working on projects. Unable to manipulate the therapist, as they have done with previous adults, children in the group turn to their peers and begin to make genuine and intimate contacts with each other, something which they previously found difficult. This strategy of the therapist also promotes social cooperation. Thus the therapist's "neutrality" fosters certain kinds of experiences onto the children who make up the group. While, on the one hand, he suggests that the group is theirs to do with as they please, on the other, he is present giving guidance and strength to encourage the forces of adaptation and growth.

Case A

A 10-year-old boy, referred for enuresis, social isolation, and school under-achievement, was characterized by the referring psychiatrist as a highly anxious child who constantly questions the acceptability of his actions. Compulsive and phobic devices were found to be only partially successful in binding anxiety.

An 11 year old who harbored strong feelings of inadequacy and was doing poorly in school was a second member of the group. He was characterized by his parents as a conforming child who readily accepts limits and has never been a behavior problem at home or school.

A third member of the group was described by his teachers as a moody and active 11 year old. Academically he was doing fine, but he had few friends in class and tended to have intense but short-lived relationships with age mates. In the neighborhood he liked to play with children who were 2 or 3 years his senior, and often would come home complaining that one of the teenagers pushed him around.

A 10-year-old obese, slovenly child was another member of the group. He was loud, boastful, and deprecatory of the activities of other children, for example by telling them how much better he could have done something or that "the one we have at home is ten times nicer or better."

An inhibited 9 year old who found it difficult to approach children but was responsive to their overtures was a fifth member of the group. He was a tense, angry child who had trouble relating to authority figures and discharged his aggression in passive-aggressive ways. His poor school performance resulted from his inability to complete assignments or to remember to hand in what little homework he was assigned in fourth grade. According to his parents he found it difficult to "tell the truth" and was prone to "find things that didn't belong to him."

The sixth member of the group was a tall 11 year old. He would have in-frequent temper outbursts in class and occasionally get into fights with students in his class. His teachers always reported they were unable to figure him out. As a rule they felt he was mild-mannered and liked by his classmates, but occasionally he "would let loose" and frighten both them and himself with his aggressiveness.

During the early sessions of the group, different children asserted themselves in an attempt to gain leadership. In the fifth activity group therapy session, the obese 10 year old strove for leadership of the group by swearing in an uncontrolled fashion. The other group members tried to control this behavior by voting to fine members who swore. He refused to pay as did a second member who was also fined for swearing. The tall 11 year old then suggested that the money could go towards a party. The boys also agreed that they would all have to chip in some money in addition to the money from the fines. It was agreed that whoever did not pay would not be able to share in the refreshments. The two boys paid their fines and the 9-year-old passive-aggressive child, whose parents felt he lied and stole, was entrusted with the club's money. Three meetings later a successful party took place.

Feeling trusted by the boys in the group, the 9 year old began to trust himself more, and also behaved differently with his parents. Furthermore, as they saw others trusting him they were able to give him greater responsibility. The boys provided their own solution to the group dilemma without the usual intrusions or directions of an adult, thus providing all of them with a sense of accomplishment rather than unadaptable feelings of inferiority.

Little objective information is available to adequately evaluate activity group therapy with children. Indeed Back, reviewing small-group intervention strategies during 1974, devotes virtually no space to children's groups.

An evaluation of an activity group therapy program carried out at the Rochester Mental Health Center was conducted by Kissel (1970). Follow-up information was obtained from parents, therapists, and teachers of 25 children who were no longer active. All the children were of average intelligence and diagnosed as having adjustment reactions of childhood, psychoneuroses, or personality disorders. In general, the program was found to be successful as the majority of children, about 70%, were reported as being helped by parents or therapists. However, school grades did not change, and teachers reported many of the children still showing classroom behaviors associated with emotional unrest. Those children benefited the most who were inhibited, had poor peer relationships, and came from an intact family where the father was considered to be conflicted over his own hostility but not thought to be ineffectual as a parent.

Attitude Change through Group Therapy

Similar to activity group psychotherapy, the major focus of play group therapy is on the individual child and his problems. The group is primarily a therapeutic tool and, as such, group cohesiveness is not actively fostered or are group values or aims analyzed (Ginott, 1961). This approach to group therapy is based on the idea that faulty behavior is the result of feelings and attitudes that are often unexpressed, distorted, or unavailable to the child. Such children require the opportunity to achieve a more consistent balance between "what they think," and "what really is." Ginott (1961), in part influenced by the early writings of Slavson (1943) and the philosophy of Axline (1947), outlined group play psychotherapy guided by the theoretical notion of effecting change in the child's intrapsychic equilibrium "through relationship, insight, reality testing, and sublimation" (p. 2). However, the therapeutic interaction is preponderantly verbal and reflective in nature (Rogers, 1951).

Children from nursery age through early latency, roughly from age 3 to 9, who are withdrawn, immature, phobic, or effeminate boys, and who have behavior disorders are considered appropriate candidates for group play therapy. Generally the sexes are mixed, especially in the younger ages, and the number of children included rarely exceeds five per group.

The play-oriented group therapist is considerably more active and directly involved with the children than is the activity-oriented group therapist. Materials such as clay, finger paints, and water stimulate regressive and primitive behaviors resulting in more rule setting and limit testing. While the atmosphere tends to be permissive and the therapist sanctions and promotes symbolic and verbal expression of dislike and aggression, physical aggression especially directed toward the therapist or other children is forbidden. Whenever limits are tested, the therapist initially recognizes and helps to put into words the wishes or feelings the child is attempting to express. The limit is restated, and the child is provided with alternative channels for expressing his feelings. Finally, the child is helped to express the dissatisfaction he is experiencing as a result of being restricted (Ginott, 1961). The group leader provides the children with an external authority with whom they can identify, and, as such, counteracts the child's inability to master his own impulses and fearful fantasies. As with all forms of group therapy, the composition of the group is important. When the children's attitudes are the major focus, much of the verbalization, control, and limit setting comes from the therapist. Moreover, the children in the group add sufficient "diversity of identification models to encourage corrective relations" (Ginott, 1961, p. 31).

Parents are important collaborators in this approach. First, they make the decision whether or not their child should be involved in a program of therapy and, once made, they are active participants in therapy. As with collateral intervention discussed in Chapter 6, parents are seen in groups meeting at the same time as their children. Such groups can be child-focused for helping parents understand the child-parent interaction or adult-focused in giving parents a better understanding of their own feelings and attitudes. In effect, such parent groups usually carry out both functions (Durkin, 1954, 1964).

Case B

Four boys were seen for weekly 90-minute group play therapy sessions. The following children comprised the group.

A, an 8-year-old only child was seen for psychiatric evaluation because he was "unable to sit still in class." Pediatric and neurological evaluations ruled out minimal brain dysfunction. Psychological evaluation found him to be above average in intelligence and having no perceptual or visual-motor difficulties. A was found to be a stubborn, spoiled, intolerant child who expected to get his way.

Bedwetting brought the second member of the group, a 9 year old, to the attention of a community mental health center. B had few friends and spent a great deal of time in his room reading or making rather elaborate models. Medication was tried with little success.

C, the third member of the group, was characterized as a troublemaker by his second grade teacher. He yelled out answers, wandered in the aisles, poked other children, and at times left his class to visit other rooms.

D, the last member of the group, an 8 year old whose social awkwardness, silliness, and facial grimacing made him a strange appearing boy, was shunned by other children who found reasons not to play with him. His parents stated that he was a very "sensitive child" who would withdraw from children in the neighborhood with the least bit of provocation.

Each child's behavior was viewed as a mask behind which hurt feelings were hiding. During the early sessions the children remained distant from each other, overwhelmed by the permissive atmosphere and somewhat distrustful of the therapist. However, D's mother reported that he was pleased with his new friends and eager to come to the clinic.

D: (Arrived 5 minutes late) Hello, fellows. (A and C who were together ignored D while B grunted without looking at him.)

T: Hello D.

D: (Walking to A and C) What are you doing? (Silence) Can I help?

A: Maybe later.

D. (Moves to B who is drawing a picture) How about a game of checkers?

B: Not now, I want to finish my picture.

D: Gee, there's nothing to do here today. (D starts walking around aimlessly touching things.)

T: No one wants to play with you, and you don't know what to do.

D: There's nothing to do today.

T: No one wants to play with you, and that makes you unhappy.

D: I want to do something.

T: You don't like it that no one wants to play with you.

D: If no one will play with me, I want to go home. (Walks closer to the playroom door.)

T: You're unhappy and don't want to stay here.

D: Yeah.

T: I know you are unhappy and want to leave, but we all stay here until our time is up.

D: What's there to do then?

T: You're unhappy and can't remember what you can do.

D: (Silence)

T: There are lots of things to do here, it's up to you.

D: (To B) Are you finished with your picture?

D continued to flare up and test limits during the next months, although with diminished frequency. During one of the parent sessions, D's mother reported that a neighbor boy called him to play for the first time, and his teacher felt he was relating to his classmates with considerably more confidence.

Group play therapy shares a similar fate with activity group therapy, in that little evidence is available regarding its effectiveness. Schiffer (1965), investigating the effectiveness of group play therapy in bringing about positive change in peer relationships, provided some children with this experience, while others received no formal group therapy but met with a recreational leader, and still others received no intervention of any sort. "Subjects in the treatment groups generally remain stable while during the same period of time, equated subjects who are not in treatment exhibited increased social maladjustment" (Schiffer, 1965, p. 29).

Behavior-Oriented Group Therapy

In an era of accountability both activity and play group therapy have been criticized because "they do not readily lend themselves to evaluation. Since goals are rarely set, it is not clear what has been achieved or whether permanent personality change has been brought about" (Rose, 1972, p. 19). Techniques of childhood management and behavior modification based upon the learning theory principles suggested by Pavlov (1928), Skinner (1938), and Hull (1943) have been applied to the treatment of troubled children (Ullmann and Krasner, 1965; Yates, 1970; Graziano, 1972). They have also been introduced into the group treatment of disturbed children (Rose, 1972; Marks and Keller, 1974; Riley, 1975). Rose (1972) presents the most complete description of treating children in groups using a behavioral approach. Initially, children and their parents are seen individually to obtain a description of the child's problem. It is important that the diagnostician specify the child's symptoms in behavioral terms, and Rose even suggests the child also be rated from 1 to 10 on a few selected activities, such as handicrafts, fighting, athletic skills, and assertiveness.

These ratings are used to help the therapist in composing his groups. At least two children in any group are required to be rated high in one similar area, thus assuring some commonality, yet it is also important that children have divergent ratings in order to create a heterogeneous group.

The specificity of behavior serves to give direction to the group while it also builds in a measure to determine effectiveness. For example, rather than characterizing a child as dependent, he is described as "one who remains constantly in the proximity of adults, who often asks for help with things most children his age do by themselves, and who cries whenever he is refused something he wants" (Rose, 1972, p. 55). The group therapist, in conjunction with the child, establishes very specific treatment goals which are not totally under the control of the child, e.g. making friends becomes playing games similar to those his age mates play so that change can be measured.

Influenced by the traditions of scientific psychology, the behaviorally oriented group therapist pays considerable attention to the group per se and thus actively formulates group goals with specific aims of encouraging cohesiveness and teaching positive interaction. While the therapist makes use of traditional behavior modification techniques, such as modeling, behavioral reversal, role playing, and time out to help the child either develop new behaviors, eliminate old maladaptive behaviors, or maintain adaptive ones, he provides this within the context of the group setting. In many quarters considerable emphasis is placed on the establishment of a token economy within the group.

In distinction to the barrenness of the activity group therapy room, the behavioral group therapy room is usually lined with posters, some of which provide reminders of group rules and goals, while others instruct children how to earn points, and yet others give information regarding the cumulative number of tokens earned and the value of each. In distinction to group play therapy, materials provided to children are considerably less regressive in nature and for the most part require interaction of at least two members. Cards, checkers, and table games rather than expressive materials, such as paints, clay, or water are provided.

Control, management, discipline, and responsibility are some of the repetitive words that concern parents whose children are considered appropriate candidates for such therapy. One of the key assumptions made by the behaviorally oriented therapist is that the child is capable of assuming responsibility for his own behavior and that acting out children can be helped by providing verbal controls for modifying unacceptable behavior (Rose, 1972; Marks and Keller, 1974). This will result in more effective commerce with parents, teachers, and age mates.

Parents are involved in a somewhat different way by the behaviorally oriented group therapist who prefers direct contact with the parents rather than working through collateral staff. Furthermore, contacts are not as frequent and can be either on an individual or group basis. Parents are expected to furnish the group therapist with behavioral data that he instructs them to gather. They are coached in ways to modify the child's home environment, especially the manner in which he is rewarded and punished. The therapist structures his role as that of a teacher or consultant.

Case C

The timer went off for the second time during the session. Two boys in the group were busily engaged in a checker game and each earned 2 points. Another member of the group earned 1 point as he was talking to one of the checker players about a school-based activity. Prior to watching the checker game, he had attempted to engage the remaining member of the group present for the session, but had been rebuffed. This boy, 11 years old, who was the oldest of the six members, was aimlessly toying with different objects in the room. At times he would approach the two boys playing checkers and silently watch, only to move away. His aimless behavior increased after the timer went off and he did not receive any points. When the group leader went to the tally chart to post the points the boys earned, the 11 year old said, "It's not fair." The group therapist then addressed himself to the group and reminded them of the different ways they could earn points and brought their attention to the "How to Earn Points" chart. These comments seemed to upset the boy even more. After repeating that it was not fair, he pushed the table which messed up the checker board and led to the other two boys becoming upset. The leader informed him that since he was not able to control himself he would have to go to the "time out" room for 5 minutes and then could return to the group. Once in the time out room, he kicked the door two or three times. This behavior was ignored and it quickly subsided. Five minutes later, he was permitted to rejoin the group. At the conclusion of the session, the leader tallied the points each boy earned for that session and added them to their cumulative total. Each boy was then given 2 minutes to decide whether he wanted to use his points to "buy something" that day or save them for a bigger item.

Every 5 weeks the group therapist met with the childrens' parents. Initially they were seen individually and subsequently as a group. Each child's chart was examined, and his behavior was compared to baseline. In addition, the frequent feedback helped the therapist to determine what behaviors to focus on by providing rewards for its occurrence.

Despite the aim of the behavior-oriented school, few formal evaluation studies have been done to either examine its effectiveness or compare it with other forms of group psychotherapy. Marks and Keller (1974) obtained some follow-up information on five boys between the ages of 7 and 8 who were seen for 12 sessions, and they reported improvement in the group in the specific goals set. However, they found little generalization of the same behavior to the school environment.

Despite the diversity of group therapy with children, the central role of the therapist and the group milieu remain relatively constant. All attempts to help the troubled child through group therapy insist on the importance of the composition of the group, which will be the therapeutic agent. This, they argue, requires balancing or heterogeneity within the context of some sameness in subgroupings. Thus the leader must choose the members wisely just as the travel agent attempts to match individual wishes and needs with specific travel packages to make the trip successful and rewarding. Whether the focus is on the individual within the group or on the group as an entity, the milieu is the message—to paraphrase McLuhan (1964). It is reasonable to expect that children, having difficulty interacting with their age mates, would benefit most from this form of intervention. Regardless of the expressed goals, group psychotherapy for children is basically an interpersonal therapy fostering social experiences in the sharing of attitudes and behaviors with peers. As with most forms of psychotherapy, the practitioner gravitates to the approach with which he feels most comfortable, a result of theory and technique meshing with his personality. Of course, his practice then becomes an amalgam of technique and style, a situation not limited to group therapy to troubled children. Some children, owing to symptomatology or to need for a more intensive relationship, require treatment provided within the context of a one-to-one relationship, where diversity is similarly the rule.

REFERENCES

Ansbacher, H. & Ansbacher, R. *The Individual Psychology of Alfred Adler*. New York: Basic Books, 1956.

Anthony, E. J. The history of group psychotherapy. In H. I. Kaplan & B. J. Sadock (Ed.), *Evolution of Group Therapy*. Baltimore: Williams and Wilkins, 1972.

Axline, V. *Play Therapy*. Boston: Houghton-Mifflin, 1947.

Back, K. W. Intervention techniques: Small groups. In M. R. Rosenzweig & L. W. Porter (Eds.), *Annual Review of Psychology*. Palo Alto, Calif.: Annual Reviews, 1974.

Blimes, M. The paradox of dealing with juvenile delinquents. San Francisco: American Orthopsychiatric Association, 1966.

Durkin, H. E. *Group Therapy for Mothers of Disturbed Children*. Springfield, Ill.: Charles C. Thomas, 1954.

Durkin, H. E. *The Group in Depth*. New York: International Universities Press, 1964.

Franklin, G. & Nottage, W. Psychoanalytic treatment of severely disturbed juvenile delinquents in a therapy group. *International Journal of Group Psychotherapy*, **19**, 165–175, 1969.

Freud, S. (Translated by J. Strachey). *Group Psychology and the Analysis of the Ego*. London: Hogarth Press, 1922.

Ginott, H. G. *Group Psychotherapy with Children*. New York: McGraw-Hill, 1961.

Ginott, H. G. Research in play therapy with children. In M. Haworth (Ed.), *Child Psychotherapy*. New York: Basic Books, 1964.

Graziano, A. M. Animism and modern psychotherapy. In A. M. Graziano (Ed.), *Behavior Therapy With Children*. Chicago: Aldine, 1972.

Hull, C. V. *Principles of Behavior*. New York: Appleton-Century-Crofts, 1943.

Hurlock, E. *Child Growth and Development* (2nd Edition). New York: McGraw-Hill, 1956.

Josselyn, I. Psychological changes in adolescent children. *Children*, **6**, 43–48, 1959.

King, C. Activity group psychotherapy. New York: American Orthopsychiatric Association, 1965.

Kissel, S. The shared common experience—an attribute of adolescent group psychotherapy. Mimeographed. Rochester, N.Y.: Rochester Mental Health Center, 1968.

Kissel, S. Mothers, teachers and therapist evaluate activity group psychotherapy. *Bulletin of the Rochester Mental Health Center*, **2,** 9–15, 1970.

Lieberman, M., Yalom, I. & Miles, M. *Encounter Groups: First Facts.* New York: Basic Books, 1973.

Lifton, N. & Smolen, L. Group psychotherapy with schizophrenic children. *International Journal of Group Psychotherapy*, **16,** 23–41, 1966.

McLuhan, M. *Understanding Media.* New York: McGraw-Hill, 1964.

Mandelbaum, D. G. *Soldier Groups and Negro Soldiers.* Berkeley, Calif.: University of California Press, 1952.

Marks, F. & Keller, N. A. Short term, goal-oriented latency boys group at a child guidance clinic. New York: American Association of Psychiatric Services for Children, 1974.

Moreno, J. L. *Who Shall Survive?* New York: Beacon House, 1953.

Pavlov, I. V. (translated by W. H. Gannt). *Lectures on Conditioned Reflexes.* Vol. 1. New York: International Publishing Co., 1928.

Reisman, J. M. *The Development of Clinical Psychology.* New York: Appleton-Century-Crofts, 1966.

Riley, J. Using behavior modification in activity group therapy. Private Communication, 1975.

Rogers, C. R. *Client-Centered Therapy.* Boston: Houghton-Mifflin, 1951.

Rose, S. D. *Treating Children in Groups.* San Francisco: Jossey-Bass, 1972.

Scheidlinger, S. Experimental group treatment of severely deprived latency aged children. *Americal Journal of Orthopsychiatry*, **30,** 356–358, 1960.

Scheidlinger, S. The concept of latency—Implications for group treatment. New York: American Orthopsychiatic Association, 1965.

Schiffer, A. L. *The Effectiveness of Group Play Therapy as Assessed by Specific Changes in a Child's Peer Relations.* Ann Arbor, Mich.: University Microfilms, 1965.

Serrano, A. C., McDanald, E. C., Goolish, H. A., MacGregor, R. & Ritchie, A. M. Adolescent maladjustment and family dynamics. *Americal Journal of Psychiatry*, **11,** 897–901, 1962.

Skinner, B. F. *The Behavior of Organisms.* New York: Appleton-Century-Crofts, 1938.

Slavson, S. R. Group therapy. *Mental Hygiene*, **24,** 36–49, 1940.

Slavson, S. R. *An Introduction to Group Therapy.* New York: The Commonwealth Fund, 1943.

Slavson, S. R. *Analytic Group Psychotherapy.* New York: Columbia University Press, 1950.

Slavson, S. R. *A Textbook in Analytic Group Psychotherapy.* New York: International Universities Press, 1964.

Speers, R. W. & Lansing, C. *Group Therapy in Childhood Psychosis*. Chapel Hill, N.C.: University of North Carolina Press, 1965.

Ullmann, L. P. & Krasner, L. (Eds.), *Case Studies in Behavior Modification*. New York: Holt, Rinehart & Winston, 1965.

Yates, A. J. *Behavior Therapy*. New York: Wiley, 1970.

CHAPTER 9

Techniques of Treatment for Individual Children

The idea that human behavior should make sense is of relatively recent origin. This is not to imply that there had been a lack of explanations for the peculiar passions and habits afflicting man. For ages the natural order of the life-cycle was accepted as an integral part of most theologies. Divine and demonic inspiration came in for a good share of the responsibility or blame for the extraordinary.

The Freudian revolution brought about an effective shift in the popular perception of man: from being a pawn of the gods to being his own worst enemy. Primitive origins as infant and child saddle man with drives and impulses that struggle against being bridled by parental figures. The vicissitudes of this domestication process within the individual are responsible for both adequate and problematic outcomes. Retrospective analysis of adults as a means of treating their neurotic conflict resolutions came into vogue after World War I following an obscure start around the turn of the century.

Early childhood experience had a central importance in psychoanalytic theory and technique. Quite naturally, analysts turned to the primary source of juvenile deviance and to its treatment both for confirmation of hypotheses about genesis and psychodynamics and for correction of problems at their beginnings. Some of the early child workers such as Healy (1915) and Healy and Bronner (1936) were influenced by Freudian formulations in such a way as to frequently fit the child to the theory of the unconscious, whereas others such as Klein (1932) used their investigative therapy with children to further embroider theory. It was not for some time, most notably through the efforts of Levy (1933, 1938, 1939) and Bender (1937), that more specific correlations between pathologic states in children and their treatment were considered

156

through the self-conscious use of a relationship. By 1939, Poffenberger catalogued at least 15 different therapies for children.

Although it was possible to ignore the social environment in the treatment of adults for a long time, this attitude did not prevail in child therapy. The parents and teachers had to become involved as co-workers in any treatment plan for the child, particularly since it was they who were puzzled by his actions or lack thereof. After all, as youthful dependents, children needed the intercession and protection of adults if they were to be in a client or patient role. The preceding chapters have elaborated the various methods that tie in environmental and personal supports for the troubled child. This chapter's purpose and aim is to give a rationale for individual therapy and to describe techniques used by child therapists. Since modern psychotherapy, including its derivatives, has its roots in psychoanalytic thinking about the nature of the human psyche, a brief description of Freudian and neo-Freudian postulates is in order (Erikson, 1963; Hartmann, 1950).

The genetic point of view of human development is the rockbed of psychoanalytic theory. It formulates a biologic timetable of libidinal and organizational development in circumscribed and sequential psychosocial stages, provided the necessary environmental conditions exist at the proper time for the unfolding of optimal growth potentials. Problems arise when there are deficiencies in drive or in stimulus tolerance, or the infant and child are subjected to improper care—whether in the form of understimulation, overstimulation, disorganization, or trauma—fixating development or even bringing on regression to earlier stages. The negotiation of later stages is contingent on the successful passage through the preceding ones. Failure to do so produces personality flaws related to that period of developmental life in which the anlage for further emotional maturation was aborted. Therapeutic intervention must then deal with the possibility of bringing that individual through an experience that resembles the stepping stone sequences of his psychological upbringing.

At no point in extrauterine life is the human organism free of the contrary tensions associated with self-gratification and socialization. The baby already must learn to deal with two masters, a process that eventually will govern him from within. On the one hand is the powerful drive for preservation of the self, that is of the instinctual drives of hunger and libidinal sexuality, while on the other is the social code that prescribes how these drives will be controlled and expressed. The dynamic point of view holds that the intrapsychic conflict arising out of this distinctly human condition is a basic attribute of psychic activity. It assumes that although conflict-free child rearing is unavoidable and even disastrous if it were possible, the quantity and quality of the conflict experiences are primary in giving impetus to a potentially healthy or abnormal reaction to the tension.

In order to understand the individual's regulating or feedback mechanism in the intrapsychic conflict model, another postulate had to be added. Thus the economic point of view in psychoanalytic theory speaks of psychological energy which is expended in a free flowing manner until checked by experiance and redirected or "bound" by the influence of sensory and psychic pain. The pleasure principle espouses a primary process of free flowing energy seeking discharge, whereas the reality principle holds that the energy is reflected back on the organismic system as a secondary process. This occurs when the primal discharge of energy in and of itself becomes less rewarding than a modified version that requires the partial use of the energy for restraint or other secondary behavior. Learning, therefore, can proceed only if there is exposure to the reality principle, that is to situations that are sufficiently denying and frustrating to the young organism to force him to find alternate routes for gratification.

The topographic point of view acknowledges that experience is both amorphous and particular. It explains the primitive and sophisticated as something that is unified in the makeup of each person by postulating unconscious, preconscious, and conscious subsystems of the psyche. Each person is a store of life-forces and of the experiental processes that accrue through time and space. The leading edge to this reservoir of energy is the conscious, a state of self-awareness that permits the individual to perform at a level that he can rationalize. Most of his inner experience remains hidden from understanding or even awareness under normal conditions, except in dreams or reverie. However, the unconscious, as this state of undifferentiated inner experience is called, intrudes constantly on the conscious decision making process in ways that—with some effort—can be analyzed. Through the medium of the preconscious, a sort of screening or mediating state, the individual has access to influences from the unconscious that may have some pertinence to an understanding of the self.

The structural point of view, yet another tenet of psychoanalysis, tries to answer the question of how the individual secures an internal balance of forces. The life forces of hunger and libido are designated as id or primitive drives that assert themselves heedlessly, presumably for the sake of survival. However, experience soon teaches that personal survival is also predicated on the child's ability to please adults. This he accomplishes by learning the values, prohibitions, and ideals of his parents and of their society. Eventually he makes these judgments his own in the formation of a superego, a potent check on the expression of instinctual forces. To both moderate between these two opposing interests and to make the necessary executive decisions in favor of action or inhibition stands the ego, which is all those functions at the command of the individual that subserve his information processing and reasoning capacity. Not all ego functions are devoted to arbitration between id and superego. Many are conflict-free or autonomous sensorimotor, behavioral, and integrative processes for gaining mastery over the environment. Methods for dealing with human problems have to distinguish between those stemming primarily from miscarriages in meshing impulse life with conscience and those emanating from deficiencies in autonomous coping functions. White (1963) postulates that the child's play exploration is inherently satisfying in the here and now and that it need not be secondary to drive reduction, to learning, or to conflict resolution. Yet, play is also sensitive to poorly resolving problems so that it can become a vehicle for the expression of disturbance.

In addition to the distinctions made between unconscious and conscious within the individual, an interface has to be recognized between inner and outer reality. The adaptive point of view in psychoanalytic thinking posits a continuous process whereby the individual internalizes external reality in order to achieve a workable relationship to it. The more clearly a person distinguishes his experiential roots in himself and in the world outside of himself, the better is his position to develop a creative accommodation to his existential condition. All therapy must at least perform a service of fostering sufficient reality testing to keep the individual in touch with what comes from self and what from nonself if it hopes to fulfill its promise of being a healing influence.

Finally, the psychosocial or epigenetic point of view sees an interdigitation between the developing child and the social institutions that in itself forms a unity through which mutual regulation evolves. In other words, growth occurs not only within the organism but also in a psychosocial context. The fit between the two contributes to the pace and style of both individual development and to societal evolving. Therefore individual treatment must always keep in mind the presence of the social and cultural matrix of forces in personal problems.

A therapy based on a multifaceted understanding of personality development and adaptation must, by necessity, either delve deeply into the psychological makeup of the person in order to bring about a realignment of contending psychic forces or select a specific deficit for strengthening so that a better chance for personal problem solving can come about. As a result there have been clinicians who focused on the global effects of therapy and those who concentrated on modifying selective parts of the personality or just achieving symptom relief.

As some children—and adults as well—were slow to change and others did not respond at all to verbal uncovering of psychic material, additional concepts were formulated about the nature of behavior. For example, differences in the biological substrate, both on the basis of genetic endowment and of individual idiosyncrasy, impose qualities of temperament that are fairly constant throughout a person's life. These differences may be present in drive expression, in motility patterns, in coping styles, and in defensive reactions. Then the mesh between the temperaments of the child and the parent becomes an important clue to problems that may have arisen between them. The therapist must recognize children whose special needs or stylistic approaches require the kind of understanding and handling that will support rather than undermine them.

Another area that had to be explored quite early was the communication process itself. How do children acquire language and meaning? What are the stages of symbolic usages? Through what forms of communication can children be reached most readily in therapy? The epistemologic investigations of Piaget (1973) indicated that there existed an orderly, phase-specific building up of logic and reasoning in the growing child which represented the outer limit of his understanding. This confirmed the clinical impression that the therapy situation had to accommodate itself to the child's changing capacities in comprehension, expression, and action.

A contrasting position has been taken by Bruner (1960) who looks upon the child as having a built-in capacity for learning the rudiments of all complex cognitive operations and holds that the onus for improving the communication of understanding to the child rests with the adult. The therapist then should always be on the lookout for simplifying higher level messages or meanings to bring them to a level that is within the reach of the child.

The influence on the child by his personal experience has taken on a more mechanistic explanation from the behaviorist point of view, which holds that actions are governed by their consequences. If the organism has choices or contingencies that are only discovered by trial and error behavior, subsequent actions will be those that elicit the preferred consequence. This observation has opened up a host of practical methods for dealing with thorny childhood problems that often eluded the therapist of traditionally analytic or nondirective persuasions. Increasingly, combinations of both psychotherapy and behavior modification have emerged for certain conditions (Blom, 1972).

An attempt to define classical psychotherapy with children and to delineate the principles of such treatment was undertaken by Reisman (1973). He argued that the therapist's actions and not his treatment objectives determined what the method ought to be called. With this in mind he defined psychotherapy as "the communication of person related understanding, respect, and a wish to be of help." So that the therapist might carry out his task in a professional manner he cited seven principles to guide him:

1. Diagnosis is a precondition to and an integral part of psychotherapy.
2. Listening allows for ample expression of feelings and beliefs.
3. Understanding, respect, and a wish to be of help must be communicated.
4. A purpose or goal of therapy needs to be stated.
5. What is unusual or inconsistent in the child's behavior, feelings, and beliefs deserves clarification.
6. Deviant behavior must be modified by negotiation within the system that supports and maintains the behavior.
7. Termination is worked out when the advantages of ending the meetings outweigh any gains by their continuance.

The direct treatment of the child, as we recognize it today, began when free play was substituted for the verbal communication that characterized adult therapy (Hug-Helmuth, 1921; Klein, 1932). Freud's pioneering effort to treatment endeavors for children, helping a 4 year old to overcome his horse phobia, was actually carried out by correspondence with the boy's father (Freud, 1959). Such an indirect method was clearly limited in application when one considers the broad range of problems to which the young were heir. Observation of the child and of the effects of treatment efforts on thought, feeling, and behavior were necessary before any significant contributions to the treatment of troubled children could germinate (Lippman, 1934).

As was true for adults, the relationship with a therapist soon came to be considered a crucial element in the therapeutic process. Emerging from the Victorian period, with its emphasis on the suppression of feelings and of sexual impulses, the early therapists identified most of the problems in terms of this cultural damming up of natural desires and the resulting inculcation of a sense of badness in the child. One of the first tasks of therapy, then, was aimed at decreasing the child's feelings of badness. This meant that the therapist provided opportunities for the child to ventilate his ideas, feelings, and associated actions. Encouraging the catharsis soon proved to be insufficient to treatment. Gradually therapists learned to incorporate such devices as supplying the child with information, with clarification of personal and interpersonal conflict situations, with reality testing and limit setting, and with suggestions for alternate ways of problem solving.

Case A

An 8-year-old girl was brought to the clinic by her mother after the child and a twelve-year-old girlfriend had falsely accused a teenage boy of sexually molesting them. In school the child was considered to be a mild behavior problem because she talked back to the teacher and did not complete her class assignments. In the unraveling of the family history, a number of elements came to light that seemed to have a bearing on the presenting symptomatology. The child's mother had been promiscuous and had been engaged in a long-standing feud with her own mother about this behavior. Several years earlier the girl had been molested by the maternal uncle. Moreover, just prior to the action that led to the referral the child had witnessed parental coitus. Concurrent with this episode, she had experienced night terrors.

It was thought important that, apart from therapy to be carried out with the parents, the child also required a chance for sorting out confused impressions about human relationships in the relatively benign but secure format of individual treatment.

The woman therapist's gentle explanation of the nature and purpose of sexuality were reassuring to the child. Moreover, the predictable manner in which the therapeutic encounter proceeded quickly dissuaded the child from exercising provocative testing maneuvers which she had ordinarily used to clear up ambiguity. Because she was uncertain about trusting her elders, she would immediately put those to the test who showed some liking for her by trying their patience and good will. Much of the time, of course, she found how the anger she engendered in others only seemed to confirm her suspicions that people were hypocritical.

Once the therapist had gained her trust, it was possible to discuss with the child some of the consequences of her own behavior and to entertain with her more appropriate ways of putting doubts to rest.

On the basis of differences in problems, distinct techniques were also needed for the most appropriate application of treatment. Some of the techniques related to a need for facilitating communication, others concerned symptom relief. Levy (1933, 1938) was one of the first to distinguish "relationship therapy" and "release" or "affect therapy." The former utilized the potential for support embodied in a benign and permissive therapist who created a corrective emotional experience for the child reared in a disturbed environment. The latter was applied more specifically to children suffering from anxiety brought on by traumatic happenings. In this instance the therapist relieves anxiety by taking an active role through doll play and by choosing the plot which reproduces the traumatic situation. More often than not, the children were found to use this technique quite spontaneously to better master the anxiety associated with the fearful events. For this reason, Bender (1937) advocated free choice of dramatic play between therapist and patient.

Two different emphases in the approach to play therapy prevail today. The spontaneous type where the therapist assumes a relatively passive role is probably the most prevalent style in clinical practice, whereas the controlled type is usually identified with a particular method or technique espoused by practitioners who believe in a more active role for the therapist. In the first method the child has free access to the materials of the playroom while the therapist keeps his own activity to a minimum, that is by encouraging activity and giving the child his full attention. In the use of the second method the therapist selects the material and the scope of play, e.g. by describing the situation and encouraging the child to react to it (Newell, 1941). Early spokesmen for spontaneous play therapy were Allen (1934) and Rogerson (1939), while Levy (1938, 1939), Conn (1939), and Solomon (1938) introduced specific uses of play techniques. The latter have been augmented in recent years by the contributions of Gardner (1970) and Winnicott (1971).

Paralleling analytic treatment with adults, the early methods of working with children stressed the place of regression in therapeutic undoing of faulty development. By bringing the child back to that period of his emotional upbringing when his coping strategies presumably were overwhelmed or went awry, the therapist is in a good position both to offer the necessary gratification of unmet needs and to demonstrate more effective ways of mastery (Rank, 1949). An offshoot treatment method, the nondirective therapy of Rogers (1946), recognized that an overly permissive attitude was unwise since it could lead to license and personality disintegration, or at least to excessive anxiety in the face of a seductive and unrealistic life experience. A mutual understanding of the goals of therapy as well as a positive regard for the child and his family were considered a sufficient safeguard against indulgent permissiveness. For several decades, however, both lay public and professionals mistakenly equated child therapy with an unmindful releasing of the furies thought to be buried in all children and itching to come out.

Glasser (1965) urged a return to reality therapy, that is helping children to become responsible and caring people.

Anna Freud (1928) approved of play as a medium for communication but questioned its use as a pure substitute for free association in the service of reliving the past. After all, the child is still in the process of acquiring information and of learning about life in preparation for adulthood. Present experience is as important to the child as the past. Therefore, the relationship to the therapist contains not only transference projections which must be analyzed but also the elements of a primary attachment upon which later learning is built. The therapist becomes, at least temporarily, an ego ideal who allows for "constructive sublimation," the psychoanalytic equivalent of education and socialization. Some therapists went so far as to ignore the importance of dynamic understanding of the child's problems because they felt that their influence as ego ideals would stimulate an innate capacity for effecting positive choice in their young patients (Allen, 1942; Rank, 1938). By espousing a philosophy of responsibility—by asking what the child can do about his situation—they hoped to instruct him in practicing his role for creating harmonious relations. The stress was on a confidential, trusting relationship with the therapist.

Case B

A 7-year-old boy, a second grader and the oldest of four children, was referred for treatment at the suggestion of his pediatrician after a series of episodes of increasing magnitude which hinted at an underlying plea for help. About a month prior to being seen the boy reported to the school nurse with the complaint of a sore throat. Although the pediatrician could find nothing wrong, the boy stayed out of school one week. Upon his return he made repeated trips to the nurse with the same complaint. About one week before the referral, as the parents were preparing to take the family out of town to visit grandparents, the boy destroyed a lawn mower destined to be returned to the relatives. During the visit he was found to be playing covertly with matches in the grandparents' house but denied any wrongdoing, even when caught.

He had a history of undergoing a tonsillectomy at 8 months, of head banging, of being fearful of the dark, and of having sustained a concussion at age 5 years after a fall from a bike. There was considerable marital discord in the home because the father either spent long hours away working or was uncommunicative when he was with the family.

The boy confided in the therapist that he was angry over feeling left out.

His parents had more time for other people than they did for him. Perhaps they did not care what he did. Of course, when he was sick or naughty they gave him the attention he craved. By denying wrongdoing he was most successful in focusing their concerns upon him.

The therapist listened attentively to the boy's complaints and pointed out that the parents were now worried enough to talk with someone to see what changes they could make in their conduct for improving the situation. However, the therapist also went on to ask whether there were problems or other things which the child would like to do something about. The boy then alluded to his several fears emanating from a strong sense of being overwhelmed by forces embodied in monsters and ghosts which he could not control. Therapy subsequently took the direction of helping the boy confront his fears so that he might better master them through more successful interpersonal experiences.

Not all children were subject to the positive influence of identification with the therapist. A longstanding interest in the nature of delinquency speaks to the frustration of workers with this group, particularly where environmental factors combine with faulty socialization (Levy, 1932; Tiebout and Kirkpatrick, 1932). Although some delinquency derives from neurotic conflict and is therefore discrepant with the professed family outlook or its social setting (Lippman, 1937; Johnson and Szurek, 1952), the majority of the problem cases have been the product of a disadvantaged milieu. Insecurity, powerlessness, and overcompensation by way of aggressive confrontations with an equally helpless adult environment characterize this process of grappling with unwholesome conditions. Various "corrective" therapies evolved which had to pay attention to the environment as well as to the reeducation of the delinquent's ego (Aichhorn, 1935; Healy and Bronner, 1936). Redl and Wineman (1952) developed special techniques for the management of impulse ridden children so that they might better bear up under anxiety and frustration by acquiring interpersonal skills from the inevitable crisis encounters with therapists.

Other groups of children who were difficult to reach through the more conventional individual therapies were variously described as atypical, borderline, psychotic, schizophrenic, and autistic. A number of therapist investigators developed special avenues of help. Although not always curative, these were sufficiently ameliorative to save many children from prolonged invalidism and institutionalization (Bender, 1942; Bettelheim, 1950; Bradley and Bowen, 1941; DesLauriers and Carlson, 1969; Despert, 1947;

Ekstein et al., 1958; Goldfarb, 1961; Kanner, 1943; Mahler, 1952; Potter, 1933; Rank, 1949; Robinson, 1961). More and more the gist of the therapeutic need has been formulated in terms of training procedures, that is literally building ego functions with painstaking care in children who have profound maturational lags in many developmental areas (Bender, 1942; 1956; Halpern, 1970).

Case C

At the time of his referral to a children's psychiatric outpatient service, this $3\frac{1}{2}$-year-old boy had already been diagnosed by several pediatric and mental health specialists as an atypical child with predominately autistic features. He had no recognizable speech and seemed amicably detached from all human relationships. His major attachment was to a crib blanket and to watching television commercials.

The patient, the youngest of three boys, had been easy to care for as a baby. The mother nursed the infant for 4 months but never knew whether he was satisfied. Only if he found himself in a strange place did he scream. As early as 1 year of age, he seemed to ignore people. In his second year of life he started to rock his crib so forcibly that it had to be attached to the wall to keep him from moving it across the floor. On occasion he would tear up his mattress. His favorite activity became the ripping out of pages from books. Part of his investigating repertoire was the smelling of objects. Although a few echoic words were overheard from time to time, he had no meaningful language for communication.

His entry into a day treatment program for atypical children provided him with systematic language and speech training. After $1\frac{1}{2}$ years in the program, individual therapy was added because he was now showing an increasing capacity for communicative speech. The therapist used the time to guide the child away from an exclusive fascination with the inanimate world to a greater engagement of people. After 2 years of therapy, the boy enjoyed walking the halls of the clinic in order to read the names of the occupants on the doors of offices. Eventually he associated the names with their bearers whom he assiduously pursued in order to carry on a "mini-conversation" about their names. Shortly thereafter he entered a learning disability class in a public school.

The assessment of the therapeutic potential of the child must take into account many factors that require sound clinical judgement. No pat formula or fixed criteria exist for the determination of effectiveness for individual therapy of children. A report of the Group for the Advancement of Psychiatry (1973) lists the following categories that have some bearing on clinical judgement in any decision regarding therapeutic choice:

1. Degree of central nervous system or physical impairment.
2. Areas of healthy functioning.
3. Capacity for relating to others.
4. Capacity for tolerance of anxiety.
5. Capacity for conceptualization and communication.
6. Developmental phase.
7. Personality structure including drive, conscience, and ego.
8. Frustration tolerance.
9. Duration of the problem.
10. Severity of disorder.
11. "Psychological mindedness."
12. Proportion of reactive to intrapsychic elements.
13. Degree of secondary gain.
14. Proneness to regression.

In addition to the correct evaluation of the child's strengths and liabilities, must be considered the readiness of the family and of the community to provide the child with the necessary support, stimulation, education, and recreation; the availability of mental health resources consonant with the needs of the child; the child's motivation for treatment; and the appropriateness of the fit between the child and his therapist. This means that some chronic and severe problems are suitable for individual help whereas others are not. Moreover, not all acute or mild problems are susceptible to outpatient psychotherapy.

In categorizing the current state of psychotherapy with children and youth, three major types of approaches are discernible under the headings of supportive, reparative, and corrective treatments. Each has its own techniques, but just as there may be an overlap of problem genesis in the individual so will there be some transfer of methods from one approach to another. It is in the realm of ego functioning that determinations must be made about strengths and weaknesses, about potentials and limitations, and about levels of integration and fixations before a suitable therapeutic stance can be assumed. The severest problems usually stem from early impairment of central nervous system functioning and/or from unfortunate experiences that thwart the unfolding of primary psychobehavioral growth stages. Less severe disorders tend to be byproducts of the ordinary hazards of living, from chance mishaps to mismatching of temperaments, and from developmental crises to cultural dissonance.

In any case, although general principles of psychotherapy define the platform on which the child therapist stands, the special techniques for dealing with particular problems provide the scaffolding necessary for the edifice of the helping process. The purist insists that for the sake of refining a technique and its effectiveness the clinician must be scrupulous about observing the formalities of method, whereas the eclectic who holds up pragmatism as his credo utilizes all avenues of help open to him. Yet even the eclectic finds a need to provide a rationale for the choices made. By categorizing techniques according to a scheme rooted in ego psychology, a more orderly procedure for selecting appropriate techniques can be achieved. A recent suggestion by Toussieng (1971), however, would place into the hands of the child the responsibility for setting the goals and determining the nature for every therapeutic intervention—"even to letting him decide whether any help is needed at all."

Supportive Techniques

If one assumes that every intact child is naturally impelled to establish his competence and autonomy if allowed to do so (White, 1963), then the failure to develop age-appropriate self-assertion and independence can be largely placed at the door of the child rearing agents. More often than not such factors as early loss of love objects, experiential deprivations, and serious interferences with the emergence of social efficacy contribute to the appearance of emotionally stunted, immature children. Their ego development proceeds cautiously, if at all, because confidence has been lost in the competency of the self. They look to the adult as an omnipotent source of power and supplies on whose capricious good will they must depend. The therapist to such children places himself into the role of provider of need gratification, protector from undue frustrations of instinctual drives, and promoter of growth—a truly paradoxical and quixotic position. Because treatment is often long and tedious, many therapists defer to less trained persons to be the mainstay of a supportive program. For example, Big Brother and Big Sister Programs match needy or deprived children with volunteers. When done under the auspices of a training orientation and with supervision, the approach has been called amicatherapy (Kraft, 1965; Mitchell, 1966).

When the child's background or deprivation is seen as a principal cause of his problems, the relationship with the therapist serves to capture those nurturing activities of closeness, feeding, and warmth that signal acceptance of inchoate desires. The supportive therapist attempts to reestablish the child's trust by providing a relationship that is reliable, by recognizing him as a person of worth, and by freely giving to him—no matter that ultimately there are limits to such providence. To the degree that this is unsuccessful, the helping process is bound to founder on the shallow attachments the child brings to the situation. Making the child dependent and anxious about his dependence at least offers him another chance to resume a more independent course, a replication of the oppositional or self-assertive stage of ego development so necessary for individuation. First one must feel cared for before it becomes possible to experiment with caring for one's self. Relationship therapy certainly includes those elements that permit direct training and learning to take place (Lavery and Stone, 1965; Riese, 1962).

Case D

A 5-year-old boy, the middle of three children, was brought to a clinic by his mother at the suggestion of her boyfriend because the child appeared to be indifferent to discipline, even to severe punishment with a strap. If his mother corrected him verbally or chastised him physically, he remained stonefaced. This behavior the mother interpreted to mean that the child did not love her. He was considered to be intelligent and was no problem in kindergarten.

The parents had been divorced 2 years. When the father did not take the boy for his weekly visit, the child simply announced that the man was not his father anymore since he did not live with the family. Nonetheless, there were evident signs of tension exhibited by the child such as trichotillomania, nail biting, and rhythmic foot tapping. He was demanding, suffered from a short attention span, fought with his siblings, and was prone to be overactive.

A few weeks after his birth he was hospitalized for treatment of pneumonia. An aftereffect of episodic vomiting was terminated by the mother by slapping him across the face a few times. The oldest sister had been taken care of primarily by the maternal grandmother for the 2 years prior to his birth. Since the mother had misgivings about the daughter's attachment to the grandmother, she tried to keep this child from becoming overinvolved with the grandmother. Despite this effort, a tie developed so that being deprived of a visit with the grandmother was one of the few occasions when the child shed tears.

Examination of the boy revealed a rejected and depressed youngster who was eager to solicit the therapist's approval and support. He felt that he was unlovable like his father, whom the mother had sent away. Not surprisingly the boy found it difficult to deal with ambivalent feelings, save to repress anger at all cost in order to protect himself from abandonment. In his therapy sessions he devoted much time to preparing meals for the therapist and himself. This identification with both the provider and the needy child gave some indication of his sense of isolation, which then required a solicitous, giving, and affectionate response from the therapist before the boy could show negative affect.

Not all deprived children tolerate a one-to-one relationship well because such an attachment is either meaningless or too threatening to them. Some quickly become so demanding that their neediness overwhelms the therapist who finds himself caught up in his own insufficiency for ever being able to satisfy a youngster's greedy hunger. Feeding represents adult concern for the child in its most elemental form. Food in the therapy sessions can thus serve as a reassurance that a relationship is built on this basic responsibility in the provision of caring. In general, the use of food in individual treatment of deprived children can only remain symbolic, so that the clinician arranges for a token amount of candy or food valued by the child to be regularly available in the sessions. For some children small gifts such as crayons, pencils, and coloring books, which are identified as their possessions, are the medium through which trust in a giving adult can take root. For older children and adolescents with this background, selected activities such as having a hamburger—inside or outside the consultation room—facilitate rapport (Schaeffer, 1962).

The supportive posture is communicated by "person related understanding" (Reisman, 1971). The therapist conveys his acceptance of the child through his attempts at comprehending the behavior, ideas, and feelings of the child. Although Reisman (1971) distinguishes five types of therapist statements—empathic, responsive, interpretive, interrogative, and expository—only the first two are uniquely supportive. The empathic therapist communicates readily his respect for the child by listening and trying to understand messages, reacts to the feeling tone rather than to the content of his productions, and reflects on a level appropriate to the child's situation and capacity for comprehension. His responsive statements indicate by simple expressions that he is listening and understanding what is being said to him.

Case E

A 10-year-old boy comes to clinical attention because he has temper tantrums at home and in school. Both parents work. Only the mother is interested in seeking assistance for herself, for the son, and for 2 younger daughters of 5 and 4 years who are overactive. The family lives in the home of the paternal grandmother who is of Eastern European origin and poorly acculturated to the New World. According to the mother, her husband is an alcoholic, although he had had a good employment record. The boy voices his disappointment in the father already in the initial interview:

BOY: My father's a drunk. He doesn't come home right away after work. I guess he goes to the neighborhood bar.

THERAPIST: You feel badly about your father.

BOY: He does it almost every day. When he comes home, he is a grouch.

THERAPIST: That probably makes you even more upset with him.

BOY: Sometimes I'm scared because he gets mean. Most of the time he just watches television or he goes to sleep.

THERAPIST: Either way, it seems you feel that you can't reach your father. That can be frustrating.

BOY: Yeah, I get so mad, I slam doors. Then my grandmother hollers at me. It's funny. She speaks different. I don't understand what she says.

THERAPIST: It makes you feel a little better to see that somebody like your grandmother acts upset when she doesn't understand what's going on—just like you do.

BOY: I sure wish I knew why my father is this way.

THERAPIST: Somehow that would help.

BOY: Maybe I wouldn't get mad so much. Maybe I wouldn't get into so much trouble.

The regularity of contact and the anticipation that an adult has set aside time in the week to give his undivided attention to the child builds up a relationship of confidence. Moreover, the child can choose any kind of toy or material for use in self-expression, thus minimizing the tension that might plague the interaction if only verbal exchanges were possible. If the therapist displays a child oriented understanding this in itself is salutary, because it opens up opportunities of risk taking for the child that may otherwise not be grasped. Depending on the kind of problems a child presents, the therapist may assume a passive or an active role in the play therapy. In the case of a detached child, a benevolently passive participation in the encounter encourages testing of the therapist's tolerance toward the expression of feelings and actions. By the adult's acceptance of the range of emotions shown, the child may for the first time try to forge more intimate links of an interpersonal nature by opening up communication and affirming trust. With the scattered child, the therapist usually takes a more active course designed to organize the experience in such a way as to differentiate it from most other relationships. He introduces or suggests play activities such as games (e.g. checkers) or task-oriented ventures (building models) in order to bind the child's anxieties about the relationship and to enable him to find his bearings in a structured experience. It is the reassurance, which in this instance springs from the guiding hand of the adult who introduces meaning and fulfillment to the interaction, that causes the child to appreciate the significance of the relationship. In either instance the therapist leads the child to a point where the latter takes a more active role in the play therapy.

Whether additional forms of therapeutic technique should be employed, other than the supportive, depends on the severity of fixation exhibited by the child and the degree of progress he has made as a result of relationship therapy (Bender, 1952). As the child is helped to discover his powers for self-expression, the therapist opens up other opportunities for broadening this quest. For example, an action oriented intervention that engages "the creative will of the child" (Frommer, 1972) operates on a level of consciousness where intellectual effort and personal attachments do not act as constraints on the experience. The use of artistic media in therapy such as music, dance, drama, story telling, painting, and sculpting can aid the healing process simply because they tap sources of constructive energy and fantasy outlets not reached by more classical modes of communication. In this manner the child becomes an active partner in giving form and direction to his therapy (Arlow and Kadis, 1946; Bender and Boas, 1941; Bender and Woltman, 1936; Dreikurs, 1960; Durfee, 1943; Naumburg, 1973; Reiser et al., 1957; Siegel, 1973).

Case F

The 8-year-old daughter of an unwed, obese mother on public assistance was being seen in collateral therapy. Although both mother and child were linked in a hostile-dependent relationship, it was the girl who was beginning to give evidence that she had been allowed to take control. She was moderately preoccupied with a variety of somatic complaints for which no physical cause could be found.

In play therapy she expressed her neediness as well as her creative talent for securing need gratification through the medium of art. For example, her first drawing represented a sumptuous dish of fresh fruit, foreshadowing an attitude toward the therapist as a generous provider of emotional and material resources. When she turned to the use of modeling clay, she produced a nesting bird, an act that spoke more to her self-confidence in being a generous person. Whatever vehicle of expression she chose, and there were many, it conveyed a powerful sense of pleasure in and of commitment to the process of creation. All complaints about her health disappeared as soon as she became involved in play therapy.

Often when children move into more advanced stages of emotional development as a result of treatment, the techniques of reparative and corrective therapy are selectively added. Both the form of communication and the exploration of the problems may undergo changes in keeping with the child's readiness to follow a more challenging undertaking. Even then, however, as the therapist embarks on a course whereby he encourages the child to face his potential for growth, the relationship must retain a supportive quality to a much higher degree than would be true for children other than the deprived.

Reparative Techniques

When disturbance arises in ego integration and functioning as a result of a combination of factors, from biogenetic to psychosocial influences, the child presents a picture of inner chaos for which very fundamental steps must be taken for the repair of deficient or disarrayed perceptual, coping, relationship, or linguistic capacities. Such children who are variously referred to as atypical, autistic, borderline, preschizophrenic, psychotic, schizoid, schizophrenic, and symbiotic are candidates for techniques that help them go through previously missed or unsatisfactory phases of development via a therapist who acts as an auxiliary ego. Mahler (1968) espouses three aims in the treatment of the psychotic child, namely (1) the establishment or restoration of greater body image integrity, (2) the development of object relationships, and (3) the building of vestigial or the repair of distorted maturational and developmental functions.

Methods for body image building include the identification of body parts by the use of the mirror, by touching, by active manipulation of limbs, by cuddling, by modeling of action, and by verbal labeling of organs and other physical structures on the child and on one's self. Insofar as is possible the therapist uses pleasurable activities to involve the child so that he comes to stand in loco parentis and is in a position to train the child in self-definition, in speech (Halpern et al., 1973), and in channeling of drives or socialization. In recent years intrusive methods have been added or have replaced earlier socialization approaches that aim to arouse such children to be more alert to the therapist (DesLauriers and Carlson, 1969), to confront for the sake of eroding negativism—or Z-technique (Zaslow and Breger, 1969), to condition the learning of stimulus response patterns (Lovaas et al., 1965), and to give language training to overcome a global aphasia thought to underlie many of these disorders (Rutter, 1974).

Case G

A 4-year-old boy whose communication difficulty had been diagnosed as a congenital expressive aphasia was referred to a child guidance clinic because his impulsive behavior placed him beyond the control of parents. His principal means of communication were grunting sounds and behavioral equivalents of frustration arising out of his loss for words. Because he took pleasure from physical interaction, he was capable of making good eye contact and exhibited good behavioral responses to game playing such as "Hide and Seek." He was not thought to be psychotic.

In addition to offering the parents guidelines for managing the child, individual therapy undertook to capture the child's attention for the purpose of establishing a pattern of communication that would be repetitive and predictable. The therapist limited the play space to 3 square feet and selected a few play materials that had high appeal but which could also be quickly removed from him. "Playing with the therapist" was then used as the goad for stepping up of expectations for speech production. In this manner the therapist prepared the boy to accept formal speech therapy with a speech specialist. As the potential for expressing himself grew, the behavioral management problems waned.

For older children who are borderline psychotic, Ekstein (1966) has developed treatment techniques that rely on verbal intercessions. For example, he describes "interpretation within the regression" which takes into account the child's ego state and therefore confines itself to this condition in order to preserve the therapeutic relationship. A therapist for this type of child would resort to the use of magical protective gestures in response to a panicky outcry or a heedless action.

Another device he names "interpretation within the metaphor" in order to bring about a gradual acclimatization to higher level communication and effective therapy. Because borderline psychotic children have a shaky grasp on reality and are "in constant danger of becoming temporarily flooded by archaic modes of thought" (Ekstein, 1966), the use of the metaphor serves as a momentary life line by maintaining contact between therapist and patient when the latter is at the mercy of primitive or primary process material. Indeed, the use of the metaphor is initiated by the child who is impelled to communicate in this fashion because deliberate language or thought-out speech is not available to him. When the child confronts the therapist with the declaration "I am a dinosaur," the interpretation within the metaphor would seek to maintain communication at that level rather than provide insight based on interpretation. For example, the therapist might well reply that the dinosaur was a large and powerful animal who once dominated the world and, although there is no live dinosaur today, we are still very much interested in him. Sometimes, children will use action metaphors such as setting the playhouse on fire to which the therapist may reply with a symbolic act or posture, for example setting up fire fighting equipment that will contain the fantasized blaze. Ekstein (1966) warned that the technique requires considerable self awareness in its application so that its limits and complications can be properly taken into account.

A related technique for treating borderline children goes under the name of "playing it right" (Tooley, 1973). In order to facilitate the integration of the therapist into the child's fantasy world, reality concepts are introduced in small, graduated doses by adding to the complexity of the play. The therapist challenges some unrealistic play element, for example insisting that a tow truck is needed to pull a car out of a sand pit rather than let the action proceed repeatedly along its predictably magic course of recovery. The introduction of reality rules makes their stereotyped play richer or more complex and therefore more pleasurable. Additionally, since the intrusion into the play is momentary, and since mastery of the play is returned to the child as rapidly as possible, it is a manageable unit of anxiety with which to accustom the child to the reality principle.

Those children whose ego deficits are expressed in the realm of poor impulse controls, may need a therapeutic encounter that is both secure and physically restricting. Although medication and behavior modification techniques sometimes better serve the purposes of treatment for such problems, psychotherapy can be an important adjunct. Limit setting or just the implied awareness of limits is a condition of all therapy with children. When a child consistently demonstrates his driven behavior or impulsiveness by being destructive or assaultive, the therapist views the transaction of limit setting as the most significant inroad he can make on the problem (Bixler, 1949; Barcai and Rosenthal, 1974). Several steps are considered, starting with a clarification of the child's feelings, followed by a reminder that certain actions are undesirable, and if these verbal interventions prove to no avail, resorting to physical restraint of the child. The struggles that can ensue must be anticipated by the therapist who will have to judge whether his control is going to be effective, since such confrontations may prove countertherapeutic if the child continues unrealistically to have the upper hand. If the therapist is unsure in this regard other therapeutic ploys had better be considered. The child who learns that a protective attitude governs the approach to his uncontrolled behavior, sooner or later takes comfort from the fact that the adult is in charge as an alter ego and that he will be allowed to make decisions about his actions as soon as both recognize that motivation and capability for self-control exist in the two of them.

Case H

A 7-year-old boy of Puerto Rican background refused to speak outside of his home. In school his mute and inhibited behavior was of concern to his teachers who could find no way of eliciting a verbal response from him, although he was thought to be of good intelligence. When he was sent to a special program for disturbed children, his verbal and behavioral reticence did not disappear. Tape recording of bilingual conversations among the boy, his mother, and siblings in the home gave evidence that he could be highly articulate and animated.

Individual play therapy was initiated with the expressed purpose of helping the boy speak outside the home. After several contacts with the therapist, during which period of time the child never uttered a sound, but nonetheless began to engage in circumscribed play activities, the plan was to give the youngster the choice to speak a word on cue and go home or to remain with the therapist until he did so. The family and the boy had been apprised of this strategy more than 2 weeks before its actual implementation. On the predetermined day, the interview proceeded as usual until the therapist pointed out that the child would be allowed to depart for home only if he would speak at least one word. Increasingly the boy became agitated, rocked vigorously back and forth, and cried angrily but silently. The therapist reassured him about the choice for speaking which would quickly get him home. About 4 hours later, the child stopped rocking and crying, announced that he wished to go, and was driven home by the therapist who, not knowing the exact location of the home, had to be instructed in finding it by his young guide.

In subsequent therapy sessions, there was no evidence of mutism. On the contrary, the child made verbal requests whenever the need to do so arose and he developed a warm and trusting relationship over the course of several weeks before being returned to his public school class.

In addition to cases of speech phobia (Halpern et al., 1971) this type of therapy has been extended to a number of conditions where peculiar reality testing has fostered fantasies of magic and omnipotent control over circumscribed life experiences, as in children who are afraid to leave home for school (Leventhal and Sills, 1964) or who are anorexic (Kissel and Arkins, 1973). Here the therapist takes control of these functions by placing the child into an unwanted predicament and then gives him the choice between the lesser of two evils. In order to extricate himself from the less desirable state of affairs, which is under the therapist's control, the child chooses to perform in that area which he previously abjured. A better appreciation of his true capacities emerges from these showdowns.

Another treatment orientation toward borderline children who are impulsive and behaviorally disorganized derives from observations in working with them in a controlled residential milieu. Under these circumstances, Redl's (1966) life space interviewing takes on special significance because the child requires adults to be in a mediating role to help him organize his psychological experiences. Although the interviews were originally conceived to be used on a crisis basis for child care workers, the technique has relevance for all intervention with this type of youngster. Essentially, when an on-the-spot upset occurs, two potential opportunities for therapeutic consideration are pursued. First, is there a chance for bringing a problem or pattern to the awareness of the child by a strategic clinical exploitation of the life event? Second, can in-the-moment emotional first aid drain off excess ill will, restore equanimity by putting a better perspective on the experience, and keep communications going to deter further withdrawal? Redl feels that all of us need gentle reminders to help us regulate our conduct according to agreed upon conventions. When children are so disturbed or unschooled in their awareness of social traffic, they require very active traffic cops.

Under the rubric of clinical exploitation Redl (1966) enumerates techniques with "tongue in cheek" labels such as "reality rub in," "symptom estrangement," "managing numb value areas," and "new tool salesmanship." For example, when a child must be repeatedly instructed as to the meaning of life events, either because he misinterprets constantly or because he alibies his way through all situations, he is receiving "on the spot reality rub ins." The therapist also tries to demonstrate that the child's pathologic behavior does not pay or that he pays too much for the meager secondary gain the symptoms provide. He also appeals to the child's sense of justice, recognizing that a code of "fairness" has much more acceptance than a demand for conformity. In this fashion, a conversion from impulsive action to talking takes place.

A symptom that seems to negate any helping effort is the unusually silent child or adolescent, one who falls short of being an elective mute. The tactic employed by Kaplan and Escoll (1973) advises the therapist to talk for the silent patient without angry accusations about the perceived central dynamic issues. Moreover, he asks frequent questions which, if refused an answer, can be answered by offering a list of possibilities for the patient. As the time progresses, periodic encouragement for speech is introduced to provide opportunities for talking which, when it comes, is accepted in the same sympathetic manner as the silence.

Corrective Techniques

When parents or fate have not unduly traumatized children who nonetheless have evidence of problems arising from inner disturbance, child analysis or uncovering psychotherapy are methods of choice (Freud, 1968).

For children who come to therapy because their problems relate primarily to painful life experiences that have produced unconscious conflicts as the basis of disturbed functioning, the utilization of working through techniques comes into play. In its most essential form corrective therapy enables the child to bring up thoughts and feelings distressing to him, and to exhume the buried conflicts so that these too may be better resolved. Establishing meaningful communication with the child becomes the sine qua non of such "uncovering therapy." To do this the therapist first seeks to clarify what the child feels about his visit, what he understands of its purpose, what he would like to do about his problems, and how he believes the therapist might help. Should the child be unable to speak easily to these points, the use of play materials generally facilitates communication so that a sense of mutual participation can occur. This also sets the tone for subsequent interactions between therapist and child where, on the one hand, the adult proceeds gradually with the child in his attempts to be understanding while, on the other, the child has the freedom to reveal as much as he is ready to do at any given time. Of course, the therapist has the additional task to recognize when verbal expression becomes too difficult and, on such occasions, judiciously help the child with nonverbal, projective techniques.

Case I

The mother's chief complaint about this 5-year-old girl was that she has a Jekyll and Hyde personality. She can be sweet and cooperative, but suddenly turn around to be irritable or oppositional. One day the child may make a friend among her peers only to drop her for another the very next day and even turn on the first friend for no apparent reason. She will frequently tell mother that she does not have to go to school. When she attends the kindergarten class she is rather attention seeking. The parents have been separated for 2 years, although the child sees her father regularly. She expresses the wish repeatedly that she would like to have the parents reunited. She sucks her thumb regularly.

In order to get the child to sleep at night, the mother has permitted the child to share her bed. Restlessness and sleeptalking are common occurrences during the night. When the parents were together, she had often witnessed their violent quarrels. The child accused the mother of having the police come "to take daddy away." There was a possibility that the girl had been exposed to father's extramarital affairs.

When the child was seen for individual therapy, her mood reflected the degree of family unrest just prior to the visit. When there had been no recent upset, she was talkative and active during the sessions. Should there have been an argument between the parents within a day of her coming, she was taciturn. She referred often to the parents' fighting about money and spoke of her desire to shut out the conflict by covering her ears or by running to the safety of her room. The therapist dealt with the child's confusion about being caught up in the obviously unresolved emotional separation between the parents. Through play, the girl conveyed a desire to be relieved of the tension —when the figure of the father was repeatedly omitted.

Case J

The parents of a 4-year-old boy requested help because he was a behavior problem at home and in nursery school. He frequently shoved and hit his 5-year-old sister and his age mates, and was considered to have a "mean streak." Furthermore, he did not please his parents because he was loath to follow their instructions, listened to them only selectively, and was quick to produce alibis for his behavior. There was more than the usual preoccupation with guns and violence. He had a fascination for firemen's hats. If spoken to sharply, he was likely to obey the father who was the more imposing parent.

His developmental history was quite uneventful although the pregnancy had not been desired by either parent who were then still living with the maternal grandparents. The grandfather, who had doted on this grandchild, died when the boy was 3 years old. Although the family had moved into their own home, the grandfather came to visit them daily in order to be with the grandson. At the time of the death, the boy was very upset and started to sleep with a hat his grandfather had given him. Overnight he had changed from calling himself "grandpa's boy" to "daddy's boy." The grandfather had possessed a gun collection and had fantasized about it a great deal with the boy.

The parents had recently undergone a trial separation when the boy had voiced a preference for the father. It seemed that unresolved feelings about the loss of the grandfather had become intensified when the father moved out for a month, ostensibly to go on a business trip. In addition to the marital counseling for the parents, a decision was made to give the boy the opportunity to work on his anger over the grandfather's perceived abandonment.

Case K

A 10-year-old boy, in foster care since age 4 years when the parents divorced, was working below his capacity in school and was withdrawing from peers. From time to time the mother had taken the son back into her home but then placed him again into the foster home for a variety of reasons—such as making plans for returning to college or because she hoped to remarry. The foster parents wished to adopt the youth, but he was reluctant to acquiesce, even after his parents surrendered him and he was released for adoption. Two younger siblings had returned to the mother after a number of years in foster care. The boy seemed depressed yet had not given up hope that his mother would some day reclaim him.

Individual therapy was undertaken with him so that he might relieve some of the deep hurt he had experienced. Beyond this, it was felt of value if he could come to grips with the reality of his situation and thus be in a better position to make use of his personal assets and of his environment.

These three cases illustrate how the therapist can offer a corrective therapeutic experience for children who have suffered significant loss, regardless of the circumstances surrounding the loss. In each case it was the sympathetic understanding communicated to the child rather than the materials present in the playroom that was the basis for therapeutic change.

Playrooms are equipped with materials that tend to reflect the orientation of the practitioners. Since those play therapists who use controlled play also incorporate free activity, there are fairly standard items in all playrooms. These include blocks, dolls, puppets, games, vehicles, dollhouses, play furniture, cooking utensils, rubber-tipped darts, running water, paints, plasticine, and other simple toys. Some will be well stocked with toy guns, sand boxes, baby bottles, or punching bags—if the therapist believes in the benefits of physical discharge in the abreaction of emotions. If the therapist employs certain standardized techniques, he may limit the quantity of toys in order to help the child focus on the controlled play situation. The use of a tape recorder for story telling, of puppets for dramatic exposition, or of drawing materials may then occupy the most prominent position in the playroom.

When the child is introduced to a playroom where he is expected to engage in spontaneous play, he is told that he can do what he likes, that he can make up stories about what he is doing. Some clinicians caution that the child may not hurt himself or the therapist and that the child may not intentionally break the lights, windows, or other fixtures. By giving his undivided attention, the adult sets the stage for a repeated elaboration of important themes by the child until both can gather their meaning. Ordinarily this tactic helps to develop close rapport although it takes time to do so. Furthermore, it provides opportunities to display resistances which may be necessary to the child until he gains in confidence.

If the therapist is more active he decides in advance how to set the stage with the play materials he wants the child to use in telling a story. For example, Levy (1938) told the child that they were to play a game for which they needed various family members who were engaged in a designated activity. He would then ask the child to go on with the story based on the scenario he had provided. The rationale for such controlled play, which can be introduced alongside free play, is that it reproduces those situations that caused the fears or conflicts. Therefore a more systematic desensitization to the anxiety producing elements can be undertaken. Conn (1939) arranged the doll family and toy furniture on a miniature stage or placed doll family members in a preplanned play situation and asked stimulus questions that pertained to the child's problems. For example, a child fearful of the toilet might be asked how a boy from the doll family felt after the therapist held it on the toy toilet. The subsequent interview follows a question and answer pattern with the child answering for the doll. A variation of this game is a conversation between two dolls so that the child can reveal ambivalent emotions more easily. A therapist doll was introduced by Solomon (1948) in order to give a more immediate significance to the abreaction of feelings. At the same time the therapist places himself into a better position for bringing cause and effect relationships most effectively to the child's awareness and for relieving guilt directly when feelings are steered at his effigy.

Doll play represents an enactment of conflicts over which the child can exercise control. After all, toys miniaturize the adult world and by virtue of their small size allow the child a sense of mastery over his situation. Not only does this reduce his sense of being overwhelmed by an oversize environment but it also gives the little child a chance to practice actions and problem solving skills in preparation for the future. In the context of play therapy he can pursue this process in a benign relationship with an interested adult. He can reenact conflict experiences from which he can gain relief, self-understanding, and corrective alternatives to problem resolution.

Games have become a stock-in-trade for most child therapists. Not only do they substitute for more spontaneous conversation, but they also represent a paradigm of unbalanced power struggles in which children find themselves entrapped by the very fact of their position in life. Here is an opportunity to deal with resistance to therapy (Loomis, 1957), with attitudes about competition (Meeks, 1970), and with the boredom born of routine (Gardner, 1969). Most significantly, the youngster observes adult behavior in the context of the power struggle, a paradoxic setup that can easily go awry if not well understood. Usually, the therapist has superior game playing skills. These he must use in the service of the therapeutic objectives, for example by establishing a more benign competitive set or by "playing fair."

The use of imaginative art work such as drawing, painting, and plasticine modeling can draw out children's feelings where game playing may not. Discussions are elicited about these productions when a child is asked to tell a story about the picture or scene he has created. The material may form the basis for much thematic elaboration of current and past concerns.

As already noted, no playroom is complete without dollhouse, dolls, and puppets. These approximations to the child's real world facilitate the play acting of real and imaginary scenes that convey both situational problems and core conflicts. Relationships to all the significant people in the child's life surface in doll house or puppet play (Erikson, 1963). Quite often, the transference to the therapist is acted upon through this medium when the child assigns certain puppet figures to him. This allows the therapist to offer corrective resolutions to the child's stories. However, another dimension that must not be overlooked lies in the creative aspect of dramatic play. Dressing up in costumes (Marcus, 1966) introduces similar dramatic play which, in addition to its fun aspects, also serves as a creative outlet for alternative mastery of strong emotions.

Winnicott (1971) tapped his own potential for creative playfulness by contributing the squiggle game to child therapy. After a preliminary explanation of the game, the therapist starts by making a squiggle with the pencil on a piece of paper and then tells the child to convert it into anything he wants. In return, the child makes a squiggle for the therapist to complete. On the basis of the symbolic significance of the child's completed squiggles and associated verbalizations, the therapist gets insights that allow him to produce corrective squiggle pictures and interpretations. Often the squiggle game is just a prelude to opening up a child's confidence in someone who appears to understand him.

An analogous technique has been developed by Gardner (1971). Because he considered the more traditional uses of dollhouses, drawings, and puppet play often to have a restricting effect on the child's storytelling or on his ability to channel it in very specific directions, he employed the technique of story telling within the context of a make-believe television show.

The child is asked by the therapist to be guest of honor on a make-believe program that features story telling. After the child has agreed to accept the honor the tape recorder is turned on, whereupon the master of ceremonies or therapist announces the program, its rules, and the fact that he will make up a story too, one that will have a moral. After a few more introductory questions that establish the child's identity and playing back his voice—presumably to relax him—he is asked to begin his story. At its completion the child is invited to say what lesson the story had. Obviously, the therapist has to be quite adept in clarifying for himself the symbolic significance of the various figures in the story to get an intuitive grasp of the messages. He then asks himself whether he can think of a more mature resolution to the story used by the child. Although the story he now creates for the child involves the same characters, setting, and initial situation, he will introduce appropriate alternatives to the major conflicts. His moral emphasizes the healthier adaptations he has touched upon in the story. When the mutual storytelling is completed, the therapist stops the recorder and inquires whether a playback is wanted. A playback of the message would reinforce what the therapist wished to impart. Modifications in the child's stories and in his behavior signify the effective influence of this technique.

Case L

A sulky, easily angered, small 11 year old who was the third out-of-wedlock child in a family of five children, was referred to a mental health center by the local department of social services because the foster parents were finding him difficult to control. The child told the following story during his fifth therapy session:

Once upon a time there was a prince and a black widow spider. The prince did not like this black widow spider so the black widow spider said, "If you marry me, I'll give you a million dollars." And so he married her and she gave him the million dollars. And she said, "If you give me a diamond ring, I'll give you a thousand dollars." And so he gave her a diamond ring and she gave him a thousand dollars. But then the black widow spider didn't like him anymore, and she played a dirty trick on him. She said, "If you give me a kiss, I'll give you a billion dollars." The handsome prince kissed her, and she poisoned him. Then the prince died and so she kept on wandering, looking for another one because each one she found was no good. Then one day she met this great old goat—it was about 1 million years old—and she said, "Will you please marry me and I'll give you a thousand dollars." So the goat married her and she gave him the money, but then she did not like him anymore and killed him too. She poisoned him just like she did the prince. Then she met a little white polar bear that was sitting in a tree. He said, "I'll marry you on one condition, if you promise not to poison me. Or I'll never marry you." And so the polar bear married her, and she said, "Okay, I'll not poison you." She didn't promise but said she wouldn't. The next day she put arsenic in his coffee and he said, "What's in that?" She said, "Oh, just some arsenic and soon you will die—in about ten minutes." So the polar bear began coughing and running around yelling, "I've been poisoned, let me out of here!" But all the doors were locked and he couldn't get out of a window because they were all locked also. And so he busted one window and climbed out and escaped and he went home. The moral of the story was to never marry a poisoned lady.

The therapist chose to focus on the child's conflict of not being able to adequately express his true wishes. The bear was interpreted as the figure who best represented the child, as he was the third child in his family and the bear was the third victim of the spider.

The story that the therapist created duplicated the child's with these exceptions: in response to her offer of marriage, the old goat said, "I don't think so, because I am old and I don't want to get married." When the spider approached the polar bear and said, "Polar bear, marry me," the polar bear said, "I don't think I want to marry you." The black widow spider said, "Polar bear, if you marry me, I will make you rich and give you lots of money," but the polar bear said to the black widow spider, "That's very nice of you, you must be a kind black widow spider, but I think I'd rather wait and find somebody whom I really like and then get married, even though I think you're nice. Thank you for your offer and goodbye." The moral of this story was that telling how you feel is better than holding it in.

With late latency, preadolescent and early adolescent children who require treatment, cooperation for such a course is often difficult to establish (Fraiberg, 1955). An introductory phase that consists chiefly of playing competitive games is probably necessary for holding a youngster's interest (Geleerd, 1957). Subsequently, the treatment procedure follows the general avenue for reaching feelings, concerns about relationships, and problems in mastering impulses and/or environment demands. During the middle phase of adolescence treatment begins to approximate the therapy for adults except that special care is taken not to attack unduly the adolescent's defenses except in those instances where there is an overreliance on denial and projection. When these are primary defenses, the tendency to develop poor reality testing is great and should be questioned. The therapist not only holds the adolescent to reality but also stands in for the parent "although in a reserved, restrained, and most neutral way" (Geleerd, 1957). Thus there is an alliance with the patient against those forces within him that seek to ignore or distort reality (Holmes, 1964; Meeks, 1971; Weiner, 1970). To do this the therapist establishes and enforces reasonable standards of conduct in the relationship. By setting limits, by clarifying consequences brought on by unacceptable behavior, and by establishing a climate of trust reality is defined. As Holmes (1964) pointed out, the testing of such reality is a most healthy developmental exercise. At the same time, the adolescent is helped to look into himself to report his ideas and fantasies so that he learns to distinguish thought and action. Eventually, it is reassuring to the adolescent to discover that he can enunciate strong feelings or perverse wishes without a magic incarnation of his thoughts taking place or without a retaliatory punishment following his verbalizations.

Case M

After three disciplinary transfers for violent behavior in as many schools, this nearly 16-year-old boy was suspended with the proviso that reentry into the school system was dependent on his willingness to accept psychiatric help. There was some recognition on his part that he was prone to overreact to minimal provocations from peers and that he was capable of mistaking normal social communications for nefarious signals. For example, the school expulsion that prompted the referral had occurred after he had struck another youth in a blind rage, simply because he disliked the manner in which the boy had glanced at him. He acknowledged much discomfort when in the presence of young men yet would also seek their company. In order to alleviate his tensions in these encounters, he would resort to alcohol and drugs such as hallucinogens and marijuana.

The patient was physically well-built and rugged in appearance. His academic potential was thought to be at least average if not better. He lived with an alcoholic mother and a younger adolescent brother with whom he shared a bedroom. An older brother who lived in a distant city was said to be homosexual. Shortly after he began individual therapy, an older sister returned to the mother's household after an unsuccessful venture into independent living.

Although the mother consented to her son's therapy, she refused to participate in it. The first 3 months of weekly outpatient visits were focused on the youth's panicked preoccupation with numerous self-doubts and with a concern over his sexual identity. The therapist's supportive clarification of dream content relating to conflicted passivity first began to intrigue the patient and eventually served to reassure him. He liked being understood without feeling condemned or being exploited as he had feared. On the contrary, the therapist became the patient's advocate as he was instrumental in arranging the patient's reentry into a new high school from which he graduated 2 years later without another incident.

Therapeutic style in working with adolescents may be the most crucial factor (Holmes, 1964). The conversational tone should be one of "abnormal candor," especially for acute and crisis disturbances. A direct and forthright approach should not be confused with offering unchecked interpretations. It is more a way of easing the tension adolescents feel around adults when the conversations deal with material not usually shared between them. Even falling into an arguing tone with an adolescent can have positive value. A vigorously discussed reality issue may lead the adolescent to the conclusion that he can give in without loss of self-respect. Moreover arguing, as controlled aggression, relieves mutual tensions, which arise easily enough in treatment between adults and adolescents. Emphasis on the manner in which the young person controls this relationship is another therapeutic tool that can give meaning and direction to its use (Leventhal and Sills, 1963). For those youths who are alienated drug abusers, confrontation of the self-destructive behavior and an expectation for improved performance are the hallmark of therapeutic intervention by agents who also strengthen the treatment alliance by their advocacy role (Bratter, 1973).

The therapist of the adolescent must be honest, authentic, and straight-forward without mimicking his patient's manner, in order not to overstep the intergenerational boundary (Lecker et al., 1973). He should be able to live with the ambiguities of life and be open to change. The paradox of treating adolescents lies in the need to model stability in the fluid processes of personal and cultural unheaval.

Brief Therapy

Abbreviated therapy as a specific method is applied in crisis problems for symptom relief. It encompasses all the elements of long term therapy such as support, abreaction, guidance, and reeducation but, in setting a time limit, there is the inherent promise of a quick resolution to the problems and the belief is transmitted that the child and his family have the competencies to set things right. The treatment moves are designed to uncover the immediate forces at work in the production of the symptoms, to provide the child with a high impact corrective experience through recreating some of the conflicts in fantasy play, and to suggest experimental alternatives for new solutions (Lester, 1968). Working with parents is important whenever the child is young and reacting to events in his life but becomes less crucial in the case of the older child whose difficulties are more internalized or are in response to inner conflict. Controlled play techniques lend themselves to the brief therapy method. The types of problems most suitable for time limited intervention are acute phobic conditions, regressed behavior with recent onset, sudden appearance of inhibitions or learning problems, reactive behavioral disorders, and phase-specific adjustment reactions. Less likely to benefit from brief psychotherapy are longstanding characterological problems, developmental lags, multiple and well-entrenched neurotic symptoms, and disturbances in object relationships that derive from early deprivation or faulty human attachments.

Although the number of interviews varies from clinician to clinician or from one child to the next, the fixing of a time limit is considered the significant variable. Within this temporal framework there are treatment stages that flow into each other or even overlap. At the time of the initial contact, the nature of the problem is quickly identified. The therapist deals with the child's resistances by his explanations of the interaction between them, of the play, and of the purpose for the meeting. This may be followed by interpretations of the child's defensive behavior patterns, both for insight and for opening up other avenues of adaptive coping. In the termination phase the emphasis is placed on the child's capacity for more effective organization of his inner experience and for more meaningful mastery over environmental exigencies. By turning the work back to the child and parents, the therapist expresses confidence in the family's latent resourcefulness to deal with its problems. Usually, the door is left open for the parents and child to return should their efforts prove insufficient or should new problems present themselves at a later time. In any event, there is no message given that the therapeutic overhaul of the child is the sine qua non of progress but that the therapist will stand by as a guide or mentor when the occasion for this arises (Miller, 1959; Proskauer, 1971; Rosenthal and Levine, 1970; 1971).

When human personality is looked upon as a dynamic process, the therapist's influence takes on the quality of a modest contribution. Yet, since human development is not predestined to be either good or bad, only having the potential to produce both (Erikson, 1963; Horney, 1950), the therapist, like the parent, has as his primary responsibility the communication of acceptance for the child as he is (Rogers, 1946) and of the belief in the child's capacity to make choices toward the solution of his own problems (Axline, 1947). Here the hope lies in the unfolding of positive patterns in a climate of good will and of meaningful opportunities for relating and creating.

On the other hand, when human conduct is thought to be predicated on the learning from the consequences of one's behavior or when disturbed behavior is believed to arise from disordered biochemical processes, the therapist as impersonal technician is called into play. Even technicians, however, cannot disregard the qualities of life that make for a more humane interaction with children who are their clients. The major difference in this treatment system rests in the belief that the efficacy of a particular method will give the child better control over his life situation without taking into consideration his feeling on the matter. Whether true freedom of choice exists for adult or child may become an academic issue once highly specific remedies become available. At such time the healing ethos for preventing suffering strongly reasserts itself, particularly when behavior control or medication brings prompt symptom relief.

REFERENCES

Aichhorn, A. *Wayward Youth*. New York: Viking, 1935.

Allen, F. H. Therapeutic work with children. *American Journal of Orthopsychiatry*, **4**, 193–202, 1934.

Allen, F. H. *Psychotherapy with Children*. New York: Norton, 1942.

Arlow, J. A. & Kadis, A. Fingerpainting in the psychotherapy of children. *American Journal of Orthopsychiatry*, **16**, 134–146, 1946.

Axline, V. M. *Play Therapy: The Inner Dynamics of Childhood*. Boston: Houghton Mifflin, 1947.

Barcai, A. & Rosenthal, M. K. Fears and tyranny. *Archives of General Psychiatry*, **30**, 392–395, 1974.

Bender, L. Art and therapy in the mental disturbances of children. *Journal of Nervous and Mental Diseases*, **86**, 249–263, 1937.

Bender, L. Childhood schizophrenia. *Nervous Child*, **1**, 138–140, 1942.

Bender, L. *Child Psychiatric Techniques: Diagnostic and Therapeutic Approach to Normal and Abnormal Development Through Patterned, Expressive, and Group Behavior*. Springfield, Ill.: Charles C. Thomas, 1952.

Bender, L. Schizophrenia in childhood: Its recognition, description and treatment. *American Journal of Orthopsychiatry*, **26**, 499–506, 1956.

Bender, L. & Boas, F. Creative dance in therapy. *American Journal of Orthopsychiatry*, **11**, 235–244, 1941.

Bender, L. & Woltmann, A. G. The use of puppet shows as a psychotherapeutic method for behavior problems in children. *American Journal of Orthopsychiatry*, **6**, 341–355, 1936.

Bettelheim, B. *Love is Not Enough: The Treatment of Emotionally Disturbed Children*. Glencoe, Ill.: Free Press, 1950.

Bixler, R. H. Limits are therapy. *Journal of Consulting Psychology*, **13**, 1–11, 1949.

Blom, G. E. Psychoanalytic viewpoint of behavior modification in clinical and educational settings. *Journal of the American Academy of Child Psychiatry*, **11**, 675–693, 1972.

Bradley, C. & Bowen, M. Behavior characteristics of schizophrenic children. *Psychiatric Quarterly*, **15**, 296–315, 1941.

Bratter, T. E. Treating alienated, unmotivated, drug abusing adolescents. *American Journal of Psychotherapy*, **27**, 585–596, 1973.

Bruner, J. S. *The Process of Education*. Cambridge: Harvard University Press, 1960.

Conn, J. The play-interview: A method of studying children's attitudes. *American Journal of Diseases of Children*, **58**, 1199–1214, 1939.

DesLauriers, A. M. & Carlson, C. F. *Your Child is Asleep: Early Infantile Autism*. Homewood, Ill.: Dorsey, 1969.

Despert, J. L. Psychotherapy in child schizophrenia. *American Journal of Psychiatry*, **104**, 36–43, 1947.

Dreikurs, R. Music therapy with psychotic children. *Psychiatric Quarterly*, **34**, 722–734, 1960.

Durfee, M. B. Use of ordinary office equipment in "play therapy." *American Journal of Orthopsychiatry*, **12**, 495–508, 1943.

Ekstein, R. *Children of Time and Space, of Action and Impulse*. New York: Appleton-Century-Crofts, 1966.

Ekstein, R., Bryant, K. & Friedman, S. W. Schizophrenia: A review of the syndrome. In L. Bellak (Ed.), *Childhood Schizophrenia and Allied Conditions*. New York: Logos Press, 1958.

Erikson, E. H. *Childhood and Society*. Rev. ed., New York: Norton, 1963.

Fraiberg, S. H. Some considerations in the introduction to therapy in puberty. *The Psychoanalytic Study of the Child*, **10**, 264–286, 1955.

Freud, A. *Technic of Child Analysis*. New York: Nervous and Mental Disease Publishing Company, 1928.

Freud, A. Indications and contraindications for child analysis. *The Psychoanalytic Study of the Child*, **23**, 37–46, 1968.

Freud, S. Analysis of a phobia in a five-year-old boy. In *Collected Papers*, Vol. 3. New York: Basic Books, 1959.

Frommer, E. A. *Diagnosis and Treatment in Clinical Child Psychiatry*. London: William Heinemann Medical Books Limited, 1972.

Gardner, R. A. The game of checkers as a diagnostic and therapeutic tool in child psychotherapy. *Acta Paedopsychiatrica*, **66**, 142–152, 1969.

Gardner, R. A. The mutual storytelling technique: Use in the treatment of a child with post-traumatic neurosis. *American Journal of Psychotherapy*, **24**, 419–439, 1970.

Gardner, R. A. *Therapeutic Communication with Children*. New York: Science House, 1971.

Geleerd, E. R. Some aspects of psychoanalytic technique in adolescents. *The Psychoanalytic Study of the Child*, **12**, 263–283, 1957.

Glasser, W. *Reality Therapy. A New Approach to Psychiatry*. New York: Harper and Row, 1965.

Goldfarb, W. *Childhood Schizophrenia*. Cambridge: Harvard University Press, 1961.

Group for the Advancement of Psychiatry. *From diagnosis to treatment: An approach to treatment planning for the emotionally disturbed child*. Report No. 87. **8**, 517–662, 1973.

Halpern, W. I. The schooling of autistic children: Preliminary findings. *American Journal of Orthopsychiatry*, **40**, 665–671, 1970.

Halpern, W. I., Cipolla, C. & Gold, J. Children with communication disorders: Some observations of an adjunctive program to their schooling (Abstract). *American Journal of Orthopsychiatry*, **43**, 233, 1973.

Halpern, W. I., Hammond, J. & Cohen, R. A therapeutic approach to speech phobia: Elective mutism reexamined. *The Journal of the American Academy of Child Psychiatry*, **10**, 94–107, 1971.

Hartmann, H. Psychoanalysis and developmental psychology. *The Psychoanalytic Study of the Child*, **5**, 7–17, 1950.

Healy, W. *The Individual Delinquent*. Boston: Little, 1915.

Healy, W. & Bronner, A. *New Light on Delinquency and Its Treatment*. New Haven, Conn.: Yale, 1936.

Holmes, D. J. *The Adolescent in Psychotherapy*. Boston: Little, Brown, 1964.

Horney, K. *Neurosis and Human Growth*. New York: Norton, 1950.

Hugg-Helmuth, H. V. Zur Technik der Kinderanalyse. *Internationale Zeitschrift für Psychoanalyse*, **7**, 1921.

Johnson, A. M. & Szurek, S. A. The genesis of antisocial acting out in children and adults. *Psychoanalytic Quarterly*, **21**, 323–343, 1952.

Kanner, L. Autistic disturbances of affective contact. *Nervous Child*, **2**, 217–250, 1943.

Kaplan, S. L. & Escoll, P. Treatment of two silent adolescent girls. *Journal of the American Academy of Child Psychiatry*, **12**, 59–72, 1973.

Kissel, S. & Arkins, V. Anorexia nervosa reexamined. *Child Psychiatry and Human Development*, **3**, 255–263, 1973.

Klein, M. *The Psychoanalysis of Children*. London: Hogarth Press, 1932.

Kraft, I. A. Use of trained volunteers as social work technicians in child psychiatry. *American Journal of Orthopsychiatry*, **35**, 264–265, 1965.

Lavery, L. & Stone, F. H. Psychotherapy of a deprived child. *Journal of Child Psychology and Psychiatry*, **6**, 115–124, 1965.

Lecker, S., Hendricks, L. & Turanski, J. New dimensions in adolescent psychotherapy. A therapeutic system approach. *Pediatric Clinics of North America*, **20**, 883–900, 1973.

Lester, E. P. Brief psychotherapies in child psychiatry. *Canadian Psychiatric Association Journal*, **13**, 301–309, 1968.

Leventhal, T. & Sills, M. The issue of control in therapy with character problem adolescents. *Psychiatry*, **26**, 149–167, 1963.

Leventhal, T. & Sills, M. Self-image in school phobia. *American Journal of Orthopsychiatry*, **34**, 685–695, 1964.

Levy, D. M. On the problem of delinquency. *American Journal of Orthopsychiatry*, **2**, 197–211, 1932.

Levy, D. M. Use of play technic as experimental procedure. *American Journal of Orthopsychiatry*, **3**, 266–277, 1933.

Levy, D. M. Release therapy in young children. *Psychiatry*, **1**, 387–390, 1938.

Levy, D. M. Trends in therapy: Release therapy. *American Journal of Orthopsychiatry*, **9**, 713–736, 1939.

Lippman, H. S. Direct treatment work with children. *American Journal of Orthopsychiatry*, **4**, 374–381, 1934.

Lippman, H. S. The neurotic delinquent. *American Journal of Orthopsychiatry*, **7**, 114–121, 1937.

Loomis, E. A. The use of checkers in handling certain resistances in child therapy and child analysis. *Journal of the American Psychoanalytic Association*, **5**, 130–135, 1957.

Lovaas, O. I., Schaeffer, B., Benson, R. & Simmons, J. Q. Building social behavior in autistic children by use of electric shock. *Journal of Experimental Research in Personality*, **1**, 99–109, 1965.

Mahler, M. S. On child psychosis and schizophrenia: Autistic and symbiotic infantile psychoses. *The Psychoanalytic Study of the Child*, **7**, 286–305, 1952.

Mahler, M. S. *On Human Symbiosis and the Vicissitudes of Individuation*, Vol. 1. New York: International Universities Press, 1968.

Marcus, I. M. Costume play therapy. The explorations of a method for stimulating imaginative play in older children. *Journal of the American Academy of Child Psychiatry*, **5**, 441–452, 1966.

Meeks, J. E. Children who cheat at games. *Journal of the American Academy of Child Psychiatry*, **9**, 157–174, 1970.

Meeks, J. E. *The Fragile Alliance. An Orientation to the Outpatient Psychotherapy of the Adolescent*. Baltimore: Williams and Wilkins, 1971.

Miller, L. C. Short term therapy with adolescents. *American Journal of Orthopsychiatry*, **29**, 772–779, 1959.

Mitchell, W. E. Amicatherapy: Theoretical perspectives and an example of practice. *Community Mental Health Journal*, **2**, 307–314, 1966.

Naumburg, M. *An Introduction to Art Therapy: Studies of the "Free" Art Expression of Behavior Problem Children and Adolescents as a Means of Diagnosis and Therapy*. Rev. ed. New York: Teachers College Press, 1973.

Newell, H. W. Play therapy in child psychiatry. *American Journal of Orthopsychiatry*, **11**, 245–251, 1941.

Piaget, J. *The Child and Reality. Problems of Genetic Psychology*. New York: Grossman Publishers, 1973.

Poffenberger, A. T. Trends in therapy: Specific psychological therapies. *American Journal of Orthopsychiatry*, **9**, 755–760, 1939.

Potter, R. W. Schizophrenia in children. *American Journal of Psychiatry*, **89**, 1253–1270, 1933.

Proskauer, S. Focused time-limited psychotherapy with children. *Journal of the American Academy of Child Psychiatry*, **10**, 619–639, 1971.

Rank, B. The therapeutic value of play. *Understanding the Child*, **7**, 19–23, 1938.

Rank, B. Adaptation of the psychoanalytic technique for the treatment of young children with atypical development. *American Journal of Orthopsychiatry*, **19**, 130–139, 1949.

Redl, F. *When We Deal with Children*. New York: The Free Press, 1966.

Redl, F. & Wineman, D. *Controls From Within: Techniques for the Treatment of the Aggressive Child.* New York: The Free Press, 1952.

Reiser, D. E., Stein, E. & Taboroff, L. H. Therapy of a child conducted in the setting of an automobile. *American Journal of Orthopsychiatry,* **27,** 608–615, 1957.

Reisman, J. M. *Toward the Integration of Psychotherapy.* New York: Wiley-Interscience, 1971.

Reisman, J. M. *Principles of Psychotherapy with Children.* New York: Wiley-Interscience, 1973.

Riese, H. *Heal the Hurt Child. An Approach Through Educational Therapy with Special Reference to the Extremely Deprived Negro Child.* Chicago: University of Chicago Press, 1962.

Robinson, J. F. & Vitale, L. J. Children with circumscribed interest patterns. *American Journal of Orthopsychiatry,* **24,** 755–766, 1954.

Rogers, C. Significant aspects of client-centered therapy. *American Psychologist,* **1,** 415–422, 1946.

Rogerson, C. H. *Play Therapy in Childhood.* London: Oxford University Press, 1939.

Rosenthal, A. J. & Levine, S. V. Brief psychotherapy with children: A preliminary report. *American Journal of Psychiatry,* **127,** 646–651, 1970.

Rosenthal, A. J. & Levine, S. V. Brief psychotherapy with children: Process of therapy. *American Journal of Psychiatry,* **128,** 141–146, 1971.

Rutter, M. The development of infantile autism. *Psychological Medicine,* **4,** 147–163, 1974.

Schaeffer, R. L. Treatment of the adolescent. An approach to therapy with the adolescent through selected activities. *American Journal of Orthopsychiatry,* **32,** 390–394, 1962.

Siegel, E. V. Movement therapy with autistic children. *Psychoanalytic Review,* **60,** 141–149, 1973.

Solomon, J. C. Active play therapy. *American Journal of Orthopsychiatry,* **8,** 479–498, 1938.

Solomon, J. C. Play technique. *American Journal of Orthopsychiatry,* **18,** 403–413, 1948.

Tiebout, H. M. & Kirkpatrick, M. E. Psychiatric factors in stealing. *American Journal of Orthopsychiatry,* **2,** 114–123, 1932.

Tooley, K. Playing it right. A technique for the treatment of borderline children. *Journal of the American Academy of Child Psychiatry,* **12,** 615–631, 1973.

Toussieng, P. W. Child psychotherapy in a new era. *American Journal of Orthopsychiatry,* **41,** 58–64, 1971.

Weiner, I. B. *Psychological Disturbance in Adolescence.* New York: Wiley-Interscience, 1970.

White, R. W. Ego and reality in psychoanalytic theory. A proposal regarding independent ego energies. *Psychological Issues,* **3** (3), monograph 11, 1963.

Winnicott, D. W. *Therapeutic Consultations in Child Psychiatry*. New York: Basic Books, 1971.

Zaslow, R. W. & Breger, L. A theory and treatment of autism. In L. Breger (Ed.), *Clinical-Cognitive Psychology: Models and Integration*. New Jersey: Prentice-Hall, 1969.

CHAPTER 10

Behavior Modification

The speed with which behavior modification has captured the imagination of providers of human services to children can be likened to a revolutionary about-face in therapy. More than 10 years ago Colby (1964) prophesied an upheaval in the popularity of psychotherapy after reviewing the state of the art, which he characterized as chaotic and in transition. As with most revolutions a series of diverse but related background events were important contributors.

The unrealistic therapeutic promises of the 1940s and 1950s that psychoanalysis and insight oriented psychotherapy could halt the spread of psychiatric suffering were not fulfilled. Children were failing in schools at an alarming rate, and juvenile delinquency was increasing. Levitt (1957, 1963, 1971), thrusting home the views of Eysenck (1952) regarding the ineffectiveness of traditional psychotherapy, marshalled an abundance of impressive data that cogently questioned the value of child therapy.

Even if this form of treatment had demonstrable value, the limited number of trained practitioners was insufficient to treat the magnitude of the problem. The shortage of trained professionals to deal with the burgeoning mental health problem led the Joint Commission on Mental Illness and Health (1963) to suggest that "every effort must be made then to provide nonpsychiatrically trained personnel in many fields with as much knowledge of mental illness and principles of its treatment as possible" (p. 123). The recommendation was taken to heart and a number of programs for training nonprofessionals to function as therapists evolved. Rioch and her co-workers (1963) trained housewives to function as psychotherapists; Holzberg (1963) instituted companion therapy whereby college students provided a one-to-one relationship to hospitalized mentally ill patients. Cowen (1971) used nonprofessional women to become sympathetically involved with at-risk children in the schools. Reducing staff shortages by broadening the base of mental health deliverers also was found to be an ineffective solution to the problem. The greater the number of health providers, the greater the demand for such services. Innovative programs and new conceptions of man, and of mental illness and health, were proposed (Smith and Hobbs, 1966; Szasz, 1961). The apparent simplicity of behavior modification with its relatively few major assumptions and easily explicable principles made it a logical candidate for giving impetus to much new programming.

Championing a Hobbesonian image of the child, Ullmann (1971) suggested man need not be viewed with the Freudian pessimism or as basically good in the Rogerian sense but ". . . that he is alive, and he is what he learns to be." Such an outlook carried the idea that actions are not necessarily normal or abnormal, only that they are outcomes of previous experiences. Furthermore, it suggested that a child's present activity is more important than his past experiences and that those who influence children consider the advantages gained by guiding the child's behavior. They needed, thus, to focus on observable action rather than ponder the defensive mysteries of behavior. A highly functional view was formulated which provided the basis for a technical but yet efficient approach to the treatment of maladaptive behavior.

Child guidance clinics were being criticized for their ineffectiveness and for their inefficiency in meeting the needs of parents and their troubled children (Barten and Barten, 1973; Kissel, 1974; Leventhal and Weinberger, 1975; Reisman and Kissel, 1968). Parents were clamoring for greater direction, advice, and more frequent opportunities to talk with their child's therapist. Direction was demanded from an expert who was perceived as an authority rather than someone who saw parents as partners in the search for therapeutic solutions.

In addition to the scientific and professional strains rising to the surface in traditional clinical treatment enclaves, the Zeitgeist favoured behavior modification for sociopolitical reasons as well. An authority-oriented, technocratic leadership was increasingly endorsed to combat growing crime on the streets; signs of social disorganization accompanying economic, cultural, and technological changes; and the deauthorization of parents, teachers and other traditional power brokers. Behavior modification provided a return of control to those who could master its principles.

Such are some of the several controversies that have influenced the rise of behavior modification as a major intervention strategy and have brought it to its current prominence. Of course, as with most radical departures, leveling takes place, but what preceded begins to be assimilated rather than being entirely dismissed. This seems to be occurring in the practice of behavior modification. Earlier claims for its effectiveness, efficiency, and economy have faded as a greater number of practitioners become familiar with the techniques, modify them, and apply behavior therapy to a wider range of maladaptive and malevolent conditions (Breger and McGaugh, 1965; Bergin and Suinn, 1975). For the most part, the early application of behavior modification, a term credited to Lindsley (1953), dealt with mentally retarded children and withdrawn schizophrenics and was carried out under well-controlled conditions. This approach followed the teachings of Skinner (1938). However, even earlier, clinicians had been suggesting that the principles of learning theory could be applied to abnormal behavior of man. During the 1920s Watson and Rayner (1920) and Jones (1924) applied Pavlovian principles to children's fears. In the 1930s Dunlap (1932) introduced negative practice to counteract faulty habits, such as tics, and Mowrer and Mowrer (1938) provided impressive data to support the treatment of enuresis according to learning principles. During the 1940s and 1950s greater interest was shown in restating psychodynamic and psychoanalytic formulations of neurosis into the language and conceptual framework of learning principles (Dollard and Miller, 1950; Shoben, 1949). While there was much preoccupation with translating internal states into the language of Hullian learning theory, Graziano (1971) suggested that the long term effect was to usher in a rethinking of the neuroses, with a greater stress on the significance of overt behavior: "To Dollard and Miller, neurotic behavior is symptomatic of the internal neurotic conditions; for Eysenck, Wolpe, Lazarus, . . . neurotic behavior itself is the neurotic condition" (Graziano, 1971, p. 12).

The 1960s and 1970s saw a proliferation of behavior therapy. Periodicals appeared such as *The Journal of Applied Behavior Analysis* and *Behavior, Research and Therapy*, as well as myriads of books and articles applying behavior modification principles to such problems as autism (Anthony, 1958; Cowan et al., 1965; Ferster and DeMyer, 1962; Yates, 1970), juvenile delinquency (Schwitzgebel, 1969; Davidson and Seidman, 1974), mental retardation (Astrup et al., 1967; Bijou et al., 1966), learning disabilities (Buckley and Walker, 1970; Simpson and Nelson, 1974), elective mutism (Halpern et al., 1971) and anorexia nervosa (Blinder et al., 1970; Kissel and Arkins, 1973; Stunkard, 1972). Comprehensive reviews of the appropriateness, effectiveness, and application of behavior modification can be found in the writings of Franks (1969), Graziano (1971), Grossberg (1964), Krasner (1971), Ross (1972), Werry and Wollersheim (1967), and Yates (1970).

The application of behavior modification to disorders of childhood rests on the use of operant (instrumental) or respondent (classical) conditioning for new learning or relearning to take place. Mowrer (1960) attempted to explain complex human behavior by combining both respondent and operant conditioning into a two factor theory of learning. Yet Ross (1972) points out that "the pragmatic behavior therapist bases his work on the principles derived from respondent and operant conditioning without much concern as to the adequacy of currently held formulations for the epistemologic soundness of a two factor theory of learning" (p. 275).

Operant conditioning specifies that a child's behavior is either weakened or strengthened as a function of the reinforcing consequences that follow the behavior. The child acts on the environment and as a result of external reinforcement, the child's actions come under control of the environment (such as parents, teachers, or age mates). It is extremely important to clarify and specify the behavior to be modified in observable and definable components so that a consistent and systematic program of reinforcement can be introduced. Reinforcement can be either positive or negative, primary or secondary. Positive reinforcement following an action will encourage its repetition, while negative consequences following an action will lessen the likelihood of its occurrence. When a response is ignored, that is, neither positively nor negatively reinforced, it becomes extinguished. Primary reinforcements are conditions that are unlearned and inherently have a tendency to influence behaviors they follow, whereas secondary reinforcers must acquire their ability to have an effect on behavior. Money, for example, becomes an effective reinforcer only as it becomes associated with a primary reinforcer, such as food. Not only is a child required to perform in a desired manner but also the assumption is made that the behavior that is to be conditioned is available to the child. When the behavior is not immediately available to the child, a procedure called successive approximation, or shaping, is utilized. The child is initially reinforced for actions that only approximate the final response desired. Internal motivational states such as frustration, needs, or anxiety are not considered as necessary for learning to take place and, therefore, little attention is paid to them in this model of treatment. The operant model has had its major application in controlled environments such as schools or institutional settings. Operant procedures have less frequently been applied to children seen in outpatient clinics. In these settings relatively young children with evidence of rather specific developmental difficulties like language disabilities, or specific target symptoms such as enuresis and encopresis, have been treated following the operant paradigm.

In classical or respondent conditioning, two conditions or stimuli are paired—one a seemingly neutral one and the other having the ability to elicit a particular reaction. Pavlov's classic experiment with hungry dogs learning to salivate to a bell as the result of the stimulus being continually paired with the presentation of food was the prototype for respondent conditioning. Ross (1972) suggested that "If the response is in the vascular-visceral-autonomic realm, the respondent conditioning paradigm seems to hold the greatest explanatory power" (p. 275). Thus, it becomes particularly relevant to the learning and unlearning of emotionally based behaviors and conditions.

In contrast to intervention strategies built on the operant approach, practitioners using respondent conditioning for altering maladaptive behavior consider internal states such as anxiety, fear, and arousal in their treatment efforts. The reciprocal inhibition treatment model introduced by Wolpe (1954, 1958, 1966) has provided the major impetus to applying the respondent conditioning paradigm to the understanding and treatment of neurotic behavior. For the most part, however, these procedures have been used with neurotic or character disturbed adults. For example, Graziano's (1971) recent book, one of the few devoted entirely to behavior therapy with children, presented 39 papers of which more than two-thirds dealt with an instrumental approach to treating children's maladaptive behaviors. This is not surprising in light of the basic components involved in the use of reciprocal inhibition. The repeated pairing of anxiety (rapid respiration, raised blood pressure, increased muscle tension, heart palpitation), elicited by having the patient fantasize conditions associated with anxiety provoking situations, with a relaxed state leads to a reduction in anxiety, which in turn results in a cessation of the neurotic, maladaptive activities. Systematic desensitization involves three major operations: (1) The patient is trained in deep muscle relaxation. (2) A habit or anxiety hierarchy is elicited whereby the patient lists in descending order those situations that generate decreasing increments of anxiety. (3) The patient is asked to imagine the least disturbing scenes in the hierarchy while he is relaxed so that it no longer elicits anxiety, and then gradually works through the entire list in this fashion.

More often than not, the motivation for changing a child's maladaptive behavior rests with the child's parents. This may contribute to the child's un cooperativeness and poor motivation. The effectiveness of reciprocal inhibition techniques assumes the patient to be motivated for change. Furthermore, adolescents and adults have acquired formal operational structures (Inhelder and Piaget, 1958) and thus are more proficient in the use of thought and imagery than are children. Often latency age children who show maladaptive behaviors have strong concerns regarding losing control of their impulses. Requiring them to "let themselves go and relax" can inadvertently introduce more anxiety into the situation.

Some attempts have been made to modify the systematic desensitization procedures for children. Lazarus and Abramovitz (1962) and Obler and Terwilliger (1970) have altered the anxiety inhibiting response. The former have used emotive imagery in which a child's heroes, such as TV personalities, are strategically introduced into a series of scenes which the child is asked to imagine. These scenes include both the hero and the fearful event. The sequence of the imagined stories follow a hierarchal similarity to that suggested by Wolpe. Obler and Terwilliger (1970) placed the child in direct contact with the fear-producing object, but used the therapist as a buffer between the two. In this method the child is required initially to look at a picture of that which is feared and then is exposed to the actual object in vivo. The child is constantly praised for moving closer and closer to the feared object in the presence of the therapist. Taking into consideration the difficulty preadolescent children have using imagery (Elkind, 1966; Elkind et al., 1969), Kissel (1972) suggested yet another alteration in the systematic desensitization procedure used with children. Scenes that contained the anxiety inducing stimuli were presented in a multisensory fashion as an aid to the evolving and concrete imagery processes of children. Tape recorded scenes of the child's own voice and stories were used to accomplish this. Homework was introduced, such as having the child draw pictures of the feared object or constructing two and three dimensional representations of the object. This counteracted possible attempts to avoid the feared situation in deed or thought away from therapy.

Despite divergent theories or techniques, all behavior oriented therapists subscribe to a common code which can be encompassed by the following three key concepts: (1) Overt behaviors rather than underlying central conditions are the major focus of therapy. (2) Knowledge of the principles of association learning theory with particular emphasis on the systematic application of reinforcement and extinction is central to conceptualizing human behavior. (3) Behavior that is to be modified has to be observable and specific so that it can be documented and counted.

Different behaviorally oriented tactics are required to help counteract differing maladaptive conditions in childhood. Often changing children's behavior in reality is changing parents' behavior. When behavior modification aims to assist the parents to more appropriately control the antecedent and consequent conditions that stimulate or sustain a child's maladaptive behavior, such as encopresis, enuresis, speech, or eating phobias, then the child's schoolteacher or parents themselves become the major interveners while the therapist's role is that of a social engineer or strategist to them. To help his client he works through the child's surrogates. Often it is the parent, not the child, who is hurting, and this is especially true with the younger child in the nursery or during the early school years.

Children are helped with more direct involvement as they complain about being bullied by peers, express fears about dogs and the dark, or refuse to go to school. The behavior therapist directly teaches the child new responses as he helps him to overcome and extinguish his maladaptive and/or fearful behavior.

Frequently the adolescent comes to the attention of mental health specialists as a result of the family members' inability to communicate with each other. Despite the initial complaints of both adolescent and parents that it is the other's problem, the relationship between them needs to be altered. Elkind (1970) conceptualized family crises during the adolescent stage of development as a breakdown of often implicit contractual arrangements. Working with families at this developmental stage, the therapist can help the family members to become more efficient in negotiating contracts by combining some of the skills of the family therapist (see Chapter 7) with those of the behavior modifier. Contingency contracting, which requires the family to formalize both wishes, demands, and rewards more explicitly, is introduced when the therapist attempts to arbitrate conflicts between adolescent clients and their parents by formalizing the terms of the negotiations among them.

Social Engineering

The major task of the behavior therapist, when he functions as a social engineer, is to be able to specify the behavior to be controlled, to delineate objectives, and then control the pertinent consequences that follow. In essence, a program of contingency management is called for whether rewards or punishments follow the behavior. Hewett (1972) has described how such a program can be applied in school settings to help children who are having difficulty in learning (see Chapter 3). The procedures are applicable to the single child disrupting an entire class or where a large group of people, such as are found in a lunchroom, generate excessive actions that adversely stimulate a few of its members.

Case A

At the monthly teachers' meeting the complaint arose that the period immediately following lunch was a waste as the students were overly excited when returning to class. Discussion of the problem with a mental health consultant identified cafeteria noise level as a target behavior appropriate for a program of behavior modification.

Initially, baseline recordings were made to measure sound level in decibels during the three lunch periods. These recordings lasted for 2 weeks and were found to be an average of 86 decibels. The cooperation of the district superintendent, building principal, and student body were enlisted. Following the baseline recordings, students in Grades 5, 6, and 7 were informed about the program contingencies.

All students in a given lunch period would be dismissed 30 minutes early on Friday afternoon, if they reduced the average noise level on each succeeding week. After 3 successful weeks, a maximum noise level of 82 decibels was set as the payoff goal, and after 7 weeks it was decided that 80 decibels would be the established maximum acceptable level for the week, with the further stipulation that on no single day could the level exceed 82 decibels. Graphs were posted in the cafeteria and accumulated results posted daily.

Teachers had the option of eating in the teachers' lounge, or participating in the program by eating with the students in the cafeteria. They were explicitly instructed not to discipline for adverse behavior. Those teachers who participated were also rewarded with early dismissal along with the students.

The noise level was reduced by 100% during the course of the school year. This led the school to tackle other maladaptive behaviors, so that the contingency for early dismissal related to acceptable hall behavior and promptness for class attendance, focusing on such specific actions as running and boisterous behavior in the halls.

Maladaptive behaviors are at times situation specific. Children often demonstrate behavior in one environment but not another. Electively mute children speak at home with their families or in the playground with their friends, but remain silent in the classroom. Halpern and his associates (Halpern et al., 1970; Kissel et al., 1974) have conceptualized such difficulties as speech phobias and developed a contingency management intervention strategy to counter the child's maladaptive behavior.

Case B

A $7\frac{1}{2}$-year-old, the product of a 12-year childless marriage, was referred to a mental health center by the school because she would not speak in her first grade classroom. The parents were conservative in speech, manner, attitude, and outlook. They were rather isolated, generally remained aloof from family, and had few social relationships. For the most part, the mother remained quiet while her husband was the spokesman for the family to the outside world. The girl preferred to interact with her parents rather than with age mates but she did speak to friends from time to time in her neighborhood. Diagnostic examinations revealed a picture of a fearful, shy child who refused to speak to the examiner initially, but consented to nod to questions and clearly whispered "goodbye" as she left the interview.

The therapist held separate conferences with parents and the girl's teacher and principal where the behavior modification program was explained. The child was told by her teacher, in front of her classmates what would be expected of her the following day: she was to speak a preselected word before being allowed to leave the classroom for home. The girl remained in her seat until 5:00 PM before she asked to be excused. The next day 15 minutes after the class left she said the preselected word and was excused. After these successes, the teacher reported the girl occasionally asked questions and talked to other children in the classroom. A followup conference with the teacher at the end of the school year revealed that, for the most part, the girl had maintained her ability to communicate verbally in class. Furthermore, the teacher acknowledged that whenever she made her expectations that the girl speak up less explicit, there was a tendency for regression.

A rather common symptom that brings parents of preschoolers to clinics relates to faulty or untrained toilet habits. Parents are often concerned that their child will be ill-prepared to enter school or that "accidents" in school will lead to peer ostracism and thus exacerbate this difficulty.

Case C

A $4\frac{1}{2}$-year-old was referred to a mental health specialist because of encopresis. At the time of referral the parents reported the boy had been slow to train, refused to sit on the toilet because it hurt when he moved his bowels, and went days at a time without moving his bowels. Medically the boy was found to be a healthy child, and a child psychologist characterized him as an alert yet cautious child of average intelligence who was inhibited and fearful of freely expressing his impulses. He had few friends in nursery school, was not belligerent, and responded to other children when they approached him.

During a diagnostic play interview, the boy showed considerable interest in cars, which was corroborated by the mother. She was informed that the child was not severely disturbed, and the following approach was suggested: The boy was to be informed by his mother that together they were going to solve his soiling problem. The mother showed him medication that was going to make it easier for him to go to the bathroom, and when he moved his bowels in the toilet, he was to be rewarded with a toy car. After breakfast next morning, he was given Dulcolax[R], a fast acting suppository, and then placed on the toilet where he had a bowel movement within 20 minutes. This was immediately rewarded with a car. This routine was carried out for 3 successive days and then the boy was told he had to move his bowels in the toilet on 2 successive days to earn his car. Additionally, each success was praised by his mother. At the end of 1 week, the child was having regular bowel movements, and the suppositories were discontinued. After the second week the cars were also discontinued, and the mother reported that except for a sporadic accident, the boy moved his bowels in the toilet without pain or complaint.

Quite frequently contingency management is associated with token economy programs in large institutions. However, such programs have been altered to suit children living at home with their families.

Case D

A hypertensive, middle-aged woman was referred by her internist because she found it exceedingly difficult to tolerate the uncooperativeness of her 6- and 8-year-old children. Separate evaluations of the children revealed both of them to be pleasant, bright, and articulate. Evidently they related without difficulty. They each had a number of friends of their own and did well in school.

The mother was particularly troubled by the children's behavior when they returned from school each day as "they entered the house fighting," and she felt this set the tone for the rest of the day until her husband came home for dinner, when things settled down. It was decided to attempt to modify the children's behavior with positive reinforcement for acceptable behavior, and extinguishing unacceptable acts through ignoring such behavior.

The mother was instructed to sit down with both children and discuss with them her concerns regarding their behavior of yelling at each other, shouting, and crying as they entered the house from school. Additionally, she was asked to enlist their involvement in the program by determining with them what special things they would like. The 8-year-old expressed an interest in models and matchbox cars while the 6-year-old wanted costume jewelry and play make-up. The mother informed the children they would both be given a check for each school day they entered the house without fighting with each other. If either one yelled, screamed, or cried, neither would receive a check.

Three weeks later the mother was glowing in her reports of success, but wondered if she would have to give the children "toys for the rest of their lives!" She was then instructed to require more work from the children for the same reward, that is 8 checks, and after 2 additional successful weeks, 10 checks for the car or jewelry. In addition to praising her for the progress she had made with the program, the therapist stressed that it was important for her not only to continually praise the children for their efforts, but also to help them see the functional benefits from cooperating with each other, such as playing with each other when their other friends were not available, more readily sharing toys, and having more fun together.

In each of the examples presented the therapist, in collaboration with responsible adults, clearly delineates the behavior to be targeted for change. He then designates a program that provides positive rewards to the children for emitting specific behaviors, while structuring the environment so that it does not reward other behaviors that would interfere with the child's learning of the adaptive response. The therapist, however, spends little time analyzing the wishes of the participants or their motives for persisting in maintaining their maladaptive states, nor does he attempt to provide the child insights into his current functioning.

The Behavior Therapist as Teacher

Fear of failure, of dying, of the dark, of animals, and of going to school or of separating from parents are common to growing children. While it is often difficult to state when a fear becomes a phobia, a "fear that is persistent and without sound grounds or without grounds accepted as reasonable by the sufferer" (English and English, 1958, p. 388), the desensitization approach is appropriate and the one most often chosen to alter such circumstances. Parents are counseled in the appropriate handling of mild and/or developmentally appropriate fears, such as children's initial fear of separation or mild unrest with sleeping alone in a darkened room. The principles of systematic desensitization in conjunction with the principles of contingency management are taught to parents to aid them in coping with their child in the home environment. However, when the behavior has reached proportions such that it either causes concern in the child, causes embarrassment, or causes excessive worry for parents, the family may seek more specific help from private practitioners or child guidance clinics.

Case E

An 11-year-old fourth grader was the oldest and the only girl in a working-class family consisting of mother, father, and three younger siblings. Kindergarten was started one year late, and she repeated the first grade. School believed her to be "shy and lacking confidence" but not intellectually retarded. During the past several years the girl had made a few friends, both in school and in the neighborhood, although when she was younger her parents did not permit her to play with other children. The girl was referred to a mental health center because she was terrified of dogs.

For the initial meeting she appeared quite apprehensive but was able to separate from her mother and accompany the therapist to the office. She expressed worry that she might be presented with a large dog. The girl readily discussed her fear of dogs and hoped she would be able to overcome it. She also told the therapist that her mother had been afraid of dogs when she was younger but had overcome it. The girl attributed her fear of dogs to the following traumatic incident: She was about 2 years old and remembered an aunt visiting her and throwing an oversized stuffed bulldog into her playpen. She began yelling, screaming, and ever since has been fearful of dogs.

At the initial session she was reassured she could be helped to learn to overcome her fear of dogs, that when she did, she would be able to pet a dog and then she would receive a reward, which was to be a mutually agreed upon transistorized portable radio. At the following session the girl was given some books that had pictures of dogs and which were shown to her page by page. She was instructed to point to every picture of a dog she saw while the therapist kept score. Three books were used and were presented in a hierarchical fashion with the initial book having the lowest number of pictures of dogs. At the conclusion of the session she was instructed to write a story about a dog at home.

At the third session the girl was asked to read the story which was tape-recorded and then played back to her while she imagined what was happening. She then was asked to describe the events and imagine the story again as they listened to it. This time the therapist added more fearful components at the conclusion of her story while she continued with the imagination process. She made up a story in which she was walking in the park with some friends and saw a dog on a leash. Added to this story was the fact that the dog ran off the leash and began playing with her and she enjoyed it. Subsequent elaborations included the dog licking her, eating from her hand, etc.

Homework assignments were also given in a hierarchical fashion. Her second assignment required that she make a scrapbook about dogs. Sessions four, five, and six were similar in format to the earlier ones. The girl was asked to create a story about a dog for the tape recorder and then listen to her story play back while going over the images in her mind.

Therapy was terminated after six sessions. Two weeks prior to termination the girl's mother informed the therapist that the child was able to walk by a dog with considerable less fear. One year later, she had maintained this level of mastery over her fear of dogs.

The case illustrates some modifications in classical desensitization techniques necessitated by the child's developmental state. Imagery of targeted fears is bolstered by more concrete and perceptually based presentations of stimuli while anxiety reduction fostered by the interest and helpful support of the therapist in relaxing quarters counters its disturbing influence. Eliciting in a graduated fashion that which is feared and pairing it with a stimulus that is anxiety-reducing are the main features of desensitization.

The more traditional techniques of desensitization have been followed with adolescents. Often they come to the attention of clinics as a result of actions that get them into difficulty within the community. Desensitization effectively helps them to eliminate their behaviors while learning more socially acceptable substitutes.

Case F

A 15-year-old male was placed on probation and ordered to apply for psychotherapy at a mental health center. In addition to being an ungovernable child at home, he was a chronic school truant and a shoplifter.

At the initial meeting he was sullen and highly unresponsive. In school the boy received high grades during the elementary years, but during the two years preceding his court involvement he had failing grades. The therapist confronted him with his attitude and informed him that if he did not learn to overcome his maladaptive behavior he would go to jail. It was emphasized that the choice was his. The therapist suggested he could help him by using a process of desensitization. The boy would have to use his imagination, which was one of his assets, and learn how to relax. When he agreed to proceed the boy was taught muscle relaxation initially. Four sessions were devoted to this while simultaneously a list of six usual situations that had led him to shoplift were constructed. Finally, the boy was asked to practice imagining himself overeating spoiled food to the point of making him nauseous and feeling like throwing up. This was accomplished in two additional sessions. During the second of these sessions, the boy ran from his chair to the sink because he feared he might throw up.

Six additional meetings followed in which the boy was asked to relax deeply, and then to imagine one of the scenes, e.g. standing in front of an unprotected candy counter, and just as he was about to shoplift he was to think of throwing up. He was then asked to relax and this time reimagine the scene but with a prosocial solution provided by the therapist, e.g. standing in front of an unmanaged candy counter but walking over to another counter to pay the clerk for the candy. Both scenes were repeated three times during a session. Therapy was completed at the conclusion of the sixth session.

At a one year follow-up, he had not appeared in court; his school reported improved attendance and academic performance.

The major component of systematically pairing two conditions was present even though adversity was introduced to help eliminate that which is anti-social while associating the prosocial with pleasure. While impressive claims for the effectiveness of desensitization procedures have been made by Lazarus (1963), Paul (1965), and Wolpe (1958). Yates (1970) in surveying the bur- geoning literature concluded that "the weight of evidence does suggest that behavior therapy may be successful very rapidly with monosymptomatic phobias but that polysymptomatic phobias will be a much harder nut to crack" (p. 146).

The Therapist as Arbitrator

Behavior contracting, while appropriate for use at all stages of development, is particularly relevant for the handling of conflicts between adolescents and their parents. Using contingency contracting to solve family problems be- tween adolescents and their families (1) places the relationship at the heart of the problem, (2) provides recognition of the growing maturity of the youth, (3) upholds the parents' rights to expect something from the child, (4) and helps to open up communication among all parties by defusing a highly charged situation. Homme (1970), Lundell (1972), and Stuart (1971) have been in the forefront of developing this approach for parents, teachers, and therapists.

Case G

A mother requested an evaluation of her teenage daughter who had been in and out of individual psychotherapy for a considerable number of years because she was doing poorly in school. A number of deficiency reports had been sent home, suggesting that while she was well above average intelligence, she was failing almost all of her tenth grade subjects. During an initial family interview, it became clear that it was extremely difficult for family members to communicate with each other. They tended to interrupt each other and listened with preconceived ideas. The daughter accused her parents of constantly nagging while they defended their behavior because of her deficiency reports.

Behavioral contracting was suggested to alleviate the problem. As a first step the therapist stated that a contract be worked out around parents' nagging and the girl's homework behavior. Each family member was asked to give some thought to the matter separately. At the next meeting they wrote a contract that stated that the girl would do 1 hour of homework each day and that the homework would be considered successful when the number of problems she agreed to do matched the assignment which she brought home and had shown to her parents prior to beginning her homework. The parents agreed furthermore that they would not remind her of her work, but did agree to permit her to stay out an additional 2 hours on Friday nights for the successful completion of four homework assignments. That is, if she did her work from Monday through Thursday, then on that Friday or possibly Saturday evening, she could stay out the additional 2 hours. All parties signed the contract and, additionally, the therapist signed as a witness.

The following week, parents commented that the house was considerably quieter, and their daughter told the therapist, with a smile, that she chose to see the "late movie with friends" rather than going to the early show.

The rapidity with which behavior intervention strategies have been adapted by providers of help to troubled children and youth has left a wake of controversy. At the heart of the controversy has been the criticism of the medical model as applied to emotional suffering. Symptoms or overt behaviors and not internal conflicts between mental structures, hidden wishes and subterranean worries are the expressions of neurotic and psychotic problems. Thus, the surface manifestations need to be focused on when intervening for change. Controversy, however, has found its way among adherents of the behavioral point of view as well. Mathews (1971) and Wilson and Davidson (1971) have seriously questioned whether it is necessary for the pairing of a phobic stimulus with a fear inhibiting state for desensitization to take place. They suggest it is only important for the fear to be exposed and that it will dissipate after repeated exposure without the presence of reinforcement.

The apparent ease with which the procedures can be taught can have the obverse effect of creating pseudotherapists instead of parents who may substitute poorly understood concepts of child rearing or formulae for an empathetic understanding of their children. The professional practitioner of whatever persuasion is guided by not only a theoretical orientation to an image of the child, but also by a set of ethical standards set down by his professional association and by rules of law. Whereas he can be held accountable for his performance, it will be more difficult to supervise those who misapply his work as they become further and further removed from him in applying the principles of learning theory to change and control of children's behavior.

REFERENCES

Anthony, J. An experimental approach to the psychopathology of childhood autism. *British Journal of Medical Psychology*, **31**, 211–225, 1958.

Astrup, C., Sersen, E. A. & Wortis, I. Conditional reflex studies in mental retardation: A review. *American Journal of Mental Deficiency*, **71**, 513–530, 1967.

Barten, H. H. & Barten, S. S. (Eds.), *Children and Their Parents in Brief Therapy*. New York: Behavior Publications, 1973.

Bergin, A. E. & Suinn, R. M. Individual psychotherapy and behavior therapy. In M. R. Rosenzweig and L. W. Porter (Eds.), *Annual Review of Psychology*. Palo Alto, Calif.: Annual Reviews, 1975.

Bijou, S. W., Birnbraver, J. S., Kidder, J. D. & Tague, C. Programmed instruction as an approach to teaching reading, writing, and arithmetic in retarded children. *Psychological Record*, **16**, 505–522, 1966.

Blinder, B. J., Freeman, D. M. & Stunkard, A. J. Behavior therapy of anorexia nervosa: Effectiveness of activity as a reinforcer of weight gain. *American Journal of Psychiatry*, **126**, 1093–1098, 1970.

Breger, L. & McGaugh, T. L. Critique and reformulation of "learning theory" approaches to psychotherapy and neuroses. *Psychological Bulletin*, **63**, 338–358, 1965.

Buckley, N. K. & Walker, H. M. *Modifying Classroom Behavior*. Champaign, Ill.: Research Press, 1972.

Colby, K. M. Psychotherapeutic processes. In P. R. Farnsworth (Ed.), *Annual Review of Psychology*. Palo Alto, Calif.: Annual Reviews, 347–370, 1964.

Cowan, P. A., Hoddmott, B. A. & Wright, B. A. Compliance and resistance in the conditioning of autistic children: An exploratory study. *Child Development*, **36**, 913–923, 1965.

Cowen, E. L. Emergent directions in school mental health: The development and evaluation of a program for early detection and prevention of ineffective school behavior. *American Scientist*, **59**, 723–733, 1971.

Davidson, W. S., II & Seidman, E. Studies of behavior modification and juvenile delinquency. *Psychological Bulletin*, **81**, 998–1011, 1974.

Dollard, J. & Miller, N. E. *Personality and Psychotherapy*. New York: McGraw-Hill, 1950.

Dunlap, K. *Habits: Their Making and Unmaking*. New York: Liveright, 1932.

Elkind, D. Conceptual orientation shifts in children and adolescents. *Child Development*, **37**, 493–498, 1966.

Elkind, D. Exploitation and the generational conflict. *Mental Hygiene*, **54**, 490–498, 1970.

Elkind, D., Medvene, L. & Rockway, A. S. Representational level and concept in children and adolescents. *Developmental Psychology*, **2**, 85–89, 1969.

English, H. B. & English, A. C. *A Comprehensive Dictionary of Psychological and Psychoanalytical Terms*. New York: Longmans Green, 1958.

Eysenck, H. J. The effectiveness of psychotherapy: An evaluation. *Journal of Consulting Psychology*, **16**, 319–324, 1952.

Ferster, C. B. & DeMyer, M. K. A method for the experimental analysis of the behavior of autistic children. *American Journal of Orthopsychiatry*, **32**, 89–98, 1962.

Franks, C. M. (Ed.), *Behavior Therapy: Appraisal and Status*. New York: McGraw Hill, 1969.

Graziano, A. M. (Ed.), *Behavior Therapy with Children*. Chicago: Aldine/Atherton, 1971.

Grossberg, T. M. Behavior therapy: A review. *Psychological Bulletin*, **62**, 73–88, 1964.

Halpern, W. I., Hammond, J. & Cohen, R. A therapeutic approach to speech phobia: Elective mutism reexamined. *Journal of the American Academy of Child Psychiatry*, **10**, 94–107, 1971.

Hewett, F. M. Educational programs for children with behavior disorders. In H. C. Quay and J. S. Werry (Eds.), *Psychopathological Disorders of Children*, New York: Wiley, 1972

Holzberg, J. D. The companion program: Implimenting the manpower recommendations of the Joint Commission of Mental Illness and Health. *American Psychologist*, **18**, 224–226, 1963.

Homme, L. *How to Use Contingency Contracting in the Classroom*. Champaign, Ill.: Research Press, 1970.

Inhelder, B. & Piaget, J. *The Growth of Logical Thinking from Childhood to Adolescence*. New York: Basic Books, 1958.

Joint Commission on Mental Illness and Health. *Action for Mental Health: Final Report*. New York: Basic Books, 1963.

Jones, M. C. Elimination of children's fears. *Journal of Experimental Psychology*, **7**, 382–390, 1924.

Kissel, S. Systematic desensitization therapy with children: A case study and some suggested modifications. *Professional Psychology*, **3**, 163–168, 1972.

Kissel, S. Mothers and therapists evaluate long-term and short-term child therapy. *Journal of Clinical Psychology*, **31**, 296–299, 1974.

Kissel, S. & Arkins, V. Anorexia nervosa reexamined. *Child Psychiatry and Human Development*, **3**, 255–263, 1973.

Kissel, S., Klosterman, E. & DeAmicis, M. Interpersonal aspects of behavior modification: A case study of a "failure." New York: American Association of Psychiatric Services to Children, 1974.

Krasner, L. Behavior therapy. In P. H. Mussen and M. R. Rosenzweig (Eds.), *Annual Review of Psychology*. Palo Alto, Calif.: Annual Reviews, 1971.

Lazarus, A. A. The results of behavior therapy in 126 cases of severe neurosis. *Behavior Research and Therapy*, **1**, 69–80, 1963.

Lazarus, A. A. & Abramovitz, A. The use of "emotive imagery" in the treatment of children's phobias. *Journal of Mental Science*, **108**, 191–195, 1962.

Leventhal, T. & Weinberger, G. Evaluation of a large scale brief therapy program for children. *American Journal of Orthopsychiatry*, **45**, 119–133, 1975.

Levitt, E. E. The results of psychotherapy with children: An evaluation. *Journal of Consulting Psychology*, **21**, 189–196, 1957.

Levitt, E. E. Psychotherapy with children: A further evaluation. *Behavior Research and Therapy*, **1**, 45–51, 1963.

Levitt, E. E. Research in psychotherapy with children. In A. Bergin and S. Garfield (Eds.), *Handbook of Psychotherapy and Behavior Change*. New York: Wiley, 1971.

Lindsley, O. R. *Studies in Behavior Therapy: Status Report III*. Waltham, Mass.: Metropolitan State Hospital, 1954.

Lundell, K. T. *Behavior Contracting Kit*. Linden, N. J.: Remediation Associates, 1972.

Mathews, A. M. Psychophysiological approaches to the investigation of desensitization and related procedures. *Psychological Bulletin*, **76**, 73–91, 1971.

Mowrer, O. H. *Learning Theory and Behavior*. New York: Wiley, 1960.

Mowrer, O. H. & Mowrer, W. M. Enuresis—a method for its study and treatment. *American Journal of Orthopsychiatry*, **8**, 436–459, 1938.

Obler, M. & Terwilliger, R. F. Pilot study on the effectiveness of systematic desensitization with neurologically impaired children with phobic disorders. *Journal of Consulting and Clinical Psychology*, **34**, 314–319, 1970.

Paul, G. L. *Insight Versus Desensitization in Psychotherapy: An Experiment in Anxiety Reduction*. Palo Alto, Calif.: Stanford University Press, 1965.

Reisman, J. M. & Kissel, S. Mother's evaluation of long-term clinic services. *Bulletin of the Rochester Mental Health Center*, **1**, 13–18, 1968.

Rioch, M. J., Elkes, C., Flint, A. A., Usdansky, B. S., Newman, R. G. & Silber, E.

National institute of mental health pilot study in training mental health counselors. *American Journal of Orthopsychiatry*, **33**, 678–689, 1963.

Ross, A. O. Behavior therapy. In H. C. Quay and J. S. Werry (Eds.), *Psychopathological Disorders of Childhood*. New York: Wiley, 1972.

Schwitzgebel, R. L. Preliminary socialization for psychotherapy of behavior-disordered adolescents. *Journal of Consulting and Clinical Psychology*, **35**, 71–77, 1969.

Shoben, E. J. Psychotherapy as a problem in learning theory. *Psychological Bulletin*, **46**, 366–392, 1949.

Simpson, D. D. & Nelson, A. E. Attention training through breathing control to modify hyperactivity. *Journal of Learning Disabilities*, **7**, 274–283, 1974.

Skinner, B. F. *The Behavior of Organisms: An Experimental Analysis*. New York: Appleton-Century-Crofts, 1938.

Smith, M. B. & Hobbs, N. The community and the community mental health center. *American Psychologist*, **21**, 499–510, 1966.

Stuart, R. B. Behavioral contracting within the family of delinquents. *Journal of Behavior Therapy and Experimental Psychiatry*, **2**, 1–11, 1971.

Stunkard, A. J. New therapies for the eating disorders. *Archives of General Psychiatry*, **26**, 391–398, 1972.

Szasz, T. *The Myth of Mental Illness*. New York: Hoeber-Harper, 1961.

Ullmann, L. P. The major concepts taught to behavior therapy trainees. In A. M. Graziano (Ed.), *Behavior Therapy with Children*. Chicago: Aldine/Atherton, 1971.

Watson, J. B. & Rayner, R. Conditioned emotional reactions. *Journal of Experimental Psychology*, **3**, 1–14, 1920.

Werry, J. S. & Wollersheim, J. P. Behavior therapy with children: A broad overview. *Journal of the American Academy of Child Psychiatry*, **6**, 346–370, 1967.

Wilson, G. T. & Davidson, G. C. Process of fear reduction in systematic desensitization: Animal studies. *Psychological Bulletin*, **76**, 1–14, 1971.

Wolpe, J. Reciprocal Inhibition as the main basis of psychotherapeutic effects. *AMA Archives of Neurology and Psychiatry*, **72**, 205–226, 1954.

Wolpe, J. *Psychotherapy by Reciprocal Inhibition*. Palo Alto, Calif.: Stanford University Press, 1958.

Wolpe, J. & Lazarus, A. *Behavior Therapy Techniques*. Oxford: Pergamon Press, 1966.

Yates, A. J. *Behavior Therapy*. New York: Wiley, 1970.

CHAPTER 11

Pharmacotherapy

Chemical modification of the internal environment of a human organism for purposes of improved functioning is looked upon with a mixture of hope and dread. The expectation of finding effective and noncostly substances that can ameliorate or even remove suffering and malfunctioning has been given impetus in recent years by breakthroughs in psychopharmacologic investigation of central nervous system metabolism and response patterns. At the same time, the realization has grown that new problems appear in the wake of these discoveries which cannot always be anticipated in the nascent stages of their development. The potential for serious side effects, a rise in iatrogenic disease, drug overuse and abuse, and the creation of a climate of psychological control through the use of chemical restraint and/or stimulation are some of the problems created.

For children in particular the issue is doubly hazardous since they generally are passive recipients of whatever the adults consider important for them. Much like Aldous Huxley (1932) envisioned "soma" in *Brave New World* as a chemical means of maintaining a docile population, so may parents, teachers, and other child caretakers yearn for a drug to keep children tractable. This accusation has already been hurled at those who prescribe medication for behavior management of children in the classroom. It is quite important, therefore, that indiscriminate use of medication be avoided if children who can benefit from drug therapy are to remain eligible for it. On the other hand, an overzealous restriction of the pharmacotherapeutic modality would also create unnecessary hardship for children, parents, and our society, which must atune itself simultaneously to high density living and to promotion of creative expression.

One of the major changes in psychiatric care in the last 30 years has been the impact of psychotropic and other drugs on the ability of the community to care for its acutely ill and on the growing capacity of the disturbed person to adapt to noninstitutional living. This implies enormous savings in cost and in waste of human potential. In children, the prevention of serious malfunctioning in adulthood as a result of poorly treated childhood problems becomes of paramount significance. However, a correlation has yet to be established between the relief of symptomatology through the use of drugs and later good adjustment, or of enhanced generativity and creativity. The tension inherent in the maintenance of checks and balances between the right to be different and the necessities of the social contract at this juncture in history will be expressed through a continuing controversy about the scope of drug use for behavioral and emotional symptomatology. With children the issues have already been debated on the highest levels of government (Office of Child Development, Department of Health, Education and Welfare, 1971) because the opportunities for abuse are grave. Yet, in the face of benefits that derive from the appropriate and judicious use of medication, it would not seem wise to become fanatically opposed to this form of medical treatment in the absence of other more effective modalities of help.

Folk medicine has included the application of physical substances to psychologically disturbed people since ages immemorial. Only the refinement of modern technology has been added to a human propensity for seeking medicinal balms to give the whole enterprise a much more sinister character than might have been true in an earlier day. Proprietary medicines of the worst type were once liberally fed to children without any controls exercised by governmental authorities. Such factors as the cost of treatment, new evidence for remedies specific for certain symptoms or entities, and the discovery of brain nutrients such as memory enhancers will influence the spread of drug use (Kety, 1970). In the final analysis the demands placed on the caretakers of children that cannot be met by other means than medication will determine the growth of drug utilization.

As has been true with adults, the movement away from institutional care to normalization in the community has also affected the children's area. Hospitalization of disturbed children, in contrast to adults, has reportedly increased (U.S. Government Printing Office, DHEW, 1971–1972), but may belatedly be leveling off or declining during a period of economic hardship and a swing to "normalization" (Department of Health, Education and Welfare, 1975). The availability of psychotropic drugs has been a major influence in implementing this trend. Medicating with tranquilizers and stimulants has made it possible for a sizeable number of troubled children to be contained in regular and special classes of the public schools. The adaptation to the school then permits a greater positive involvement in the community and is less likely to lead to sequestering troubled students in isolated academic settings and institutional placements. Drugs may frequently make it possible for community based programs to work effectively with children who would otherwise be too aggressive, self-injurious, or inattentive for non-institutional routines. For those who are hospitalized, the return to out-patient or day treatment status is quickened by enabling the children to be more self-controlled through medication.

Often, drug therapy must be combined with other approaches, which are the primary treatment agents, ranging from psychological counseling to behavior modification or from personal tutoring to special group instruction. The day may come, however, when many emotional problems will yield to highly specific chemotherapy. Gilles de la Tourette's disease or "maladie des tics" is illustrative of a syndrome that is now successfully relieved by chemo-therapy, whereas a few years ago psychodynamic explanations customarily elucidated the disease on emotionally based terms (Ascher, 1948). For most problems the complex interplay of temperament, biorhythms, mood swings, central nervous system dysfunction, experience, and idiosyncratic response patterns will probably impede the development of high specificity in pharma-calogic management of behavior and emotion except in well-circumscribed pathological entities.

Widening research in the biochemistry of the brain has illuminated the possible mechanism for affective and psychotic disorders in particular. Neurotransmitter substances called serotonin, dopamine, norepinephrine, histamine, and acetylcholine are implicated in various explanations of brain action (Eveloff, 1966). Another area of investigation suggests that protein synthesis in the central nervous system regulated by ribonucleic acid provides for long term information storage (Uphouse et al., 1974). The disruption and facilitation of memory processes by chemical agents opens up the possibility of treating disordered and defective learning.

Drug therapy is also applied to problems associated with the reticular activitating system of the brain stem (Eveloff, 1966). This network of nerve cells is a transmitting station for all sensory and motor impulses traveling in and out of the brain. It facilitates and inhibits or otherwise modulates and filters sensory input and motor performance. Disorders of wakefulness and sleep are associated with the activities of this particular system.

There are unique issues in child psychopharmacology (DiMascio, 1971), when contrasted to the adult field. Because poor agreement on diagnosis and etiology exists, research findings are difficult to interpret and are sometimes contradictory (Fish, 1969). Most significant is the influence of maturation on behavior so that the treatment success over time could well be ascribed to a natural improvement from one stage to the next rather than to the efficacy of drugs. Of course, this criticism can also be leveled at all intervention techniques used for children. For this reason alone, the employment of adequate controls in experimental studies looms as an important validating factor.

Eisenberg (1971) outlined several principles of drug therapy in child psychiatry. He considered the use of medication as only a component part of a total treatment program for the disturbed child. In each case the potential risks of taking chemicals into the body must be weighed against the anticipated benefits and costs to the individual if not given. Symptomatic relief need not be disparaged if it improves a child's functioning. In any event, (1) drugs should be used only if there are firm indications for them; (2) an old drug is better than a new one unless the latter's superiority has been proved; (3) drugs should be used at the lowest effective dosage and no longer than necessary; and (4) the degree of morbidity from both use or nonuse of the drug should be taken into account in determining the cost to the well-being of the child.

Although chemotherapy has been less dramatic in child psychiatry than has been true for adults (Koupernik, 1972), some notable gains have occurred. As more becomes known about the nature of brain chemistry and of neurophysiology, a workable frame of reference for understanding the effects of drugs on behavior should facilitate the search for appropriate chemotherapeutic agents in dealing better with primary pathology. Conners (1972a) criticized the present state of the art because of several factors such as the primitive nosology in child psychiatry, the preoccupation with symptomatic treatment, and the poorly controlled variables in drug research with children. Although several efforts have been advanced to improve upon the classification system (Fish, 1969), to introduce greater precision in measuring indices of functioning (Conners, 1972a; DiMascio, 1971), to correlate biochemical changes with diagnostic categories (Cytryn et al., 1974), and to guard against the treatment of psychiatric labels or symptoms rather than of the underlying function (Irwin, 1968), the practitioner is still too often left with the choice of treating symptoms with drugs on a trial and error basis or to fall back on alternatives devoid of drug use. With these limitations of current pharmacotherapy well in mind, only a pragmatic classification that fits the existing reality of practice can be undertaken. A threefold categorization suggests itself for utilization of medication in children: (1) tension relief; (2) nonspecific modification of mood and behavior; (3) modification of target symptoms.

What must be kept in mind is that the treatment of children is further influenced by the attitudes of parents, teachers, peers, and others. For example, there are medication accepting and medication rejecting families (Knobel, 1962) who can have considerable impact on outcome. Since some children must take pills in school, the attitude of school administrators and teachers has a similar significance with regard to effectiveness. Another concern is the self evaluation of the medicated youngster and the question of emerging sociological problems related to drug use by children (Cole, 1975). In all likelihood, however, the clinician will be increasingly called upon to consider medication as one of the viable treatment options.

Treatment for Tension Relief

Perhaps one of the more debatable points in the widespread use of drugs today is the easy acceptability of anxiolytic agents to the adult population. Whatever the source of tension or of anxiety, this state of feeling is recognized as one difficult to bear for prolonged periods. This century is often referred to as the Age of Anxiety, although it may be difficult to document that life experiences today offer more cause for chronic tension. A complementary development has been in the discovery, production, and sale of tranquilizing agents, many of which have powerful tension reducing and anxiolytic effects. Can the downward reach of this trend to the youngest age groups be condoned under any circumstances? Does the early introduction of such treatment lead to later drug dependence? Worrisome concerns such as these have been raised although no study has as yet demonstrated a correlation between the use of medication in childhood and later habituation or a predeliction for drug abuse.

The use of "true" or "minor" tranquilizers has had a limited application in work with children. Certainly the preferred route for relief of anxiety in children remains in the modification of responsible environmental and experiential factors or in the correction of the neurotic basis for the upset.

Prior to the discovery of tranquilizers, the medication most commonly employed for restless children was phenobarbital, which also has efficacy as an anticonvulsant. Its drawbacks relate primarily to sedating effects which, over time, can produce a form of pseudoretardation (Cordes, 1973) and to drug dependence. In some children a paradoxic reaction of overstimulation and irritability occurs in lieu of sedation.

In pediatric practice the minor tranquilizers such as hydroxyzine hydro-

chloride (Atarax[R], Vistaril[R]) and the antihistamine diphenhydramine hydrochloride (Benadryl[R]) have replaced phenobarbital as the stopgap measure for
treating "mild restlessness of childhood" (Eveloff, 1966; Fish, 1968; Piuck,
1963). The effectiveness of these medications is insignificant and may well be
accounted for by a placebo effect on the parents. Meprobamate (Miltown[R],
Equanil[R]), chlordiazepoxide hydrochloride (Librium[R]) and diazepam
(Valium[R]), among others, are also resorted to for brief periods when anxiety
is the main symptom, but they have not proven to be helpful unless combined
with other treatment modalities such as parent counseling and child psychotherapy (Kraft, 1968).

Nonspecific Modification of Mood and Behavior

Children with moderate to severe adjustment problems or with chronic behavioral difficulties benefit from measures that reduce their tendencies to be
overreactive, hypersensitive, or impulsive. Their attitudes and actions become self-defeating and consequently prove to be a source of considerable
irritation to their families and schools. When their acceptance in both spheres
is jeopardized, urgent intervention in the form of medication is considered
beneficial to save a deteriorating situation. While some of the children may
have neurotic problems, others can be considered prepsychotic or suffering
from a poorly defined organic brain syndrome which usually requires multiple forms of supportive help. Because the child's global behavior rather
than a circumscribed or well-defined function is deviant, the selection of
neuroleptic drugs for broad symptom control is the pharmacologic treatment
of choice. Of these the phenothiazine derivatives have proven to be the most
popular despite their slowing down learning and cognitive skills, their having
undesirable neurologic and hemovascular side effects, and their contribution
to obesity (Helper et al., 1963; McAndrew et al., 1972).

Chlorpromazine (Thorazine[R]) was the first of this group to be tried (Fish,
1969; Hunt et al., 1965; Korein et al., 1971). This medication as well as a
succession of other antipsychotic agents has been given to atypical young
children, whether autistic or schizophrenic, without anything more than
transient symptomatic improvement reported (Campbell et al., 1972a). Perhaps the most effective drug of this type is thioridazine (Mellaril[R]) which
helps the highly excitable and impulsive young patient who may be mentally
retarded to keep himself under better control (Alexandris and Lundell, 1968;
Pavig et al., 1961). In older children and adolescents, problem behaviors

including those encompassed by delinquency and schizophrenia may be alleviated by such neuroleptics as perphenazine (Trilafon[R]) (Molling et al., 1962), trifluoperazine (Stelazine[R]) (Fish et al., 1966), and thiothixene (Navane[R]) (Campbell et al., 1970; Waizer et al., 1972). For example, good effects from thiothixene on schizophrenic outpatients include significant improvement in motor activity, stereotypic behavior, coordination, sleeping, affect, exploratory behavior, concentration, eating habits, and communication skills (Waizer et al., 1972), which may say more about the nonspecificity of this medication effect than about its healing potential for a particular mental disorder.

Case A

Well into the second half of first grade, a 6-year-old boy suddenly developed a reluctance to attend school, became obsessed with smells, and carried out several avoidance rituals such as not wishing to touch his food. His panic was intense when his mother persisted in taking him to school. He voiced a wish to die. His mother found him with a knife in his hand as if he were contemplating injury to himself.

The boy had been doing well in school but was considered to have perfectionistic tendencies which caused him no end of worries. He played with other children, was popular, and yet was also happy when he needed to amuse himself alone. The parents had considerable marital difficulties as well as problems with a 14-year-old son.

The child was brought to a mental health center during this crisis, about 10 days after its onset. There was a formidable separation problem between the mother and the child, with the child exercising considerable control over the mother. The anxiety in the boy seemed to stem from an unrealistic perception of himself as an omnipotent person who was forced to tyrannize others in order to maintain an illusion of control.

In addition to play therapy for the boy and marital counseling for the parents, medication was also introduced to reduce the child's anxiety to more manageable proportions and to make continued school attendance feasible. This objective was easily reached in this case by giving the child thioridazine (Mellaril) 10 mg daily.

Case B

An 8-year-old boy, the oldest of six out-of-wedlock children, was chronically in trouble at home and in school as he was moody and prone to lose self-control. In order to control his outbursts and his uncooperative attitude, the school had resorted to brief suspensions and finally had placed him on a half-day attendance program. His mother who relied on him to look after the younger children would often discipline him with beatings so that a protective intervention became necessary. Over a period of 2 years, both individual therapy and a therapeutic day school were made available to this deprived child with good results.

When he returned to public school, he quickly was embroiled again in fighting as a result of temper outbursts accompanying a tough-guy facade. He was started on thioridazine (Mellaril) 25 mg twice daily in the hope that the medication would reduce the intensity of his impulsive flare-ups in school. Although there were occasional reports of fighting with peers, the number of such episodes decreased dramatically.

Claims have been made for the efficacy of other classes of medication in behavior disorders of childhood and adolescence. The anticonvulsant diphenylhydantoin (Dilantin[R]) has been utilized for problem children and delinquents (Lindsley and Henry, 1942; Resnick, 1967; Walker and Kirkpatrick, 1947) although Pasamanick (1951) and others (Green, 1961) do not find it effective. A review by Connors (1972a) of anticonvulsant drug therapy for behavior disorders concludes that studies have been inconclusive to date.

The uses of tricyclic amines, basically developed as antidepressants, have become more diversified following a number of serendipitous observations. One of these uses, especially for imipramine (Tofranil[R]), has been its striking effect on behavior disorders in school maladjustment (Rapoport, 1965; Splitter and Kaufman, 1966; Waizer et al., 1974). Unfortunately, some of the early dramatic results in this respect have not held up (Connors, 1972a).

Hormonal agents, particularly triiodothyronine (Thyrolar[R]), have been investigated for their antipsychotic and stimulating effects in preschool schizophrenic children (Campbell et al., 1972b; Sherwin et al., 1958). However, their potential for effective treatment of these disorders awaits further validation.

The antihistaminic diphenhydramine (Benadryl) has also been employed in treating behavioral disorders (Effron and Freedman, 1953; Korein et al., 1971). Its beneficial effect probably is being mediated through its sedative influence.

Megavitamin therapy for all manner of problems has its partisan adherents (Cott, 1969) but also awaits confirmation via controlled studies. Rimland (1974) believes that certain subtypes of autisticlike children respond better to megavitamins than do others. A search is under way to define such sub-groups.

Modification of Target Symptoms

When a specific bit of behavior can be controlled or at least significantly ameliorated by a reasonably safe drug, often there follows an indiscriminate utilization of the substance for relief of problems even remotely resembling the intended symptoms. This is not too surprising since the diagnostic categorization of childhood problems is poorly contrived and quasiscientific. Because the clinician's interpretation of what he observes may differ from person to person—or the child may even behave differently with observers —criteria for pharmacotherapy are not always enlightening. Therefore, if the suspicion is sufficiently great that a symptom may be susceptible to a drug, many clinicians are tempted to prescribe it on a trial basis. This becomes most true when a target symptom or function is thought to be highly responsive to a given drug. Yet even in this domain, care must be given to a variety of factors that may alter the effect of a perfectly useful drug, whether relating to proper dosage schedules or to idiosyncratic reactions of a physical or psychosocial kind (Connors, 1972a). There are variable opinions as to what constitutes an adequate trial of medication (Fish, 1967), the range extending from homeopathic to near-toxic dosages.

Pharmacologic agents have been found for only a few target symptoms and functions. Of these, the following list represents the most common difficulties that are unusually sensitive to specific medication:

1. Hyperkinesis
2. Enuresis
3. Encopresis
4. Sleep disorders
5. Depression
6. Mania
7. Anorexia
8. Obesity
9. Tics
10. Phobias
11. Learning problems

Hyperkinesis

Nearly 40 years ago Bradley (1937) described the use of amphetamine (Benzedrine[R]), a stimulant drug, in the treatment of behavior disorders of children. Shortly thereafter dextroamphetamine (Dexedrine[R]) was found to be even more effective (Bradley, 1950). By 1953 Ginn and Hohman reported that excessive restlessness was most responsive to dextroamphetamine. Although a variety of symptoms such as short attention span, impulsiveness, temper outbursts, poor concentration, and quarrelsomeness improved concomitantly, it was chiefly the driven motor behavior that was often dramatically turned off by this drug and thus the drug came to be thought of as a specific treatment modality for the hyperkinetic syndrome (Eisenberg et al., 1963; Weiss et al., 1971). Because approximately 4 in every 100 grade school children are believed to be hyperkinetic (Millichap, 1968), the importance of the drug for classroom management and indirectly for improving academic performance was not lost on educators (Freeman, 1966). Public outcry about the potential for political abuse and social control was not far behind (Grinspoon and Singer, 1973).

Stimulant drugs are considered a proper modality of treatment for hyperkinetic children if integrated into a total treatment program that addresses itself to the child in his situation rather than to solely symptomatic activity (Eisenberg, 1971; 1972a). Since the syndrome may encompass a variety of problems stemming from diverse causes, overreliance on one drug seems hardly realistic (Fish, 1971). Moreover, the differential effects of these drugs on aspects of behavior have yet to be thoroughly explored (Arnold et al., 1973).

A stimulant of a different chemical structure, methylphenidate (Ritalin[R]), has virtually supplanted the amphetamines (Campbell et al., 1971; Schleifer et al., 1975), because it has a comparable effect without being invested with the socially stigmatizing quality of "speed." Although claims have been made for fewer side effects with methylphenidate, there is some doubt about this earlier position. Like dextroamphetamine, it tends to cause insomnia, depressed appetite, and reduced physical growth (Safer et al., 1972; Safer and Allen, 1973) although the last finding has been refuted in a retrospective study of adolescents (Beck et al., 1975). Dextroamphetamine is more likely to be utilized for hyperkinetic preschoolers because a liquid preparation is available, whereas not for mephylphenidate. A third central nervous system stimulant which is structurally different from the aforementioned two drugs is pemoline (Cylert^R) which can be administered on a once daily dosage regimen. In addition to improving gross motor behavior, some positive effects on cognitive and perceptual functions have also been recorded (Connors et al., 1972; Page et al., 1974). Caffeine in the form of well-brewed coffee has had good results in the hands of one practitioner (Schnackenberg, 1973).

One of the major concerns about the introduction of stimulants in the treatment of hyperactive children has centered about the danger of habituation and later drug abuse (Koupernick, 1972; Learning Disabilities Report, 1971). All evidence over a 30-year period strongly suggests the absence of such proclivity in treated children while medicated and during several years of posttreatment observation (Beck et al., 1975; Laufer, 1971a; 1971b).

Case C

The mother of two children applied for service on the advice of her son's nursery school teacher and pediatrician because the youngster did not get along with other children. For example, he would repeatedly ride his tricycle roughshod through a group of children and seemed not to learn from the negative attention he received for this behavior. Those who observed him in the nursery and in the neighborhood believed that he liked getting into scraps. He took his parents' full attention to the point that they felt neglectful of an 11-year-old daughter who was 7 years his senior.

From birth on the boy was considered to be a much more difficult child than the sister had been. As a baby he had been fretful, colicky, and restless in the night. The parents believed that he had never slept through a night as they would often hear him get up to go to the bathroom, to drink water, or to simply busy himself in his bedroom when he was expected to be asleep. Television viewing had to be curtailed since he would become too excited with certain programs. His hyperactivity during the day was expressed in terms of "wildness" when he was unable to stop himself from running around and when his excitement interfered with his awareness of others. At age 1 he had been given phenobarbital for his irritability, but this medication had caused a paradoxic increase in wakefulness and in discomfort.

When the child was seen clinically in the office there was no sign that would lead one to suspect that he was hyperactive, least of all that he was prone to lose self-control. However, when he was observed in an open group setting or in the waiting room his driven behavior became quickly evident. The child was treated with methylphenidate (Ritalin), 20 mg being the most effective daily dose. When he entered first grade, he was teased by other children about taking a pill at noon so that the medication was changed to a long-acting form of dextroamphetamine 10 mg (Dexedrine Spansule[R]). With this regimen, he continued his improved behavior in school where he was sufficiently attentive and calm to benefit from the teacher's instructions. During vacations, the parents were supported in their desire to have the boy take a drug holiday. On follow-up visits the child indicated that he felt better about himself since he was on medication. One side effect, the fact that he cried more easily, had initially troubled the parents since they were not accustomed to his ever being weepy.

Case D

The recently divorced mother of three girls was referred for help by the school social worker in order to check out what could be done for the oldest child who was about to repeat kindergarten. This girl was described as immature and hyperkinetic. Her birth weight had been somewhat over 4 pounds. Because the mother believed her to have suffered most from the breakup of the family, she requested psychotherapy for this daughter and herself.

On being seen, the girl exhibited driven behavior and pressured speech. It was difficult to sort out the situational or reactive factors from an endogenous problem with hyperkinesis. The decision was made to at least try stimulant medication while starting a course of play therapy for the child and collateral counseling for the mother. Ritalin, 10 mg twice daily, had an immediate positive effect on the outward manifestations of overactivity, although there was good reason to continue in treatment with the child who tended to be negativistic, demanding, and manipulative. After 10 months of weekly collateral meetings, the girl was thought to be sufficiently improved so that play therapy was discontinued. However, she remained on her medication for another 2 years while she matured. One year after the medication was stopped she was reported to be making an adequate school adjustment.

The dosage schedule for these medications must be titrated to a child's idiosyncratic response. Some children show a clear-cut drop in their driven behavior with low dosages, while others require much higher amounts before there is a notable improvement. Sometimes, one of the stimulants works better than the other so that each should be considered as a potential alternative in case of poor response or of undesirable side effects.

A suggested dosage schedule for three of these drugs is given overleaf.

Ordinarily a starting dose of dextroamphetamine is 2.5 mg on arising and after lunch for preschoolers, while for older children 5 mg twice daily or 5–10 mg of methylphenidate morning and noon is recommended. These

Initial mg/kg body weight/per day

Dextroamphetamine	0.25
Methylphenidate	0.25
Pemoline	0.50

Optimum mg/kg body weight/per day

Dextroamphetamine	1.00
Methylphenidate	2.00
Pemoline	4.00

amounts may be increased until the desired improvement occurs or until side effects intrude. Furthermore, the dosage may have to be adjusted over time in keeping with the maturational changes of the child. Vacation periods are looked upon as good opportunities for cutting back or withholding medication. This is to see if the requirements for its use still exist and to obviate potentially deleterious consequences of chronic drug use such as those recorded on appetite and rate of physical growth (Safer et al., 1972). Idiosyncratic side effects have been reported (Mattson and Calverley, 1968) but are not common (Conners, 1972b)

When other methods fail the multifaceted antidepressant imipramine (Tofranil), although less efficient in the amelioration of hyperactivity than the stimulants, is thought to have some applicability in the management of this problem (Rapoport, 1974; Quinn and Rapoport, 1975). However, in the desirable dosages it may precipitate major seizures in children who have evidence of organic brain disease but who are without a history of convulsions (Brown et al., 1973). In susceptible patients in whom seizures intervene with stimulants or antidepressants, a lowering of the dosage and supplemental anticonvulsants should be used (Millichap, 1968).

Enuresis

Nocturnal enuresis or automatic bedwetting while asleep probably affects 2 to 3 million children in the United States (Muellner, 1960). Most instances stem from physiologically determined immaturity of bladder capacity and control, although psychological factors occasionally may be contributory to this symptom formation. In any event, it is a distressing problem to the child and as often to his parents if the number of drugs and devices deployed in its remediation is any sign of the anxious effort devoted to its management. In 1960 McLean reported that imipramine (Tofranil) benefited bedwetters, and since then a host of articles have appeared attesting its efficacy in this respect (Margolis, 1962; Munster et al., 1961; Poussaint and Ditman, 1965). To decrease nocturnal enuresis in children under 12 years of age, 25–50 mg of imipramine are given at bedtime for up to 2 months, when it is withdrawn. The dose may be increased to 75 mg in children over 12 years of age. At the end of this program many children have been "trained" to be dry. Some children remain poor responders or eventually escape the drug's restraint. The precise action is not known but it is believed that the anticholinergic effect of the drug brings about an increased capacity of the bladder to hold urine and that its stimulant effect on the central nervous system makes the individual more aware of a full bladder. Side reactions may include dryness of the mouth and constipation as well as greater aggressiveness (Tec, 1963) and electrocardiographic changes (Martin and Zang, 1975).

Case E

An 8-year-old boy, the middle of three children, wet his bed nightly. Medical investigation had ruled out a clear-cut organic basis for the enuresis. The middle class parents, whose two daughters were dry at night, had tried all kinds of methods to help their son with this problem, although he was not visibly upset by it. He was an alert, active child who had friends, did well in school, and seemed rather fastidious in his personal grooming. It had been noted that he was dry on the one occasion when he slept at a friend's house.

Using this pretext the parents came for help because they believed that emotional reasons only could explain the phenomenon of selective bed-wetting. When the therapist spoke with the boy, he learned that the youngster had been worried about embarrassing himself by wetting and had tried not to sleep. In all likelihood, he did not reach the deeper sleep stages during which automatic voiding usually occurs.

A trial of imipramine (Tofranil) 25 mg at bedtime served to eliminate the wetting for 2 nights only. The dosage was increased to 50 mg nightly with excellent control of the symptom. After 2 weeks the dosage was reduced and then withdrawn. When wetting recurred within a few days, the medication was again administered at the higher dosage for 1 month before being again withdrawn. The enuresis did not recur subsequently.

Encopresis

Children who have a problem with fecal soiling on a functional basis suffer even more as they often become social pariahs and a source of chagrin or embarrassment to their parents. At one time this symptom was viewed as a serious sign of underlying conflict between mother and child who were thought to be locked into a hostile-dependent relationship (Bellman, 1966; Call et al., 1963). This explanation may well have mistaken the emotional and traumatic consequence of soiling for its cause. Berg and Jones (1964) distinguished several types of retentive and nonretentive encopresis for which they outlined appropriate treatment plans, including therapy with the family and oral laxatives such as senna (Senokot[R]) for the child. Abrahams (1963) reported one child's encopresis being relieved by imipramine (Tofranil). More recently, good results have been reported for the nonretentive type with imipramine, which seems to be contraindicated in the retentive type of encopresis (Gavanski, 1971).

When retentive constipation and secondary leakage pose a problem, training or retraining of the bowels may remove the cause. An angry or frightened child or one phobic of toilets may, in withholding feces, form an impacted mass and secondarily an atonic sigmoid colon. Defecation quickly threatens to become a painful experience that the child avoids at all cost. The incontinence starts when fecal leakage occurs around the impaction. By returning control over his bowels to the child, there is good likelihood that routine toileting will be resumed. Rather than utilizing oral laxatives, the effect over which the child would have no control, using a quickacting rectal suppository will empty the bowels 15–30 minutes after insertion so that evacuation can be arranged under predetermined conditions. Usually the child is directed to sit on the commode after this procedure and is rewarded with a small gift on successful evacuation into the toilet. A safe substance for this purpose is bisacodyl (Dulcolax[R]) suppository of 10 mg, which is inserted once daily for three successive days before beginning a trial of two days without medication to see whether the child will go to the bathroom spontaneously. Rewarding the child during the suppository free period is continued, contingent on the successful moving of stool into the toilet, until the bowel habit is well established. Should retention of stool recur, a repetition of this treatment is required. Of course, associated interpersonal or phobic difficulties that might have given rise to the problem in the first place need to be attended to concurrently through appropriate psychotherapy or family counseling.

Sleep Disorders

Children may undergo periods of insomnia at different stages which may be puzzling and disturbing. On the whole, hypnotics and sedatives are to be avoided except for brief intervals when relief needs to be offered to the child and to the parent. Chloral hydrate (Noctec^R) and diphenhydramine (Benadryl) are commonly employed for this response. Some hyperactive children do well with a bedtime dose of their stimulant medication as they may experience a rebound effect after the daytime medication has worn off (Laufer, 1971).

Sleep walking or somnambulism is estimated to afflict 15% of all children between 5 and 12 years of age at least once and is related to the shifting sleep stages from "nonrapid eye movement" (NREM) to "rapid eye movement" (REM) sleep in the neurologically immature child. A related phenomenon is pavor nocturnus, or night terrors, whereby a child is aroused into a panic state while remaining asleep. No specific psychological etiology has been demonstrated. Although these phenomena, really disorders of arousal, usually disappear spontaneously with age, the use of diazepam (Valium) at bedtime has been helpful in controlling them (Anders and Weinstein, 1972).

Narcolepsy, or involuntary dropping off into sleep, is very responsive to central nervous system stimulants, which are considered symptomatic treatment for the disorder usually starting in childhood. Methylphenidate (Ritalin) 10–20 mg three times per day before meals is preferred to dextroamphetamine (Dexedrine) or Methamphetamine (Desoxyn^R) since it is reported to have fewer side effects (Yoss and Daly, 1960).

Depression

Affective disorders in childhood are generally masked by behavioral problems. Presumably if depressive states of childhood are to be better delineated, the discovery of biochemical correlates would prove most helpful in their identification (Cytryn et al., 1974) since antidepressant drugs like imipramine (Tofranil) can be most effective (Frommer, 1967). Their use in adolescents is no different from that of adults.

Mania

There is some evidence that mood disorders with manic or cyclic stages occur before adolescence (Feinstein and Wolpert, 1973). Lithium carbonate (Eskalith[R], Lithane[R], Lithonate[R]) is the drug of choice for abatement and prevention of mania (Annell, 1969). Blood serum levels must be monitored between 0.5–1.5 mEq/1 which is considered the effective range short of toxicity. Campbell et al. (1972a) noted that a child's autoaggressive and explosive behavior ceased on lithium when all other methods failed.

Case F

A 16-year-old high school student, the son of a lawyer, dropped out of school in order to travel. When he was arrested for possession of marijuana, he appeared unusually "high." At first his behavior was looked upon as drug related, but when the youth persisted on advertising himself fervently as mankind's savior, he was brought to psychiatric attention.

On examination he was hypomanic, suspicious of all authority other than his own, and expansive about his powers of understanding people. The history revealed a similar episode two years previous when the youth had run away from home for the first time after rejecting the control of home and school. During the two-month absence, while he had lived a marginal existence in a hippie community, he became depressed and had returned home. He had looked upon this excursion as a defeat and awaited the magical age of 16 to strike out again independently.

The diagnosis of a mood disorder of the manic-depressive type was entertained and lithium carbonate prescribed to attenuate the manic behavior. Within days after this regimen was instituted he became less pressured in speech and action, dropped his allusions to being a spiritual power, and began to make more realistic plans for himself. He returned to school and graduated one year after his classmates while remaining on a daily maintenance dose of 600 mg lithium and requiring only periodic follow-up visits.

Anorexia

A condition characterized by food aversion and associated weight loss of serious proportions has come in for much clinical attention as a result of its refractoriness to treatment. All manner of regimens and therapies have been advanced, each reaching some patients in positive ways but clearly not reversing the process for all. What works in some, seems anathema to others. A treatment approach that uses multiple modalities in keeping with the dynamics of the patient offers most hope (Tolstrup, 1975). Some clinicians look upon food as something that can be prescribed like medicine. The patient's weight is determined daily, and only evidenced weight gain leads to the granting of desirable privileges (Galdston, 1974). Neuroleptics of the phenothiazine group such as chlorpromazine (Thorazine[R]) have been recommended to promote appetite (Dally and Sargant, 1966).

Obesity

Lorber (1966) recommends that drug therapy be used with utmost restraint for exogenously overweight children. In grossly obese children, only when all previous dietary treatment has not been adhered to, a trial of anorectic drugs is indicated. Even then, long-term results are poor unless the whole family can also be treated, sometimes aided and abetted by high incentive group effort or mutual support. Unlike the case in adults, the use of a slow release amphetamine (Dexedrine Spansule) or prolonged action phenmetrazine hydrochloride (Preludin[R]) in children affords short-term weight loss without causing restlessness, excitability, habit formation, or withdrawal symptoms.

Involuntary Tics and Other Movements

A syndrome of involuntary tics and utterances that may be coprolalic was first described in 1885 by Gilles de la Tourette. Its onset occurs usually between the second and sixteenth year, more often in boys, and may persist for months or years. An organic attribute of unknown etiology contributes to its unfolding, but psychological factors may also influence its expression (Stevens and Blachly, 1966). In its major form the manifestations of the syndrome have a devastating impact on the child's social adjustment and on his academic life (Rosenthal et al., 1975). Triflupromazine (Vesprin[R]), thioridazine (Mellaril), diazepam (Valium), and haloperidol (Haldol[R]) benefit in bringing on a remission of symptoms although the last drug seems to be preferred (Challas and Brauer, 1963; Chapel et al., 1964; Lucas, 1964; Stevens and Blachly, 1966). Initial dosage will vary with age and weight, with increases occurring until symptoms are controlled.

On occasion a child suffering from Sydenham's Chorea or St. Vitus' Dance surfaces in a mental health facility (Halpern, 1974). The peculiarities of behavior can easily mislead the clinician to perceive the problem in purely psychological terms. Early diagnosis and treatment of the rheumatic nature of this disease, including an antibiotic regimen, prevents long-range physical disability which can occur in up to 75% of untreated choreic children. The involuntary choreic movements of the extremities and of the face, not commonly associated with vocal tics, are secondary reactions to streptococcal infection in children from ages 5 to 13 years and are more prevalent in girls.

Case G

An 8-year-old boy was referred to a community mental health center by his pediatrician after the sudden onset of "nervous" traits and habits. He was said to shake parts of his trunk, blink frequently, jerk his head to one side, and fidget in other unusual ways. Along with this behavior, he had become irritable, was often in tears, and was sleepless. Moreover, he began hiding himself so others could not observe his motions. He had told his parents that he was aware of the movements but that he could not do anything about them. The parents felt that this child had always been a tense youngster.

The history revealed that the boy had had multiple streptococcal throat and ear infections for several years until a tonsillectomy was performed about a year prior to the onset of the current symptoms. Two weeks before the present illness, the patient and a younger brother had complained of earaches but there had been no treatment for this condition.

When the boy was examined the most prominent sign was an involuntary head-shaking tic. There was some minor movement of the shoulders. His overall actions were fast and jerky as if he did not have good control over his body.

All laboratory tests were normal except for an elevated AS-O titer which was presumptive evidence for a previous streptococcal infection. A diagnosis of Sydenham's Chorea or St. Vitus' Dance was entertained, and a course of penicillin was prescribed by the pediatrician. About 3 months after the onset of the symptoms, all involuntary movements had virtually disappeared. The boy's functioning had returned to his premorbid condition of inoffensiveness.

Several British authors have reported successful treatment of stutterers with haloperidol (Haldol) (Barker, 1975; Wells and Malcolm, 1971).

Phobic States

The treatment of phobic children with antidepressant drugs appears to be practiced more commonly in Great Britain (Kelly et al., 1970) than in the United States where psychotherapeutic or behavior management methods are preferred. A report about a multidiscipline treatment program of school phobic children (Gittelman-Klein and Klein, 1971) revealed that imipramine (Tofranil) in dosages of 100–200 mg per day was superior to placebo in obviating the principal symptom. However, the high dosage required introduces risks of side effects which makes this approach an alternative after other methods have been unsuccessful. Librium was used successfully to return children to school by one investigator (D'Amato, 1962).

Learning Problems

There is a growing emphasis on the search for drug facilitated learning or specific help for the underachieving or learning disabled child. The psychic energizers such as methylphenidate (Ritalin) and pemoline (Cylert) in particular seemed to have some effect on cognitive functioning (Alexandris and Lundell, 1968; Page et al., 1974; Sprague et al., 1970; Rapoport et al., 1974). Even for hypoactive and schizoid children with learning problems, stimulants may be effective in ameliorating some of the dysfunction arising out of subtle developmental deviations (Fish, 1971). Nonetheless, the long-term appropriateness of drug use for this purpose requires further investigation before psychopharmacologic therapy for special learning handicaps can be recommended. Antidepressants have been given to high school underachievers with good results, although it is not certain whether the mood elevating property or the mild tranquilization or both are responsible (Splitter and Kaufman, 1966). If the claims for improvement in this complex target symptom by any number of chemical agents can be believed, there need hardly be any young person who should not progress on one or another medication. Only the major tranquilizers, like chlorpromazine (Thorazine), have actually been found to have a deleterious influence on learning (Baker, 1968; Hartlage, 1965; McAndrews et al., 1972).

There has been practically no support for pharmacologic treatment of children outside of the total management concept, which also includes individual, collateral, or family therapy. This stands in marked contrast to the orientation to adults, for whom medication alone is recommended more often than not as the therapy of choice. Several reasons account for the difference. To begin with, the young rarely report the changes they experience as a result of drug ingestion. Altered behavior, function, and mood must be observed by parents and teachers. This requires their cooperation for both perceptive observation and for accurate reporting. In turn, their attitudes and behavior affect the child's symptomatology. How regular and at ease are the parents in administering the medication to the child? Do they discontinue medication prematurely because they are pleased or frightened by the effects? Are their expectations too high or too skeptical?

In addition, the young child undergoes changes normally over time so that problem behavior may disappear spontaneously and not require further medication. A continuing assessment of the situation keeps track of this possibility through direct involvement with the child and his therapist. On the other hand, growth may outstrip effective dosages for earlier periods of development so that medication amounts must be revised upward, again mandating close monitoring of the young patient and of his contacts.

Of course, drugs by themselves are not capable of imparting knowledge and wisdom or of initiating changes in a nonsupporting environment. They may be helpful in bringing about optimal conditions so that the child faces his adaptive and learning tasks with the least amount of impedance. Since psychological, interactional, and sociocultural factors also intrude upon the child's manifestation of the problem, both in a causative and in a reactive fashion, it behooves the clinician to take a broad if not global treatment perspective rather than to depend on the curative or maintenance powers of drugs alone. For some conditions the synergistic effect of medication and behavior modification or of psychotherapy is superior to a single method. Even environmental intervention, whether school or home-based, can be strengthened by the prudent use of medication. Obviously, the clinician will try to identify all those factors that contribute to the child's problem and, in the absence of clear-cut indications, reach for medical palliatives only as ancillary to other therapeutic efforts. Eisenberg (1972a, 1972b) has repeatedly made the point that the hungry, breakfast-deprived child's restlessness or lethargy in the classroom should not be treated with drugs when a correction of his poverty and his poor dietary habits are called for.

In time innovations that have already surfaced and others still hidden will enrich the field of chemical and physical therapy for disturbed children and youth while others will pass into oblivion along with such modalities as electroconvulsive treatment and psychosurgery for children. Some methods have appeal to small groups of devotees but have not found their way into general use as yet, e.g. biofeedback (Sheer, 1975), dietary control (Feingold, 1975), and hypnosis (Kaffman, 1970). A breakthrough in the search for memory enhancing substances may bring radical and unforeseen reverberations in psychopharmacology. In many ways pharmacotherapy is an area that remains a mental health frontier.

REFERENCES

Abrahams, D. Treatment of encopresis with imipramine. *American Journal of Psychiatry*, **119**, 891–892, 1963.

Alexandris, A. & Lundell, F. Effect of thioridazine, amphetamine and placebo on the hyperkinetic syndrome and cognitive area in mentally deficient children. *The Canadian Medical Association Journal*, **98**, 92–96, 1968.

Anders, T. F. & Weinstein, P. Sleep and its disorders in infants and children: A review. *Journal of Pediatrics*, **50**, 311–324, 1972.

Annell, A. L. Lithium in the treatment of children and adolescents. *Acta Psychiatrica Scandinavica*, **207**, 19–30, 1969. Supplement.

Arnold, L. E., Kirilcuk, V., Corson, S. A. & Corson, E. O'L. Levoamphetamine and dextroamphetamine: Differential effect on aggression and hyperkinesis in children and dogs. *American Journal of Psychiatry*, **130**, 165–170, 1973.

Ascher, E. Psychodynamic considerations in Gilles de la Tourette's disease (Maladie des Tics): With a report of five cases and discussion of the literature. *American Journal of Psychiatry*, **105**, 267–276, 1948.

Baker, R. R. The effects of psychotropic drugs on psychological testing. *Psychological Bulletin*, **69**, 377–387, 1968.

Barker, P. Haloperidol. *Journal of Child Psychology and Psychiatry*, **16**, 169–172, 1975.

Beck, L., Langford, W. S., Mackay, M. & Sum, G. Childhood chemotherapy and later drug abuse and growth curve: A follow-up study of 30 adolescents. *American Journal of Psychiatry*, **132**, 436–438, 1975.

Bellman, M. Studies on encopresis. *Acta Paediatrica Scandinavica Supplement*, **170**, 1–151, 1966.

Berg, I. & Jones, K. V. Functional faecal incontinence in children. *Archives of the Diseases of Childhood*, **39**, 465–472, 1964.

Bradley, C. The behavior of children receiving Benzedrine. *American Journal of Psychiatry*, **94**, 577–585, 1937.

Bradley, C. Benzedrine and dexedrine in the treatment of children's behavior disorders. *Pediatrics*, **5**, 24–36, 1950.

Brown, D., Winsberg, B. G., Bialer, I. & Press, M. Imipramine therapy and seizures: Three children treated for hyperactive behavior disorders. *American Journal of Psychiatry*, **130**, 210–213, 1973.

Call, J. D., Christianson, M., Penrose, F. R. & Backlar, M. Psychogenic megacolon in three preschool boys. A study of etiology through collaborative treatment of child and parents. *American Journal of Orthopsychiatry*, **33**, 923–928, 1963.

Campbell, M., Fish, B., Korein, J., Shapiro, T., Collins, P. & Koh, C. Lithium and chlorpromazine: A controlled crossover study of hyperactive severely disturbed young children. *Journal of Autism and Childhood Schizophrenia*, **2**, 234–263, 1972a.

Campbell, M., Fish, B., David, R. Shapiro, T., Collins, P. & Koh, C. Response to triiodothyronine and dextroamphetamine: A study of preschool schizophrenic children. *Journal of Autism and Childhood Schizophrenia*, **2**, 343–358, 1972b.

Campbell, M., Fish, B., Shapiro, I. & Floyd, A. Thiothixene in young disturbed children. *Archives of General Psychiatry*, **23**, 70–72, 1970.

Campbell, S. B., Douglas, V. I. & Morgenstern, G. Cognitive styles in hyperactive children and the effect of methylphenidate. *Journal of Child Psychology and Psychiatry*, **12**, 55–67, 1971.

Chapel, J. L., Brown, N. & Jenkins, R. L. Tourette's disease: Symptomatic relief with haloperidol. *American Journal of Psychiatry*, **121**, 608–610, 1964.

Challas, G. & Brauer, W. Tourette's disease: Relief of symptoms with R1625. *American Journal of Psychiatry*, **120**, 283–284, 1963.

Cole, S. O. Hyperkinetic children: The use of stimulant drugs evaluated. *American Journal of Orthopsychiatry*, **45**, 28–37, 1975.

Conners, C. K. Pharmacotherapy of psychopathology in children. In H. C. Quay and J. S. Werry (Eds.), *Psychopathological Disorders of Childhood*. New York: Wiley, 1972a.

Conners, C. K. Psychological effects of stimulant drugs in children with minimal brain dysfunction. *Pediatrics*, **49**, 702–708, 1972b.

Conners, C. K., Taylor, E., Meo, G., Kurtz, M. A. & Fournier, M. Magnesium pemoline and dextroamphetamine: A controlled study in children with minimal brain dysfunction. *Psychopharmacologia*, **26**, 321–336, 1972.

Cordes, C. K. Chronic drug intoxication causing pseudoretardation in a young child. *Journal of the American Academy of Child Psychiatry*, **12**, 215–222, 1973.

Cott, A. Treating schizophrenic children. *Schizophrenia*, **1**, 44–49, 1969.

Cytryn, L., Gilbert, A. & Eisenberg, L. The effectiveness of tranquilizing drugs plus supportive psychotherapy in treating behavior disorders of children: A double-blind study of eighty outpatients. *American Journal of Orthopsychiatry*, **30**, 113–129, 1960.

Cytryn, L., McKnew, D. H., Logue, M. & Desai, R. B. Biochemical correlates of affective disorders in children. *Archives of General Psychiatry*, **31**, 659–661, 1974.

Dally, P. & Sargant, W. Treatment and outcome of anorexia nervosa. *British Medical Journal*, **2**, 793–795, 1966.

D'Amato, G. Chlordiazepoxide in management of school phobia. *Diseases of the Nervous System*, **23**, 292–295, 1962.

DiMascio, A. Psychopharmacology in children. In S. Chess & A. Thomas (Eds.), *Annual Progress in Child Psychiatry and Child Development*. New York: Brunner-Mazel, 1971.

Effron, A. & Freedman, A. The treatment of behavior disorders in children with benadryl: A preliminary report. *Journal of Pediatrics*, 42, 261–266, 1953.

Eisenberg, L. Principles of drug therapy in child psychiatry with special reference to stimulant drugs. *American Journal of Orthopsychiatry*, 41, 371–379, 1971.

Eisenberg, L. The hyperkinetic child and stimulant drugs. *New England Journal of Medicine*, 287, 249–250, 1972a.

Eisenberg, L. The clinical use of stimulant drugs in children. *Pediatrics*, 49, 709–715, 1972b.

Eisenberg, L., Lachman, R., Molling, P. A., Lockner, A., Mizelle, J. D. & Conners, C. K. A psychopharmacologic experiment in a training school for delinquent boys: Methods, problems, findings. *American Journal of Orthopsychiatry*, 33, 431–447, 1963.

Eveloff, H. H. Psychopharmacologic agents in child psychiatry. A survey of the literature since 1960. *Archives of General Psychiatry*, 14, 472–479, 1966.

Feingold, B. F. *Why Your Child is Hyperactive*. New York: Random House, 1975.

Feinstein, S. C. & Wolpert, E. A. Juvenile manic-depressive illness. Clinical and therapeutic considerations. *Journal of the American Academy of Child Psychiatry*, 12, 123–136, 1973.

Fish, B. Drug use in psychiatric disorders of children. *American Journal of Psychiatry*, 124 (February Supplement), 31–36, 1968.

Fish, B. Problems of diagnosis and the definition of comparable groups: A neglected issue in drug research with children. *American Journal of Psychiatry*, 127, 900–908, 1969.

Fish, B. The "one child, one drug" myth of stimulants in hyperkinesis. Importance of diagnostic categories in evaluating treatment. *Archives of General Psychiatry*, 25, 193–203, 1971.

Fish, B., Shapiro, T. & Campbell, M. Long-term prognosis and the response of schizophrenic children to drug therapy: A controlled study of trifluoperazine. *American Journal of Psychiatry*, 123, 32–39, 1966.

Freeman, R. D. Drug effects on learning in children. A selective review of the past thirty years. *Journal of Special Education*, 1, 17–44, 1966.

Frommer, E. A. Treatment of childhood depression with antidepressant drugs. *British Medical Journal*, 1, 729–732, 1967.

Galdston, R. Mind over matter: Observations on 50 patients hospitalized with anorexia nervosa. *Journal of the American Academy of Child Psychiatry*, 13, 246–263, 1974.

Gavanski, M. Treatment of non-retentive secondary encopresis with imipramine and psychotherapy. *Canadian Medical Association Journal*, 104, 46–48, 1971.

Ginn, S. & Hohman, L. The use of dextroamphetamine in severe behavior problems of children. *Southern Medical Journal*, 46, 1124–1127, 1953.

Gittelman-Klein, R. & Klein, D. Controlled imipramine treatment of school phobia. *Archives of General Psychiatry*, **25**, 204–207, 1971.

Green, J. B. Association of behavior disorder with EEG focus in children without seizure. *Neurology*, **11**, 337–344, 1961.

Grinspoon, L. & Singer, S. B. Amphetamines in the treatment of hyperkinetic children. *Harvard Educational Review*, **43**, 515–555, 1973.

Halpern, W. I. St. Vitus' dance: Psychological symptoms as masquerade for physical illness in children. *Bulletin of the Rochester Mental Health Center*, **6**, 2–10, 1974.

Hartlage, L. C. Effects of chlorpromazine on learning. *Psychological Bulletin*, **64**, 235–245, 1965.

Helper, M., Wilcott, R. C. & Garfield, S. L. Effects of chlorpromazine on learning and related processes in emotionally disturbed children. *Journal of Consulting Psychology*, **27**, 1–9, 1963.

Hunt, B. R., Frank, T. & Krush, T. P. Chlorpromazine in the treatment of severe emotional disorders of children. *American Medical Association Journal of Diseases of Children*, **91**, 268–277, 1956.

Huxley, A. *Brave New World.* New York: Harper, 1932.

Irwin, S. A rational framework for the development, evaluation, and use of psychoactive drugs. *American Journal of Psychiatry*, **124**, 1–17, 1968 Supplement.

Kaffman, M. Hypnosis in child psychiatry. *Current Psychiatric Therapies*, **10**, 46–51, 1970.

Kelly, D., Guirguis, W., Frommer, E., Mitchell-Heggs, N. & Sargant, W. Treatment of phobic states with antidepressants. A retrospective study of 246 patients. *British Journal of Psychiatry*, **116**, 387–398, 1970.

Kety, S. S. The biogenic amines in the central nervous system: Their possible role in arousal, emotion, and learning. In F. O. Schmitt (Ed.), *The Neurosciences: Second Study Program.* New York: Rockefeller Press, 1970.

Knobel, M. Psychopharmacology for the hyperkinetic child. *Archives of General Psychiatry*, **6**, 198–202, 1962.

Korein, J., Fish, B., Shapiro, T., Gerner, E. W. & Levidow, L. EEG and behavioral effects of drug therapy in children: Chlorpromazine and diphenhydramine. *Archives of General Psychiatry*, **24**, 552–563, 1971.

Koupernik, C. Chemotherapy in child psychiatry. *British Medical Journal*, **3**, 345–346, 1972.

Kraft, I. A. The use of psychoactive drugs in the outpatient treatment of psychiatric disorders of children. *American Journal of Psychiatry*, **124**, 1401–1407, 1968.

Laufer, M. W. Long-term management and some follow-up findings on the use of drugs with minimal cerebral syndromes. *Journal of Learning Disabilities*, **4**, 54–58, 1971.

Laufer, M. W. Long-term management and some follow-up findings on the use of drugs with minimal brain syndromes. *Journal of Learning Disabilities*, **4**, 518–522, 1971.

Lindsley, D. B. & Henry, C. E. The effect of drugs on behavior and the electroencephalograms of children with behavior disorders. *Psychosomatic Medicine*, **4**, 140–149, 1942.

Lorber, J. Obesity in childhood: A controlled trial of anorectic drugs. *Archives of Diseases in Childhood*, **41**, 309–312, 1966.

Lucas, A. R. Gilles de la Tourette's disease in children: Treatment with phenothiazine drugs. *American Journal of Psychiatry*, **121**, 606–608, 1964.

McAndrew, J. B., Case, Q. & Treffert, D. A. Effects of prolonged phenothiazine intake on psychotic and other hospitalized children. *Journal of Autism and Childhood Schizophrenia*, **2**, 75–91, 1972.

MacLean, R. E. G. Imipramine hydrochloride (Tofranil) and enuresis. *American Journal of Psychiatry*, **117**, 551, 1960.

Margolis, L. H. Control of enuresis with imipramine. *American Journal of Psychiatry*, **119**, 269–270, 1962.

Martin, G. I. & Zang, P. Electrocardiographic monitoring of enuretic children receiving therapeutic doses of imipramine. *American Journal of Psychiatry*, **132**, 540–542, 1975.

Mattson, R. H. & Calverley, J. R. Dextroamphetamine-sulfate-induced dyskinesias. *Journal of the American Medical Association*, **204**, 108–110, 1968.

Millichap, J. G. Drugs in management of hyperkinetic and perceptually handicapped children. *Journal of the American Medical Association*, **206**, 1527–1530, 1968.

Molling, P. A., Lockner, A., Sauls, R. J. & Eisenberg, L. The impact of perphenazine and placebo in committed delinquent boys. *Archives of General Psychiatry*, **7**, 70–76, 1962.

Muellner, S. R. Development of urinary control in children: A new concept in cause, prevention, and treatment of primary enuresis. *Journal of Urology*, **84**, 714–716, 1960.

Munster, A. J., Stanley, A. M. & Saunders, J. C. Imipramine (Tofranil) in the treatment of enuresis. *American Journal of Psychiatry*, **118**, 76–77, 1961.

Office of Child Development, U.S. Department of Health, Education and Welfare. *Report of the conference on the use of stimulant drugs in the treatment of behaviorally disturbed young school children*. Washington, D.C.: U.S. Government Printing Office, 1971.

Page, J. G., Janicki, R. S., Bernstein, J. E., Curran, C. F. & Michelli, F. A. Pemoline (Cylert) in the treatment of childhood hyperkinesis. *Journal of Learning Disabilities*, **7**, 498–503, 1974.

Pasamanick, B. Anticonvulsant drug therapy of behavior problem children with abnormal electroencephalograms. *Archives of Neurology and Psychiatry*, **65**, 752–766, 1951.

Pavig, P., Deluca, M. A. & Ostenheld, R. G. Thioridazine hydrochloride in the treatment of behavior disorders in epileptics. *American Journal of Psychiatry*, **117**, 832–833, 1961.

Piuck, C. L. Clinical impressions of hydroxyzine and other tranquilizers in a child guidance clinic. *Diseases of the Nervous System*, **24**, 483–488, 1963.

Poussaint, A. F. & Ditman, K. S. A controlled study of imipramine (Tofranil) in the treatment of childhood enuresis. *Journal of Pediatrics*, **67**, 283–290, 1965.

Quinn, P. O. & Rapoport, J. One-year follow-up of hyperactive boys treated with imipramine or methylphenidate. *American Journal of Psychiatry*, **132**, 241–245, 1975.

Rapoport, J. Childhood behavior and learning problems treated with imipramine. *International Journal of Neuropsychiatry*, **1**, 635–642 1965.

Rapoport, J., Quinn, P. O., Bradbard, G., Riddle, K. D. & Brooks, E. Imipramine and methylphenidate treatments of hyperactive boys. A double-blind comparison. *Archives of General Psychiatry*, **30**, 789–793, 1974.

Resnick, O. The psychoactive properties of diphenylhydantoin: Experiences with prisoners and juvenile delinquents. *International Journal of Neuropsychiatry*, Supplement Number 2, **3**, S30–S48, 1967.

Rosenthal, J. H., Nicholson, R. & Collier, E. The syndrome of Gilles de la Tourette· *Journal of Learning Disabilities*, **8**, 38–40, 1975.

Rimland, B. An orthomolecular study of psychotic children. *Orthomolecular Psychiatry*, **3**, 371–377, 1974.

Safer, D. J. & Allen, R. P. Factors influencing the suppressant effects of two stimulant drugs on the growth of hyperactive children. *Pediatrics*, **51**, 660–667, 1973.

Safer, D., Allen, R. & Barr, E. Depression of growth in hyperactive children on stimulant drugs. *New England Journal of Medicine*, **287**, 217–220, 1972.

Schleifer, M., Weiss, G., Cohen, N., Elman, M., Cvejic, J. & Kruger, E. Hyperactivity in preschoolers and the effect of methylphenidate. *American Journal of Orthopsychiatry*, **45**, 38–50, 1975.

Schnackenberg, R. C. Caffeine as a substitute for schedule II stimulants in hyperkinetic children. *American Journal of Psychiatry*, **130**, 796–798, 1973.

Sheer, D. E. Biofeedback training of 40 Hz EEG and behavior. In N. Burch (Ed.), *Behavior and Brain Electrical Activity*. New York: Plenum Press, 1975.

Sherwin, A. C., Flach, F. F. & Stokes, P. E. Treatment of psychoses in early childhood with triiodothyronine. *American Journal of Psychiatry*, **115**, 166–167, 1958.

Splitter, S. R. & Kaufman, M. A. A new treatment for under-achieving adolescents: Psychotherapy combined with nortriptyline medication. *Psychosomatics*, **7**, 171–174, 1966.

Sprague, R., Barnes, K. & Werry, J. Methylphenidate and thioridazine: Learning, activity, and behavior in emotionally disturbed boys. *American Journal of Orthopsychiatry*, **40**, 615–628, 1970.

Stevens, J. R. & Blachly, P. H. Successful treatment of the maladie des tics. Gilles de la Tourette's syndrome. *American Journal of Diseases of Children*, **112**, 541–545, 1966.

Tec, L. Unexpected effects in children treated with imipramine. *American Journal of Psychiatry*, **120**, 603, 1963.

Tolstrup, K. The treatment of anorexia nervosa in childhood and adolescence. *Journal of Child Psychology and Psychiatry*, **16**, 75–78, 1975.

Uphouse, L. L., MacInnes, J. W. & Schlesinger, K. Role of RNA and protein in memory storage: A review. *Behavior Genetics*, **4**, 29–81, 1974.

U.S. Department of Health, Education and Welfare. *Residential Psychiatric Facilities for Children and Adolescents: United States, 1971–1972*, DHEW Publication No. (ADM) 74–78. Washington, D.C.: U.S. Government Printing Office.

U.S. Department of Health, Education and Welfare. Statistical Note 115, DHEW Publication No. (ADM) 75–158. Washington, D.C.: U.S. Government Printing Office, 1975.

Waizer, J., Hoffman, S. P., Polizos, P. & Englehardt, D. M. Outpatient treatment of hyperactive school children with imipramine. *American Journal of Psychiatry*, **131**, 587–591, 1974.

Waizer, J., Polizos, P., Hoffman, S. P., Engelhardt, D. M. & Margolis, R. A. A single-blind evaluation of thiothixene with outpatient schizophrenic children. *Journal of Autism and Childhood Schizophrenia*, **2**, 378–386, 1972.

Walker, C. F. & Kirkpatrick, B. B. Dilantin treatment for behavior problem children with abnormal electroencephalograms. *American Journal of Psychiatry*, **103**, 484–492, 1947.

Weiss, G., Minde, K., Douglas, V., Werry, J. & Sykes, D. Comparison of the effects of chlorpromazine, dextroamphetamine, and methylphenidate on the behavior and intellectual function of hyperactive children. *Canadian Medical Association Journal*, **104**, 20–25, 1971.

Weiss, G., Minde, K. & Werry, J. S. Studies on the hyperactive child VIII. Five-year follow-up. *Archives of General Psychiatry*, **24**, 409–414, 1971.

Wells, G. H. & Malcolm, M. T. Controlled trial of the treatment of 36 stutterers. *British Journal of Psychiatry*, **119**, 603–604, 1971.

Yoss, R. E. & Daly, D. D. Narcolepsy in children. *Pediatrics*, **25**, 1025–1033, 1960.

CHAPTER 12

Choices

Troubled families expect their encounters with trained professionals to be built more on scientific investigation than on mere personal whim. They trust that the prescriptive treatment will be appropriate and effective. In other words, they may well believe that the strategy selected for them or for their child is at least rooted in therapeutic optimism and is also based on tested evidence for success.

There is an expanding research literature concerned with the question of effectiveness in mental health intervention with children (Halpern, 1968; Levitt, 1971; Mellsop, 1972; Robins, 1972). In a recent review on psychotherapy and behavior change Levitt (1971) observed that "few conditions have been definitely established as requisite or even advisable for the treatment of the child patient." He summarized follow-up data from almost 10,000 children and concluded that the effectiveness of child psychotherapy was not evident from the data. This impression rested on the finding that no significant distinction could be made in terms of outcome between treated and untreated children. Robins (1972), after reviewing follow-up studies about behavior disordered children, also came to the conclusion that

"at the present time, unfortunately, there is no substantiated evidence that childhood psychosis or antisocial behavior can be either prevented or treated successfully. All carefully controlled studies have agreed in showing poor results no matter what techniques have been attempted. It is, however, encouraging that follow up methods provide us with a technique for evaluating our attempts at prevention and treatment that produces clear and consistent answers. When we do find successful techniques for preventing or modifying childhood disorders, we can expect follow up studies to demonstrate their effectiveness as dramatically and consistently as they now demonstrate our present failures in prevention and cure" (pp. 445–446).

Research in and evaluation of children's maladaptive reactions and behaviors are complicated by a number of factors such as differences in diagnosing and labeling among evaluators, contamination of psychopathology by developmental variability, and faulty control groups. This last factor, generally under the guise of comparing groups of treated and nontreated children, has been the main argument about the ineffectiveness of psychotherapy (Eysenck, 1965; Levitt, 1957). Since the outcome for both groups is thought to be roughly equal, a spontaneous remission effect had to be postulated as operating strongly across all categories of childhood problems. Bergin and Suinn (1975) suggested however, that the spontaneous remission argument is a weak one since research over the last 20 years has not supported that position. On the contrary, a reanalysis of the data originally compiled by Eysenck (1952), which he used to buttress his assertion that over time two thirds of disturbed patients change for the better irrespective of treatment, was not corroborated. Whether behavior modification will fare better than traditional psychotherapy in achieving a higher improvement rate is still to be demonstrated. The empirical research in family therapy outcome has also been disappointing so far (Wells et al., 1972). What seems to be emerging is that therapy accelerates change and that the more efficient the treatment is the more accelerated the change (Bergin and Suinn, 1975).

In short, outcome research has not been helpful to the decision making process of the clinician in his daily job. A most cumbersome task faces the practitioner who must recommend a course of action for each of the diverse childhood problems he encounters. Only a guide to general criteria in the selection of treatment modalities, or the constraints placed upon them, can be suggested. Clinical judgement must remain an important tool in treatment choice until a better method comes along. This implies that the clinician keep abreast of the growth in his field and become acquainted with newer methods. Education for choice, although still too elementary to be subsumed under a rational system, is rapidly acquiring the characteristics of necessity in an overly providential therapeutic society (Lipowski, 1972). Neither ignorance about the growth of one's craft or avoidance of choice through parochialism will long hold up in today's marketplace. Indeed, Eisenberg (1975) warns that "with the range of treatments available, it is no longer tolerable to have 'schools' of exclusive salvationism whose practitioners fit all comers onto a Procrustean couch, whatever their disorder."

In determining a course of treatment the clinician relies on the patient data in his possession, on the knowledge he has of treatment choices, and on the educated judgement he hopes to exercise in fitting one to the other (Avallone et al., 1973). The preceding chapters have presented some highlights about the major modalities of current therapies for children and their families in the belief that the clinician will want to be acquainted with his options before reaching for a treatment plan. This is not to imply that the task of choosing the most appropriate regimen is always made simpler by an awareness of alternative treatment methods or of an all encompassing knowledge of this field. Sometimes making choices among nearly equally attractive methods is more burdensome than if alternatives did not exist. Neither will it negate the natural tendency to follow personal preferences, to repeat the familiar, and to identify with the prevailing practices of one's profession or discipline. Despite these qualifications, the principle still holds that effective help for children can best be achieved in the long run only through widely disseminated under-standing of available treatment options.

Obviously, in any consideration of this topic, attention must be given at the very least to the age of the child, to the conditions of his environment' and to the assets and liabilities of both. For optimal growth and adaptation to take place, his developmental age and his temperament require a commen-surate response from the surrounding human medium. When problems arise we conceive the child and his environment to be out of phase. Etiologically the disharmony may arise within the child, in the parents and their surro-gates, or at the interface between them. In any event, the diagnostic and treatment efforts are attempts at realigning forces that trouble one or more of the participants in the child-rearing experience. It follows then that inter-vention assists the return to a more manageable life for both child and parents. Only that effort necessary for bringing about this goal ought to be applied, since a parsimonious approach is least likely to create iatrogenic complications. With our present knowledge of treatment effectiveness, only an empiric disposition can be proposed. This means that what works in one situation may not easily generalize to all seemingly similar cases, and may be even totally out of place in some. If a child presents with idiosyncratic be-havior for which no clear-cut explanation can be formulated, that help is extended which reduces disability and promotes a more positive outlook while holding undesirable effects to a minimum. Not to act in the face of uncer-tainty and ambiguity may turn out to be a negative choice when it means foregoing the chances of potential help to disturbed children.

In the organization of the preceding chapters we have traversed the various layers of the support system for children, from the basically external medium of history and society to the inner circle of the family and finally to the bio-social realm within the individual. The analogy of peeling away the layers of an onion is not meant to convey that one method has primacy over another or that one has more value, except as each has a special position in a total Gestalt that does not harbor a precious core. Nevertheless, each approach—

comparable to each layer of the onion—has different dimensions and has a unique place in the total organization.

We can make only a few generalizations for distinguishing treatment choices without resorting to too many qualifiers. Although not meant to be an exhaustive list, the following statements appear axiomatic to us.

1. In any therapeutic endeavor, the younger the child the greater the involvement of parents.

2. Environmental manipulation is a desirable technique if it has protective or preventive implications, if it serves as an instrument of respite, and if reality dictates its use when alternatives are fruitless.

3. Environmental manipulation is to be avoided or held to a minimum as long as the likelihood for improvement from other treatment techniques continues to exist.

4. Changing or modifying natural systems such as the family or the school in order to broaden the therapeutic scope and identifying children at risk for appropriate intervention is preferable to dealing with victims of adaptive struggles.

5. For children who need achievement oriented success, a psychoeducational program yields the greatest promise for accomplishing this therapeutic goal.

6. Children who have trouble processing information in one or more spheres of learning require training directed at their handicaps.

7. When the problems are closely tied to faulty child rearing, to disturbed communication, or to conflicted relationships, the work with parents takes on major significance.

8. Although working with families as units can be carried out for all manner of problems, it presupposes a modicum of family group cohesion and the cooperation of at least one adult member to be of practical use.

9. When problems with peers comprise the major complaint about a child, group therapy can be a good corrective device.

10. Although most children gain something from individual psychotherapy, its effectiveness is greatest for those who allow themselves to be involved in the therapeutic process and who perceive the therapist as more potent than themselves.

11. Circumscribed behavior problems and well-defined symptoms lend themselves most easily to the systematic treatment methods of behavior modification.

12. Chemotherapy for symptom relief or for behavior control in children

has specificity for only a limited number of problems, but it is most often used as an adjunct to other treatment methods and also when other methods cannot be implemented or when they fail.

Beyond such broad guides for discrimination lurk the much more critical tasks of hammering out treatment plans whose formulations are anchored in biology, psychosocial development, family life, community organization, and sociocultural reality Every occasion for planning a course of action demands a comprehensive and integrated point of view about the child, his situation, and the available resources.

We picture the child as unfolding in a recognizable organismic pattern along four dimensions. First is the biological rhythm that is uniquely his. The strength of his drives, the timing of his inner clock, and the integrity of his self-regulating system determine the nature of a given temperament. Both the child and those who deal with him must learn to accommodate to his genetic disposition. The proper meshing of people rests in large measure on such an accommodation, something often overlooked in arriving at treatment plans.

A second dimension of this pattern relates to the stages through which each child must pass in order to progress. These stages of development have temporal predictability, must be navigated sequentially in a determined order, and lay the groundwork one for another. Because a child's problems may be stage specific, the therapist cannot dismiss the role of developmental complications.

In childhood the thrust of this progression is from primitive to more complex and more highly differentiated stages, an effect that resembles a positive spiral toward maturity (Kissel, 1967). Yet we know that growth and decline, the third dimension, have a reciprocal relationship and are also coexistent in life, thereby giving rise to an existential paradox. From this frame of reference it follows that, in treating children, emphasis must be placed as much as possible on the facilitation of growth by holding in check those negative factors that can cause a premature foreclosing on life or even an early decline into death.

Finally, the child is not alone in time and space but is connected to particular people, values, and traditions that give meaning and continuity to his life and to that of others. Consequently, intervention also tackles issues ranging from personal survival to the quality of existence in a psychohistorical perspective. In his work, the therapist not only affirms the right of the young for a good life but also respects the supporting organizational matrix as a valid instrument for socialization.

REFERENCES

Avallone, S., Aron, R., Starr, P. & Breetz, S. How therapists assign families to treatment modalities: The development of the treatment method choice. *American Journal of Orthopsychiatry*, **43**, 767–773, 1973.

Bergin, A. C. & Suinn, R. M. Individual psychotherapy and behavior therapy. In M. R. Rosenzweig and L. W. Porter (Eds.), *Annual Review of Psychology*, Palo Alto, Calif.: Annual Review, 1975.

Eisenberg, L. The ethics of intervention: Acting amidst ambiguity. *Journal of Child Psychology and Psychiatry*, **16**, 93–104, 1975.

Eysenck, H. J. The effects of psychotherapy: An evaluation. *Journal of Consulting Psychology*, **16**, 319–324, 1952.

Eysenck, H. J. The effects of psychotherapy. *International Journal of Psychiatry*, **1**, 99–178, 1965.

Halpern, W. I. Do children benefit from psychotherapy? A review of the literature on follow up studies. *Bulletin of the Rochester Mental Health Center*, **1** (1), 4–12, 1968.

Kissel, S. The positive spiral in parent-child relationships. *Mental Hygiene*, **51**, 21–23, 1967.

Levitt, E. E. The result of psychotherapy with children: An evaluation. *Journal of Consulting Psychology*, **21**, 189–196, 1957.

Levitt, E. E. Research in psychotherapy with children. In A. Bergin and S. Garfield (Eds.), *Handbook of Psychotherapy and Behavior Change*, New York: Wiley, 1971.

Lipowski, Z. J. The problem of Buridan's ass: Psychotherapy for choice. *Current Psychiatric Therapy*, **12**, 18–26, 1972.

Mellsop, G. W. Psychiatric patients seen as children and adults: Childhood predictors of adult illness. *Journal of Child Psychology and Psychiatry*, **13**, 91–101, 1972.

Robins, L. N. Follow-up studies of behavior disorders in children. In H. C. Quay and J. S. Werry (Eds.), *Psychopathological Disorders of Children*. New York: Wiley, 1972.

Wells, R. A., Dilkes, T. C. & Trivelli, N. The results of family therapy: A critical review of the literature. *Family Process*, **11**, 189–207, 1972.

Author Index

Subject Index